The Death Proclamation of Generation X

To Denise,

Thank you for your interest and support.

Marvin 2010

The Death Proclamation of Generation X

✦

A Self-Fulfilling Prophesy of Goth, Grunge and Heroin

Maxim W. Furek

iUniverse, Inc.
New York Bloomington Shanghai

The Death Proclamation of Generation X
A Self-Fulfilling Prophesy of Goth, Grunge and Heroin

Copyright © 2008 by Maxim W. Furek

All rights reserved. No part of this book may be used or reproduced by any means, graphic, electronic, or mechanical, including photocopying, recording, taping or by any information storage retrieval system without the written permission of the publisher except in the case of brief quotations embodied in critical articles and reviews.

iUniverse books may be ordered through booksellers or by contacting:

iUniverse
1663 Liberty Drive
Bloomington, IN 47403
www.iuniverse.com
1-800-Authors (1-800-288-4677)

Because of the dynamic nature of the Internet, any Web addresses or links contained in this book may have changed since publication and may no longer be valid.

The views expressed in this work are solely those of the author and do not necessarily reflect the views of the publisher, and the publisher hereby disclaims any responsibility for them.

ISBN: 978-0-595-46319-0 (pbk)
ISBN: 978-0-595-50558-6 (cloth)
ISBN: 978-0-595-90614-7 (ebk)

Printed in the United States of America

Copyright information follows for the lyrics quoted in this volume and are gratefully acknowledged.

Portions of the chapter "Hollywood on Dope" have appeared in *Counselor, The Magazine for Addiction Professionals* in a somewhat different form.

Portions of the chapter "Woodstock Burning" have appeared in *Professional Counselor Magazine* in a somewhat different form.

Grateful acknowledgement is made for permission to quote from the following copyrighted material:

"Angry Chair," written by Layne Thomas Staley. Copyright 1992 by Jack Lord Music (ASCAP). All rights reserved.

"Emma," written by Errol Brown and Tony Wilson. Copyright 1974 by Finchley Music Corporation (ASCAP). All rights reserved.

"God Save the Queen," written by Paul Thomas Cook, Stephen Philip Jones, Glen Matlock and Johnny Rotten. Copyright 1977 by Universal Music Careers (ASCAP). All rights reserved.

"Golden Boy," written by Natalie Merchant. Copyright 2001 by Indian Love Bride Music (ASCAP). All rights reserved.

"Hello 2 Heaven," written by Christopher J. Cornell. Copyright 1991 You Make Me Sick I Make Music. (BMI). All rights reserved.

"Heroin, written by Lou A. Reed. Copyright 1967 by Oakfield Avenue Music LTD (BMI). All rights reserved.

"Jane Says," by Eric Adam Avery, Perry Farrell, David Michael Navarro, Stephen Andrew Perkins. Copyright 1988 by I'll Hit You Back Music/Bubbly Orange Stuff Music/Embryotic Music/Swizzle Stick Music/Irving Music (BMI). All rights reserved.

"Junkhead," words and music by Jerry Fulton Cantrell Jr. and Layne Thomas Staley. Copyright 1992 by Buttnugget Publishing/Jack Lord Music (ASCAP). All rights reserved.

"Loser," by Beck David Hansen and Karl F. Stephenson. Copyright 1994 Adler Dance Music Publishing and Cyanide Breathmint (ASCAP). All rights reserved.

"Man of Golden Words," written by Jeffrey Allen Ament, Bruce Ian Fairweather, Greg A. Gilmore, Stone C. Gossard and Andrew Wood. Copyright 1990 Stardog Music (ASCAP). All rights reserved.

"Night Prowler," written by Ronald Belford Young, Angus McKinnon Young and Malcolm Mitchell Young. Copyright 1979 by J. Albert & Son (USA) Inc. (ASCAP). All rights reserved.

"Perfect Day," words by Lou A. Reed. Copyright 1972 by Oakfield Avenue Music LTD (BMI). All rights reserved.

"Reach Down," written by Christopher J. Cornell. Copyright 1991 You Make Me Sick I Make Music (BMI). All rights reserved.

"River," words and music by Natalie Merchant. Copyright 1995 by Indian Love Bride (BMI). All rights reserved.

"Satan's Bed," by Stone C. Gossard and Eddie Jerome Vedder. Copyright 1994 by Write Treatage Music/Innocent Bystander/Jumpin' Cat Music/Scribing C-ment Songs/Pickled Fish (ASCAP). All rights reserved.

"Smells Like Teen Spirit," by Kurt D. Cobain, David Eric Grohl and Krist Anthony Novoselic. Copyright 1991 by The End of the Music/MJ Twelve Music/Murky Slough Music/Primary Wave Tunes/Songs of Universal Inc. (BMI). All rights reserved.

"Suicide Solution," words and music by Robert John Daisley. John Osbourne and Randy Rhoads. Copyright 1981 and 1986 by Essex Music International Inc., New York, NY and Kord Music (ASCAP). All rights reserved.

"Then The Night Comes," written by William M. A. Broad and Mark A. Smith. Copyright 1993 by Boneidol Music/Chrysalis Music/EMI April Music Inc./Marked Man Music/WB Music Corp (ASCAP). All rights reserved.

"Would," written by Jerry Fulton Cantrell Jr. Copyright 1992 by Buttnugget Publishing (ASCAP). All rights reserved.

"Hey, Hey, My, My (Into The Black)," by Jeff Blackburn and Neil Young. Copyright 1979 by Broken Arrow Music Corporation (ASCAP). All rights reserved.

This book is dedicated to the two most important women in my life. My wife Patricia, a model of patience, who stood by me throughout this entire process of elation, frustration, action and inaction until finally, after almost a decade, the possibility of a finished project was within reach. And to my step-daughter Heather, a Gen Xer, who with passion, energy and vision, taught me that it was impossible to stereotype her generation as they continued to defy categorization. Thank you ladies for your love. Thank you for believing in me. Only because of you has this book been possible.

Contents

Acknowledgments .... *xiii*

Introduction .... *xix*

Chapter 1   The Dark Prophesy 1

Chapter 2   The Lost Tribes of Generation X 8

Chapter 3   Kurt Donald Cobain 20

Chapter 4   The Culture of Goth 45

Chapter 5   River Jude Phoenix 73

Chapter 6   Hollywood on Dope 95

Chapter 7   Heroin Chic 110

Chapter 8   Woodstock Burning 130

Chapter 9   Anna Nicole Smith 139

Chapter 10 Post Columbine 154

Chapter 11 Concerning their Legacy 167

The 1990's Political and Sociocultural Timeline *179*

References *205*

About The Author *231*

Acknowledgments

Many people encouraged the writing of this manuscript and there have been numerous individuals who have played key roles in the research and development of the final product. I wish to acknowledge all of them and to recognize the value of their contributions. As a Baby Boomer (1946-1964) I have always felt a fascination, affinity and connection to the younger demographic group known as Generation X. As part of my attempt to learn as much as I could about this group I poured over countless volumes of magazines, publications and newspaper articles that detailed the exploits of the various tribes of Generation X. A large number of friends and associates shared articles and information during this data-gathering process. Too, I visited tattoo parlors and tattoo conventions, medieval stores and Goth citadels and entered into conversation with those who dabbled in matters of Goth, grunge and all things Generation X. There were many who helped along the journey.

I am indebted to such individuals as Cultural Anthropologist Dr. Anne Bolin of the Department of Sociology and Anthropology at Elon University who breathed new life and expectation into this project with her sage comments and critical direction. Dr. Barbara Basron, who validated a basic tenet of cultural anthropology and the "modern primitives" with her personal insight, is yet another who shared of their time, energies and generous wisdom.

A special "thank you" to Nancy Sponeyberger who initially requested that I develop a training addressing tattoos and body modification for the Pennsylvania Department of Health which begat further information on this topic and the resulting "Tattoos and Body

Modification: Blood, Pleasure and Pain" workshop. I am grateful to organizer Mark Fairchild and his *Inking the Valley Convention* for allowing me to film and document his Wilkes-Barre, PA. event and for introducing me to countless others in that special artistic community. A special note of gratitude to Little John's Infinite Art Tattoos for sharing his historic expertise and perspective and also to the Association of Professional Piercers for their sage advice. I acknowledge the contributions of Charles Coleman who introduced me to the collective works of Douglas Kent Hall's *Prison Tattoos*. I am also thankful for the comments from numerous other tattoo and piercing parlors, including Buffalo Bill's Totem Tattoo and Elmer Lewis' Elmer's Tattoos, in Philadelphia, Pittsburgh and cities in-between who collectively attempted to explain the public fascination of their craft and the "modern primitives movement."

Very special thanks go to Trinka Porrata, President of Project GHB and author of *"G'd Up" 24/7: The GHB Addiction Guide* for all of her comprehensive and detailed information regarding Billy Idol and the Hollywood underground and specific background information on River Phoenix and the sensational GHB controversy surrounding his death. Too, I enjoyed spending time and sharing thoughts with Trinka, a retired LAPD narcotics detective, at the 2004 St. Louis Health and Fitness Expo where we both presented our anti-drug message to the masses of humanity.

During his visit to Northeastern Pennsylvania Doug Pray, director of the independent film *Hype* provided me with explicit information about the Seattle-based grunge sound and earlier rock acts that begat the unique Seattle genre. His documentary allowed many of us increased insight into the strange musical collective of Nirvana, Mudhoney, Soundgarden, Pearl Jam, The Gits, 7 Year Bitch, The Fastbacks, The Melvins and numerous others who influenced an entire generation.

As a former music critic and avid student I listened to music of the genre. I attempted to understand and appreciate what these songs had to offer, songs including grunge, rap, heavy metal and the so-called "angry female rockers." I strived to decipher the code, listening to Nirvana's "Smells Like Teen Spirit" and TuPak's "Brenda's Got A Baby," to experience for myself the words, rhythm and attitude of this music. I am indebted to numerous disc jockeys for opening their vast libraries to me and introducing me to the world of hip hop, techno pop and trance music. I am indebted to those who shared with me their collection and understanding of music.

I wish to recognize and extend my appreciation to John Fodar a.k.a. Johnnie Floater of Hollywood's GM Media Live 365 who helped immensely by opening up many music industry doors, so important to this work. I owe a debt of gratitude to Mel Lawrence, the 1969 and 1999 Woodstock Director of Operations. Mel's fresh perspective helped provide me with a much-needed counter-balance to this project. Special thanks to Darryl Morden, music critic, radio writer-producer and *Buzzine Music* Editor. Darryl has walked the worlds of broadcast, print and the Internet for more than two decades and was a writer/producer for syndicated radio programs heard around the globe, including American Top 40 with Casey Kasem. Darryl's music and interviews have appeared in a wide variety of entertainment and trade publications, including the *Hollywood Reporter*. His upcoming rock'n'roll detective novel is titled *Interstate City*. I am appreciative to, among others, Robert T. Wiemers, a.k.a. "Hippy Bob," for his insight into the Woodstock phenomena and the evolution of rock from the old to the new and also to metal aficionado Joshua Siegfried for his impressive body of knowledge regarding heavy metal and his personal account and reflections of the controversial and ill-fated Woodstock '99.

In the realm of psychological and sociological variables I received valued feedback from such personalities as John G. Messer, President of the Susquehanna Institute; Barry J. Jackson, Professor and Director of DAWN, Bloomsburg University and Pat Torcella who took the time to literally walk me through various phases of this project. I am indebted to her for her interest and support of this book. Also, my thanks to Ken Dickinson, M.S., R.Ph., Gaudenzia Eastern Region

Consultant, for his data on, among other things, Complex PTSD and evolving drug trends.

A special "thank you" to motivational speaker Linda Talley who had attended my presentation on Generation X several years ago in Erie, PA. and demonstrated an incredible curiosity and interest in this topic. I wish to thank Rev. Dr. David L. Hain of Etsah Ministries and Rev. John Baumgartner IV, Sr. Pastor/Counselor of Heritage Baptist Church and Reformers Addictions Program for their friendship, optimism and spiritual insight.

There were many who educated me on the obscure Goth musical genre and culture. I wish to thank Sebastian Dante Giovanni, aka Carl NiCastro and The Gothic Arts Society of Harrisburg for introducing me to the realm of the Vampyre and the lands of the undead. Many others shared with me the esoteric sounds of Goth through the music of Bauhaus, Advent Sleep, Seraphim Shock, Play Dead, Usherhouse, The Damned, Nosferatu, The Shroud, The Last Dance, Kill Sister and Black Tape for a Blue Girl.

The world of the drug user, hidden from the mainstream, was another dark corner that needed to be illuminated. I am indebted to so many individuals who allowed me to interview them as a means of furthering my education. I appreciate the efforts of Georgia Fourlas, and to "Adam," "Rose," "A.J." and "Barbie" and so many others all in varied stages of addiction, withdrawal or recovery, for sharing their personal journey. Thanks to Scott Lynn, Montour County Coroner for his insights on Ketamine and Heroin and to Jack McCann, US Attorney's Office, for his impressive body of knowledge on heroin and current street substances.

There were so many supportive colleagues from the Pennsylvania Department of Health, Bureau of Drug and Alcohol Programs, Pennsylvania Certification Board and Institute for Research, Education and Training in Addictions who I especially wish to thank. Among them are such luminaries as Tom Brown, Robert Burhannan, Debra Browning, Amy Shanahan, Holly Hagle, Kathy Coleman, Kristine Pond, Susan Edgar, Katie Polachek, Tonya Welshans, Mary Jo

Mather, Tom Baier, Terri Wray, Peg McCloskey, Crystal Thomas, Rich Raynak, Heather Casner, Cheri Lare and Mary Jane Woods. Michael Heisey, former BDAP employee who initially suggested that I research obscure street drugs, such as MDMA, Ketamine and GHB, helped to guide me in the proper direction as I embarked on what was to become a long and strange trip into unchartered waters. I thank every one of you as you have taught me well.

My proofreaders I must profoundly thank for their efforts in making this work such as it is. To Michael Merrits, thank you for your contributions. You have served Generation X well. Karen DeFrancesco of Susquehanna University did much to encourage me with her positive message to keep pushing forward. Dr. Ted Billy for his attention to detail and insistence upon clear and precise communication, nothing vague, obscure, assumed was the strong and steady anchor. Ted was there to help me remain calm, even during times of chaos, anxiety and panic. And to Libby Beiler for keeping me in a single time zone without vacillating between the present and past in my literary time-travel discourse and for her positive and uplifting Leo spirit that buoyed me on so many occasions.

I am grateful to Brent DeFranco of Lakeside Graphix.com for his dramatic and immediate book cover design and subsequent website, and too, as an expert on the aforementioned Generation X, I appreciated much of Brent's personal feedback and observations of this tribe. And also to The Mark Sullivan Studio for their creative endeavors in making the final book design one of eye-catching excellence.

Many thanks to two special colleagues whose perspective and input has been invaluable. Phillip Rouse, PhD, thank you so much for opening my eyes to the works of Alice Miller, Roberto Assagioli, Phillip Zimbardo, David Presti and so many others. And to Raymond Nelson Loftus, perhaps the most accomplished and effective existential psychologist I have known. Thank you Ray for keeping me poised, focused and pointed in the right direction. You have been a good listener and a true friend and for that I have been truly blessed.

Introduction

This project was formally initiated on December 6, 1998, after presenting three seminars entitled "The Substance Abuse of Generation X" for the Pennsylvania Bureau of Drug and Alcohol Programs and IRETA (the Institute for Research Education Training). [I must point out the actual chronology of this book and explain why it has taken so long to complete. My research and writing took a slight 14-year detour after I began to publish *Steele Jungle Publications*, a magazine tabloid that advocated against dangerous ergogenic drugs including anabolic steroids, human growth hormone, Tetrahydrogestrinone and Erythropoietin. After that long and strange trip, from 1992 to 2005, reached its conclusion, I immediately began to scan over my Generation X manuscript and seriously attempted to finalize this project.] I was acquainted with the various substances of abuse that were appearing on the streets but, as I prepared for these seminars, I realized that there was a host of key information that was lacking. Missing from the cryptic puzzle was the exciting cultural piece, something that belonged to another unique group. Generation X'ers were different than my Baby Boomer roots. My family of origin was blessed by having an intact family structure, a mother who stayed at home and nurtured her three children, and a father who, with an eighth-grade education, relentlessly pursued anything he could to bring food and clothing and shelter to his family. I was raised in that atmosphere where faith and hard work begat reward. I believed, as my family did, that I would go on to pursue a college education and reap the rewards of the American Dream.

If any decade represented the unique cultural fabric of Generation X, it was without question the ten-year span of the turbulent 1990's. This time period witnessed the Rodney King beating, the Amadou Diallo killing and the hate-crime murder of James Byrd Jr. Beginning with the death of obscure grunge rocker Andrew Wood, a "dark prophesy of heroin" revisited that horror over and over again with the deaths of Kurt Cobain, Layne Staley, Shannon Hoon, Jonathan Melvoin and River Phoenix. Hollywood acknowledged the heroin trend by releasing violent drug-ridden films such as *Natural Born Killers, Pulp Fiction, Trainspotting and The Basketball Diaries*. The mass-murder of school students that culminated in the Columbine tragedy began an unsettling trend that has continued to this day. The homegrown terrorism of Eric Rudolph, "Unabomber" Ted Kaczynski and Terry Nichols and Timothy McVeigh forced us to admit that the enemy was lurking in our midst. We watched in horror at the ritualistic killings of the Heaven's Gate cult and sang along to the music of Lilith Fair and Lallapolooza. And just as the decade awoke to the firelit skies and anarchy of the L.A. Riots, it ended with the ill-fated violence, sexual assault and propane tank explosions of Woodstock 1999. For better or worse, this was the decade that belonged to Generation X.

Intended to be an introspective and intelligent look at a sensitive topic, *The Death Proclamation of Generation X* visits the alienation, frustration and angst of a scapegoated generation. In this work the decade of the 1990's is explored to better understand the essence of this generation through the eyes of icons such as Andrew Wood, Kurt Cobain, Layne Staley, Marilyn Manson, Anna Nicole Smith and River Phoenix. For some it may appear dark and gloomy, "edgy," as one colleague stated, and in that regard reflects aspects of pain, suffering and death. But, too, this book is the celebration of all those things that members of Generation X can proudly claim as their own powerful and positive attributes—characteristics often shunned by the popular media.

As they were scapegoated, marginalized and forgotten, the experience and expectation of Generation X were considerably different from that of the Baby Boomers. X'ers had little of the optimism, expectation and promise that embraced previous generations. But, like hunter-gatherers of pre-history, Generation X forged Maslovian tribal structures that established identity and safety. Their mission, in a hostile postmodern universe, was merely to survive. Both Goth and grunge were pathways to develop strength amongst like-minded tribal members allowing X'ers to ultimately endure and ultimately thrive. Heroin, for some, became an accepted way to deaden the pain despite the dangers of overdose and addiction. According to Join Together there was significant growth in heroin use in the United States during the 1990s with an estimated number of heroin users increasing from 68,000 in 1993 to 325,000 in 1997. From 1990 to 1996, heroin-related emergency room visits rose more than 150 percent. Much of this book is an attempt to understand the evolution of heroin from the underground to the cultural mainstream and the promotion of the heroin culture by members of a despondent Generation X.

This work has been an effort to piece together the complexities of Generation X. It has been a quest to determine what messages previous generations have presented them and, in turn, what messages Generation X begat their younger peers. It has been a plea, to offer insight as we attempt to optimistically prevent history from repeating itself. My purpose is not to castigate these brave Generation X individuals, but rather to acknowledge their individuality, honor their existence and to celebrate their future. They are indeed a unique group with their own identity of music, attitude and culture. The resilience of Generation X is but another example of the power of this special group of people, a group of highly skilled and adaptive individuals. It is my strong hope and belief that the observations and conclusions reached in this manuscript will mesh with those of Generation X and also help to further the reach of the drug and alcohol profession.

1

The Dark Prophesy

In the dead of night, like a muscular white stallion, it strode into town. They called it horse. *Equus caballus.* Beginning with a slow trot it swirled in a deliberate and calculated dance, then, with patient temperament, burst into full gallop. It came not as a stranger but as an invited and expected guest.

In 1990 Andy Wood, charismatic lead singer of Seattle's pioneer grunge band, Mother Love Bone, died from a heroin overdose. Wood was the first in a cadre of Pacific Northwest musicians to embrace The Dark Prophesy of Heroin and ride the horse. Black tar heroin, in a cheaper, more potent form, became the drug of choice for angry, disconnected grunge rockers. The untimely deaths of Nirvana's Kurt Cobain and the childlike film star River Phoenix signaled early on that the path Generation X had chosen would be strewn with body bags and roadside crosses. The deaths of numerous other musicians, including the possible overdose suicide of Alice in Chains lead singer Layne Staley, continued the tragic death toll.

All of the signs were there. Generation X, as they learned to crawl and then walk from the sometimes-stifling embrace of their Baby Boomer parents, was forewarned about the storm clouds ahead. It was a warning cry that went unheeded and ignored.

For members of Generation X, born between 1965 and 1978, the philosophy of their parents was a celebration of sorts. Memories of a Utopian Woodstock Nation reflected a culture they had grown to embrace: the music, psychedelic artwork, tied-dyed clothing and bell bottoms—all part of the peace and love passed down from idealistic Baby Boomers to their Generation X children. And part of that rite of passage was the expected experimentation with illegal recreational drugs. The trend, beginning with marijuana, was expected to end there, but for some continued on to hallucinogens like LSD and mescaline before embracing harder substances such as cocaine, methamphetamine and finally King Heroin.

Heroin overdoses had increased dramatically in the Pacific Northwest, fueled in part by a pessimistic and excessive music culture that accepted the use of heroin as a recreational substance. One music critic postulated, "One in four Seattle musicians is involved with heroin." The hand of death, cold and gripping, reached out to this vulnerable group; their landscape littered with scorched spoons, empty syringes and dirty needles. In Portland, OR, there was a 141 percent increase in fatalities associated with heroin and opiates from 1993 to 1999. Seattle, the grunge epicenter, demonstrated a 134 percent increase in heroin deaths from 1990 to 1999. Deaths from heroin overdose peaked in 1998, when 140 bodies were laid out at the King County morgue. (Mexican black tar [40-80 percent pure] has played a significant part in the Pacific Northwest heroin epidemic and during the 1990's was recognized as a leading cause of death among young people.

The acceptance of heroin as an acknowledged mainstream drug was unexpected, as smack had always been considered a bad drug, one that invited disease, addiction and the mathematical probability of overdose. But that possibility did little to discourage countless young individuals from experimenting with the dirty white powder. Heroin use begat the dark prophecy embraced by many in the ranks of Generation X, including Andrew Wood and Kurt Cobain, individuals who experienced heroin's sweet euphoric numbness and shared in the bizarre perception that dope held more meaning than life, more truth than hypocrisy. That dark prophecy was eerily documented in Kurt

Cobain's agonizing and misguided suicide note as it reflected Neil Young's lyrics, "It's better to burn out than fade away."

On an alternate philosophical level, heroin, a drug of isolation and solitude, was *the* perfect drug for this scapegoated group of youth. It validated the maxim that "life sucks" and, as such, was the most appropriate accoutrement for a generation of youth who had been "counted out" as worthless losers by a hostile media and other segments of an insensitive society. The use of heroin seemed a logical response to the despondency influencing the lives of Generation X, and, as rationalized by Mark Renton in *Trainspotting*, "It's the only real honest drug. It doesn't alter your consciousness. It just gives you a hit and a sense of well-being. After that, you see the misery in the world as it is …"

Shooting dope was a negotiated tradeoff of sorts, a compromise. There was the warm flushing of the skin and the familiar itching just before the nod and the *semi somnolence* before the promised land of the dream state. But then, inevitably, there was a terrible craving for the dope which, if left unleashed, brought about the horrifying sensation of muscle being ripped from aching bone and the unimaginable pain of steel needles piercing the head. That torture soon led to surrender and the realization that it was better to just fix and get well rather than to spend four days of eternity kicking the habit; four days that added up to more than 24 hours, more than 38 hours, more than 42 hours. It was the junkie's timetable, the junkie's clock of hell.

Withdrawal from heroin is a most difficult task. Junkies felt like they were dying over and over again, as they attempted to kick. And they really did die. There was always a part that would never be the same as they looked, with the constricted pupils of a dead man, into the mirror, and saw staring back a part that had died years before. Yet for some, they would rather die than get sick, would rather feel their heart and lungs give out in one last painless gasp. That too, regrettably, was all part of the deal as doing heroin underscored the philosophy of nihilism and the realization that maybe it was ok to practice self hatred and actively pursue the destruction of self. As the black curtain fell, that scenario played out for Andrew Wood, as it would soon play out for Kurt Cobain and River Phoenix and Layne Staley all those falling victim to the curse of heroin's dark prophesy.

ANDREW WOOD

Andrew Patrick Wood was raised on Bainbridge Island, WA, and began his charismatic musical journey with the band Malfunkshun. In 1983, at the age of 17, Wood's outrageous stage act, comprised of younger brother Kevin and drummer Regan Hagar, opened for the Seattle-based bands Ten Minute Warning and The Melvins.

As front man for Malfunkshun, Andrew Wood was the proverbial perfect fit. His silver suits, capes, painted face and outrageous platform shoes and motorcycle boots projected a superstar status in the making. Calling himself *L'andrew the Love Child*, Wood injected crazy, spontaneous stage antics into the musical mix. That stage presentation paid tribute to earlier Pacific Northwest bands, such as the Kingsmen and Paul Revere and the Raiders.

Steeped in themes of punk and post-1970's glam rock, Malfunkshun was all about experimentation. It was the complete package of pre-grunge energy and youthful rebellion. Philosophically, the band was a reaction against glam metal, a form of commercial heavy metal popular in the 1980's. *"Love rock"* was the term the band used to describe their persona with L'andrew the Love Child as their visual spokesperson. In the documentary *Hype*, Seattle engineer Jack Encino called Wood "The only stand-up comedian front man in Seattle." Still, Woods' vocals and audience interaction were not his strong suit; rather, it was his artistic creativity that pushed the band to the edge of stardom. That potential was left to languish on the vine. His brother Kevin knew that heroin was becoming a big part of Andrew's life: "He hung out with other people. When he started to come of age, he moved to Seattle and he started hanging out with other people that I didn't know. I didn't see him too much, except for band activities, and he hooked into some friends that were into needle drugs. I really had no idea the extent of it. This is the honest truth; I had no idea. I mean, I knew he did it every now and then because he would talk about it, but I had no idea it was such a big deal in his life."

Malfunkshun's theatrical intensity was short lived. Following several personnel changes between Green River and Lords of the Wasteland, Mother Love Bone was formed. The final hybrid consisted of Andy Wood, Jeff Ament, Stone Gossard, Bruce Fairweather and Greg Gilmore. Mother Love Bone was quickly discovered by Polygram Records, who released their EP *Shine* in 1989. All indicators were that the band, the first Seattle group of their generation to net a major record deal, was poised for national success.

But that road was paved with major obstacles, according to Kevin Wood, "He was at my house one time and he pulls out this piece of black tar heroin and says, 'look at this, this is for later'.... and I said, "Jesus Christ man, you're just about to make it big, you're just about there, don't fucking blow it." He said, "Everything is fine, I just do it every once in awhile." Then before I know it, he's back in rehab. At that time, when he was in Mother Love Bone, I didn't see him at all. He was pretty much gone all the time."

Apple, a full-length album, was scheduled to be released in early 1990 and, in preparation, the band was actively touring. Around this time Wood checked himself, once again, into a rehab and after discharge was interviewed by *RIP* magazine. The singer spoke about his ongoing battle with addiction: "It's a total struggle. When you first get out, you're on this pink cloud, and it's pretty easy. After a while things start getting more real, and you have to just stay straight a second at a time."

Staying straight was something that Andrew Wood could not do. Upon discharge he continued using heroin and, with lowered tolerance, overdosed. At this stage the singer would have experienced confusion and weakness caused by hypotension or low blood pressure. This abnormal condition, triggered when the pressure of the blood against the walls of the blood vessels during and after each heartbeat is lower than usual, resulted in cold, pale skin and blue fingertips.

Andrew Wood's central nervous system, with faint pulse and shallow breathing, was already dangerously depressed even before any possibility of being saved.

On March 16, 1990, Wood's unconscious body was discovered by his fiancée, Xana La Fuente. Unable to wake him, she called for paramedics. Wood was taken by ambulance to Harborview Medical Center and initially declared dead. He was then revived and placed on life support. For three days Wood remained in intensive care and on a respirator. His family and friends waited until Chris Cornell flew back from New York to join them. On March 19, 1990, the life support was removed and Andrew Wood was officially pronounced dead. The medical report determined that he died from a heroin overdose coupled with a cerebral hemorrhage. He was only 24. Andrew Wood's death fit the profile of classic heroin overdose fatalities. The average reported death is a male in his late twenties or early thirties. Most fatal cases have been using heroin for a considerable amount of time prior to death and are not, on the whole, novice users.

In an interview with *FIBM*, brother Kevin Wood stated that Andrew lived for a while after the overdose: "Yea, he was on life support for a little while. I don't know all the specifics, but he was on a breather for a while and he was responsive in some ways ... I mean, there was a chance that he was going to come back, but during the time they had him hooked up to life support he had a hemorrhage aneurysm and lost all brain function ... that was like the third day that he had been in there and they (doctors) said ... well you know, his brain ... there is nothing going on in there, you may as well pull the plug. So we all just stood around and watched ... you know like on TV when they have the machine, the heart monitor ... it just got slower and slower and then was just a flat line. That was it, you know."

Many of the Emerald City's close-knit artistic community were affected by the death of their good friend. Alice In Chains dedicated their CD *Facelift* (1990) "to Andrew Wood and Gloria Jean Cantrell." "Would," from the CD *Dirt*, written in 1992, was another posthumous effort from the group addressing Wood's death. Written by guitarist Jerry Cantrell, it begged for absolution: "Know me broken by my master/Teach thee on Child Of Love hereafter/... So I made a big mistake/Try to see it once my way/Drifting body its sole desertion/Flying not yet quite the notion."

Temple of the Dog (1991), a collection of ten remarkable tunes, became the "tribute album" dedicated to the memory of the band's friend Andrew Wood and introduced Temple of the Dog as the world's first grunge super group. The title of the album came from "Man of Golden Words," a song written by Wood that intoned: "Seems I've been living in the Temple of the Dog/Where would I live if I were a man of golden words/Or would I live at all"? Wood's former roommate Chris Cornell of Soundgarden wrote two songs, "Hello 2 Heaven" and "Reach Down" for his friend. The insightful lyrics "the sky was your playground, but the cold ground was your bed," came from "Hello To Heaven." And in "Reach Down," Cornell's harsh words affirmed: "Yes, love was my drug but that's not what I died of." In 1992 *Temple of the Dog* successfully broke into the lofty top ten of the album charts, a fitting tribute to their mate.

The documentary *Malfunkshun—The Andrew Wood Story*, directed by independent filmmaker Scot Barbour, premiered at the Seattle International Film Festival and captured the Best Documentary award at the 2005 FAIF International Film Festival in Hollywood. The posthumous tribute came 15 years after Wood's fatal drug overdose.

2

The Lost Tribes of Generation X

Canadian writer Douglas Coupland has been credited with coining the term Generation X. In his 1991 book entitled *Generation X: Tales For An Accelerated Culture,* Coupland painted a picture of generational outcasts, unfocused and unproductive. They were the perceived "slackers," with few goals or aspirations other than to hang out at the malls, spend their parents' money and acquire materialistic goods. Coupland spoke of youths envisioning their "mental ground zero," their location at the exact moment the atomic bomb was dropped. It was fitting that he chose the cryptic symbol *"X"* to name a generation of youth that the world would not easily accept, nurture or understand. There was something painfully tragic about Coupland's lost tribes of Generation X. Even their name is obscured in a murky confusion. For those who still wonder, the debate endures about the genesis of the term "Generation X." The letter X is the mathematical symbol for the unknown. It indicates an unfamiliar, amorphous quantity, but also means "to cross out or mark with an X." By definition then, Generation X represented an unknown group that could be, or is apt to be, discarded by society.

The actual demographics of this "amorphous" group are confused and nebulous. Some have identified Generation X as those individuals born between the 20-year span of 1961 to 1981. Not everyone agrees on this tight interpretation, as the Cox News Service pointed out, "there are no definitive years on which everyone agrees." Some groups like American Demographics do not even list a "Generation X," but note such groupings as Baby Bust (1965-1976), Baby Boomlet (1977-1994) and Echo Bust (1995-). There are other demographic organizations that take a slightly different perspective, but for our purposes we have considered Generation X as those individuals born between 1965-1978. This generation represented 46 million people, placing them in the minority when contrasted against the larger Baby Boomers (80 million) and Generation Y (76 million).

Like lab rats in a wire-mesh Skinnerbox, X'ers were subjected to a Pavlovian experiment of humiliation and scapegoating. The age-old phenomenon of scapegoating is a hostile social-psychological discrediting routine by which people move blame and responsibility away from themselves and towards a target person or group such as Generation X. It is also a practice by which angry feelings and feelings of hostility may be projected, via inappropriate accusation, towards others. The target feels wrongly persecuted and receives misplaced vilification, blame and criticism and they are likely to suffer rejection from those whom the perpetrator seeks to influence.

Simon Crosby, founder of The Scapegoat Society, described scapegoating as a projective defense used by both individuals and societies where responsibility is transferred from the perpetrator onto the target. Scapegoating allowed the discharge of aggression, freed the perpetrator from self-dissatisfaction and provided some narcissistic gratification. It may also relieve the perpetrator's feelings of guilt and shame according to Crosby.

Researcher Lynne Namka further argued that the dreadful practice of scapegoating caused anxiety and misery for the target group. They experienced exclusion, ostracism and even expulsion within their society. The target, viewed as weak and vulnerable, felt insecure and began to develop a victim mentality as evidenced by the art, pessimism and negative expectations of Generation X—especially in their despondent music. Rich Lowery of the *National Review* described the grunge sound: "Grunge is for the most part shorn of ideals and the impulse for political action. Whereas 1960's student rebels were mostly the product of middle-class two-parent families, the defining family for grunge kids is the broken home, a consistent theme in their music."

The widespread negativity and scapegoating emanated from all quarters of society—from the scientific community to the popular press, with every aspect of the social order, including church and state, participating. None of it was optimistic. Most was critical. Consider the sordid propaganda that the media systematically imposed on this group of individuals during the 1990's. They were called by *The Washington Post* "A generation of animals" and "The Doofus Generation," and by *The New York Times* "The Numb Generation" and "The Unromantic Generation." *Time Magazine* called them "The Tuned Out Generation" and "an unsung generation, hardly recognized as a social force or even much noticed at all." "The Blank Generation" was the term they received from *The San Francisco Examiner*.

After the scapegoating, this group was literally sent to their corner, and then shamefully ignored. Caught between the neglect of Baby Boomer parents and overbearing Boomer Yuppies, X'ers were overwhelmed by the sheer force of greater numbers. Those with louder voices and larger economic clout soon usurped the X'ers unique cultural agenda. Bronwyn Lance Chester, in a commentary entitled "Time Gen-X wakes up, smells Starbucks," explained: "Among political age groups in America, we are the smallest—through fate—and least powerful—through indifference. But unless we wake up and realize there's more to life than Starbucks and plasma TVs, we're in for a harsh lesson about letting others take the reins of our future."

The Baby-Boom Echo, created by Boomers who postponed childbirth until their 30s and 40s, became the all-important Generation Y (also known as the Millennial Generation, Echo-Boomers and Generation Next) and represented a possible correction of past mistakes in child-rearing. From the beginning, Generation Y was expected to be, unlike their war-protest Boomer parents, more civic-minded like the

GI Generation (1901-1924) of Jimmy Carter, Gerald Ford, Lyndon Johnson, John F. Kennedy, Richard Nixon and Ronald Reagan. Still, this group harbored more than just political aspirations. Generation Y, raised on MTV and reality shows such as *The Anna Nicole Show* and *The Osbournes*, sought out the financial stability and security of corporate America as they aspired to amass wealth and fame. A 2007 Pew Research Center telephone survey found that the top life goals among Generation Y, 18 to 25 year-olds, were to be rich (81 percent) and famous (51 percent), as compared with a 1967 survey of Boomer college freshmen where 85.8 percent stated that developing "a meaningful philosophy of life" was their main concern. In 2002, as confirmation of this possibility, Forbes magazine ranked Generation Y 21-year-old pop singer/actress Britney Spears, who had sold over 70 million albums, as the "most powerful celebrity in the world."

OMINOUS ECONOMIC HARBINGER

That financial optimism did not connect with Generation X, however, as the doomsday bell soon resonated from the White House and from a Boomer Chief Executive. President William Jefferson Clinton made that point dramatically clear as he emphasized the plight of this "Doomed Generation." He stated, "Years of neglect have left America's economy suffering from stagnant growth and declining incomes … they have left a mountain of debt and a federal Government that must borrow to pay more than a fifth of its current bills. Perhaps most sadly, they have left the great majority of people no longer dreaming the American Dream. Our children's generation may be the first to do worse than their parents." The fate of the Social Security System remained an unknown variable. Although many politicians have attempted to resolve the Social Security issue, as it stands currently, the fund will be exhausted before Generation X has retired. In another three decades the massive wave of retired Baby Boomers will have depleted the fund. They, unlike Generations X and Y, are guaranteed to inherit the rewards of the Social Security System as their sheer numbers rapidly surpass age 60 and enter into retirement. Since 1996, every eight minutes a Baby Boomer has turned age 50, with that trend expected to continue until 2014. Currently there is a ratio of 3.4 to 1 of workers to retirees, but that ratio will dramatically decline to 2 to 1 in about 15 years. Trustees for the fund predicted that the social security surplus would dissipate by the year 2037. Those statistics should be of concern to every member of Generation X.

In addition to that ominous economic harbinger was the realization that a larger disparity between the wealthiest and poorest segments of society was encroaching on the middle class. X'ers worried that they would not share in the prosperity that had enveloped their parents and, most likely, would be worse off than the upbeat, postwar Boomers. At the beginning of the decade, a large majority of Americans bought into that doomsday mindset as a shroud of gray encapsulated our national consciousness. A Gallop Poll, released in January 1990, reported that about 75 percent of Americans feared that their personal financial situation would become worse by the year 2000. Another 64 percent believed that it would be harder for young people, including college graduates, to find adequate employment. Yet another 79 percent predicted that retirement would be more difficult and more costly, while 81 percent anticipated that it would be harder to afford a house, as the American Dream, sought after by generation upon generation, appeared to have vanished into the ether. For some, the ideal of the American Dream had become an impossible quest, a fairytale belonging to another time.

This cloud of doom, like a constant swirling blur, was one of numerous portents looming in front of the X'ers. Part of the national despondency was a direct result of slanted media coverage. A 1996 study by George Washington University tracked the national evening news for a 100-day-period. That finding revealed 6,500 negative news items reported, as opposed to a scant 370 positive news stories. The warnings about global warming, pollution, the depleted ozone layer, weather-related disasters and extinct species also began to take hold as we internalized the sensory news overload and message that our planet was dying. Many felt impotent and fatalistic and, to that end, the collective mindset of Generation X became one of pessimism, their view of the future steeped in fear, suspicion and cynicism. Beck's 1994 Cajun-rap song "Loser," from his successful debut album *Mellow Gold*, spawned a Generation X catch phrase with its explicit lyrics and fatalistic proclamation "I'm just a loser baby, so why don't you kill me?"

Of that cynicism, and clearly articulated in an internet essay titled *Talkin' bout our Generation*, an anonymous writer explained: "We are not a monolith. We do not share a brain, or any one set of opinions. What binds Generation X is the cultural climate in which most of us grew up, and the realities that we face as we come to adulthood under less than ideal conditions." For this group, that cultural climate of "less than ideal conditions" was one that took a walk into the gloom. Generation X was reared on 1980's musical excess and 1990's musical angst. Furthermore, consider a cultural landscape that embraced crack cocaine, the acceptance and celebration of heroin, AIDS, holes in the ozone layer, the cult of punk nihilism and the despondent philosophy of grunge coupled with a soaring national debt and American manufacturers relocating to Taiwan and China. This was the unique cultural landscape that the vulnerable Generation X inherited.

Generation X'ers grew up during a phase of extreme disharmony in their family unit. Included in this chaotic period was an unprecedented rate of divorce and broken homes, latchkey kids fending for themselves, homelessness, grandparents raising grandchildren and the conspicuous absence of the father. This dramatic change in the complexion of the traditional American family emerged when, in 1963, *The Feminine Mystique* by Betty Friedan introduced a new feminist perspective to women and an opportunity to explore new roles in society. The Students For a Democratic Society (SDS) proffered an agenda "to promote justice, peace, equality and personal freedom" for those on the fringes of society, which included racial minorities, America's poor, and America's women. Those cluster of events begat the feminist movement that empowered women and challenged their traditional roles in the family and the institution of marriage. The 2000 U.S. Census Bureau noted that since 1990, the number of families headed by single mothers [7.5 million] had increased 25 percent while single fathers headed an estimated two million households. During this period about one third of all babies were born to unmarried women. In 1992, a female headed almost 50 percent of black families and 68 percent of live births among blacks were born to unwed mothers, one of the poorest segments of our society. An obsessive work ethic, driven by capitalism and consumerism, led many parents to place more importance on careers and materialistic goals than family. The resulting turmoil led to an acceptance of divorce, reflected in a liberalization of divorce laws and the reduction in the cost of divorces via no-fault divorce. A recent Demographic Profile of American Baby Boomers produced by the MetLife Mature Market Institute observed that boomers had a higher divorce rate (14.2 percent) than prior generations. The divorce rate for the pre-boomer generation, those 65 years of age and older, stood at 6.7 percent, while the percentage of boomers who never married (12.6 percent) was three times higher then prior generations. As a result, the extended family system, that all-important neighborhood safety net, began to fade away as our sense of social cohesion also dissipated.

Although there has been much focus on their well-publicized alienation, substance abuse, and perceived violence, it has been difficult to define the soul of this traumatized generation. Like the intellectually curious beatniks and self-enlightened hippies of yesterday, X'ers questioned the meaning and fairness of life in an attempt to make sense of their bleak world. One Generation X spokesman was a despondent Kurt Cobain, leader of grunge-group Nirvana, who, even as he voiced constant complaints of opiate abuse, attempted to rationalize his addiction: "It might be time for the Betty Ford clinic or the Richard Nixon Library to save me from abusing my body any longer," Cobain said. "I decided to use heroin on a daily basis because of an ongoing stomach ailment that I had been suffering from for the past five years. (After drug rehabilitation) I instantly regained that familiar burning nausea and decided to either kill myself or stop the pain. I bought a gun but chose drugs instead," he explained in an inarticulate deadpan manner. A self-confessed "emotional wreck," Cobain described his anti-social persona as his "need not to belong." Cobain often spoke of personal suffering and his search for a warm and secure family unit. He also voiced his animosity towards the relentless paparazzi. The cult of nihilism and subsequent suicide surrounding Kurt Cobain's life helped influence part of his generation's "loser" attitude just as previous generations had received their varied cues from Dylan, Kerouac, Hemingway and the like.

The influence of a handful of music celebrities upon their target demographic group was an important yet hard-to-define variable. The life and death drama of individuals such as Andrew Wood, and later Kurt Coban and Layne Staley, had a significant impact on countless members of Generation X who followed their careers, listened to their musical output and absorbed the dark grunge philosophy of nihilism. Gladwell's *The Law of the Few*" described how individuals from specific social groups influenced others. Gladwell postulated that a trio of individuals—connectors, mavens and salespersons—have the ability to create connections among their audiences. Acting as *salespersons*, music celebrities have the ability to persuade audiences and subconsciously alter perception. In the case of grunge music the message predominately was one of misery, lowered self-esteem and the self-destruction surrounding heroin use.

Elaborating on this theme Teisha-Vonique Hood, in her article "Teen Icons: Cultural Images and Adolescent Behavior," noted that emulating music and film icons was a safe way for individuals to discover themselves through this type of external cultural experimentation. Hood stated, "Accordingly, images from popular culture often provide the external basis from which teenagers will benchmark their thoughts, opinions and associations. Indeed, adolescents will forge their identities largely in conformance with these pop culture images. They perceive such images as the social norm and, thus, as a means to attain the social acceptance that is so vital to their personal maturation."

To fully understand this troubled and scapegoated group one must realize that Generation X did not stand alone. They shared notable similarities with The Lost Generation, that comparable demographic group born mainly in the Gay Nineties and prominent in the post-World War I era, a generation passionately documented by Ernest Hemingway in *The Sun Also Rises*. Published in 1926 and considered to be Hemingway's best work, the novel followed a group of aimless American expatriates numbed by alcohol and devoid of optimism. Born between 1883 and 1900, The Lost Generation demonstrated an alarming self-destructive quality as evidenced by their high suicide rate and prolific use of bathtub gin, marijuana, chloral hydrate and cocaine. This group also endured unthinkable obstacles. The Lost Generation watched as 675,000 individuals, ages 20 to 40, died from a lethal virus known as The Great Influenza of 1918, America's deadliest epidemic, and an epidemic that may have claimed as many as 40 million victims worldwide. The Lost Generation, called "uncivilized" and "delinquent bad boys," shared other traits with the scapegoated Generation X. Despite a 65-year-span, there is an interesting literary correlation between the writings of Hemingway and the song lyrics of Cobain, one attempting to metaphorically define a post-war society and the latter attempting to comprehend his era of post-modernism.

COLLECTIVE MISTAKE

Even as Generation Y was expected to become our national heroes, many apparently viewed Generation X as our collective mistake. This group, symbolic of things gone wrong, became the Baby Boomers' uncomfortable penance. Concerning Generation X, expectations were not high for this group of individuals. At least part of the gloomy prophecy stemmed from a fascinating book by William Strauss and Neil Howe. In *Generations: The History of America's Future 1584 to 2069*, the authors proffered a theory that American history was in step with a recurring cycle of actions and reactions. The most current examples, as cited by the authors, include these specific groups: # 10 Civic (The G.I. Generation), #11 Adaptive (The Silent Generation) #12 Idealist (Baby Boomers) and # 13 Reactive (Generation X.) The so-called Generation X group was listed as the Reactive Type and its group members viewed as nuisances and problems for society. They were, during their youth, generally discarded and shared this sentiment with the authors group # 9, The Lost Generation. But, as the Reactive Theory went, Generation X will be called upon in middle age to provide steady leadership during a great historic crisis yet to be identified.

The Idealistic Baby Boomers have been commonly known as the demographic group born between the years of 1946–1964. (Note: Demographics are not an exact science and looks at sundry variables including culture and population booms to identify select groupings. As a case in point, Baby Boomers had been identified by the *New York Times* as "80 million Americans born from 1945 to 1963," a slight departure from our numbers.) The years 1946 to 1964 represented, respectively, the celebration of our victory in World War ll and the passage of the Civil Rights Act, both important dates for the Boomer generation. This group represented the largest demographic group and, perhaps, because of their greater numbers and appeal to marketing agencies, the most influential. Both Presidents William Jefferson Clinton and George Walker Bush were Baby Boomers. Numerous indicators acknowledge that the boomers possessed more disposable income and cash flow that were directed to leisure pursuits than any other group, including their parents. U.S. Census Bureau officials have estimated that the median family income for a head-of-household individual, ages 45 to 54, had risen from $23,170 (adjusted for inflation) in 1947 to $61,833 in 1998. This generation, the most affluent generation in U.S. history, also had the highest standard of living ever. In 2000, the poverty rate for boomers was 7.3 percent, lower than for any other segment of the population. The boomers have indeed lived larger and longer with their life expectancy reaching 76.

The friction, created at the point where boomers were to pass the torch to Generation X, was not unexpected, as there were many philosophical problems between these competing groups. Boomers witnessed the birth of the Free Speech Movement under their watch. In 1964 demonstrations at California's radical Berkeley campus began a long string of college protest: loud, organized and militant. It was one of the variables that helped bring an end to the Vietnam War, but also one of the personality traits that defined many of the Boomer protest-generation. That Boomer attitude has been under assault with the current trend for younger managers in their 20's and 30's to be supervising older employees. In 1999, 14 percent of top executives were members of Generation X, according to Dun and Bradstreet estimates. It was something that caused discord among the more experienced and seasoned boomers who had their own perspective on organizational structure and implementation of process.

And unlike the Boomers who pointed to their global anti-war demonstrations, their Civil Rights participation, and their much-publicized gathering of the tribe at Woodstock, the only events that Generation X could call their own were events, shrouded in gloom and pessimism, such as the deaths of Kurt Cobain and Layne Staley and the homicides of TuPac Shakur and Notorious BIG. X'ers have never experienced the magic of their special moment, a peak event that defined their spirit and essence and echoed an inspired message to the world. They have never taken center stage and basked in their glory. The unsettling decade began with an obscure Generation X crack addict named Rodney King, whose police brutality trial on April 29, 1992 led to the insane response of the Los Angeles Riots when over 50 individuals died, over 2,000 were injured and over 8,000 were arrested for primal acts of looting, anarchy and civil disobedience. And, at the end of the decade, two students, armed with a 9-mm semiautomatic carbine, two sawed-off shotguns, one TEC-DC9 semi-automatic handgun and dozens of homemade bombs vowed to kill as many fellow students as possible as they executed the horrific bloodshed at Columbine High School. Five months later the vile images of Woodstock 1999, the celebration of music and art, presented America with vile images of exploding propane tanks against a foreboding backdrop of mindless vandalism and rampant sexual assaults. The decade of Generation X ended as it had begun, with a disenchanted society in turmoil and in the throes of senseless and unimaginable violence.

3

Kurt Donald Cobain

o o o o o o o o o o o o o o o o o o o o o o o o o

"I can't stand the thought of Frances becoming the miserable, self-destructive, death rocker that I've become ..."

—Kurt Cobain.

It wasn't right. It wasn't fair. Kurt Cobain's legacy should have been a celebration of his life and of his accomplishments. But his eulogy, told and retold so many agonizing times, only focused on the pain and suffering. His life became a tortured spirit draped in a dark, bloodstained shroud; a casket that reeked of fear, loneliness and heroin.

Cobain and his followers were betrayed. In some crazy mathematical miscalculation, their parallel universe allowed their heroes to die. It was not the stuff of Hollywood cinema where the protagonist is resurrected to a place of redemptive salvation and goes on to ride off on muscular steed into the sunset—credits rolling, and audience satiated. Not Kurt Cobain. He died as he lived, a miserable slave to the lies and emptiness of heroin.

He was not alone. There were so many others of his group. Generation X has been more seduced by the deadly powders of heroin than any before. Yes, we all remember Joplin, Hendrix and Morrison, all superstar members of the Silent Generation, all victims of heroin overdose, * but they only numbered three. Those of Generation X, those who died from heroin's chokehold were larger in number and scope. There simply can be no comparison as to the devastation of Cobain's people from this special narcotic. Generation X grunge rockers allowed heroin to become their very personal drug of choice. And like an ancient curse, it followed them, marked them, and stalked them to their grave.

(*Note: According to his death certificate, Jimi Hendrix' demise was caused by barbiturate intoxication (quinalbarbitone). It was not heroin as so many believed, but another drug, equally deadly, capable of snuffing out one more precious life. Hendrix's girlfriend, Minika Danneman, admitted that Hendrix had taken nine of her Vesperax sleeping pills prior to his death. The music star was declared dead on arrival at St. Mary Abbot's Hospital, where pathologist Prof. Donald Teale reported that death was due to "inhalation of vomit due to barbiturate intoxication." In his summing up, the coroner said: "The question why Hendrix took so many sleeping pills cannot be safely answered.")

Before he elected to end his life, Kurt Donald Cobain had become a sad caricature of the tortured, addicted artist. Miserable in the glow of success, his was a life of pain and suffering. Despite incredible talent and timing, Cobain's 27 years on earth ended in surrender and a hopeless defeat.

The life of Kurt Cobain was a modern-day Greek tragedy, a cautionary tale. He was the reluctant rock star, a successful artist who became the ambassador, albeit briefly, for a generation of wayward and unfocused youth. Unfortunately the pressures of stardom came at a high cost. His physical afflictions and inability to deal with life on life's terms led to an eventual heroin addiction. Like rock counterpart Jimi Hendrix, another Seattle luminary, the sting of a needle being slid into tender flesh momentarily held more promise than the guarantee of living.

THE PUNK MOVEMENT

The anger of disaffection, of being on the outside looking in, was not a novel innovation. The dance has gone on forever, an endless rite of passage where angst fumes, smolders and sparks to flashpoint. Modern-day versions of this social revolution began with the Beatniks of the 1950's, the hippies of the 1960's and continued with the political ranting of the Punks. This predictable and well-orchestrated pattern begat the Grunge Movement that embraced the 1990's. Punk was an important declaration made on several levels. First it was a fashion statement replete with spiked, colored hair and safety pin ornaments. Secondly, punk was a political protest, having more importance and impact in Great Britain than in the United States. Punk was fast, furious and final. Most of the songs, under two minutes in duration, contained anti-establishment messages, such as the Clash's "White Riot." Others in this company included Generation X, the Buzzcocks and the Damned but it was Johnny Rotten and his Sex Pistols' "God Save the Queen," released in 1977 during the Queen's Silver Jubilee that equated Queen Elizabeth ll with a "fascist regime" and predicted, "there is no future in England's dreaming." The British Broadcasting Company and the Independent Broadcasting Authority both banned the anti-authoritarian protest song even as the Houses of Parliament discussed the Pistols under the Treason Act. Despite lack of widespread media exposure "God Save The Queen" became the "official" underground anthem of the punk movement, emblematic of the confrontation, belligerence and anarchy that it espoused.

Spawned by relentless Baby Boomer creativity, America was the birthplace of the punk revolution. From Queens, New York, the Ramones, with lanky, leather-jacketed lead singer Joey Ramone, churned out angry teen rants that included "I Wanna Be Sedated," "Now I Wanna Sniff Some Glue," "Sheena Is a Punk Rocker " and "Teenage Lobotomy."

The Ramones' three-chord garage rock assault was the undeniable American influence on upstart, and eventually more commercial English bands, such as The Clash and The Sex Pistols. The Ramones began their tour of Great Britain on July 4, 1976—the start of the U.S. Bicentennial and the beginning of a musical revolution. Their status was not to be denied. In 2000, National Public Radio included the Ramone's "I Wanna Be Sedated" in its list of "The 100 Most Important American Musical Works of the 20th Century." Boasting a 22-year long songbook, the Ramones were inducted into the Rock and Roll Hall of Fame in 2002.

Punk did not last long. The final gasp of the movement was abrupt and uncelebrated. It came after Sex Pistol's member Sid Vicious was imprisoned in New York's Rikers Island. The bass player was charged with murdering his girlfriend, Nancy Laura Spungen. The former go-go dancer was stabbed to death in Room 100 at the Chelsea Hotel. Vicious was charged with second-degree murder. He was later released on $50,000 bail. He died of a heroin overdose, reported as an apparent suicide, on February 2, 1979. He was 21 years old.

KURT COBAIN

Grunge borrowed much from the punk movement. The pounding, unrelenting beat of grunge was a renegade musical style blending punk with metal and pop. It was punk with a hard commercial beat and a hungry mainstream audience. Grunge was successfully promoted worldwide by Jonathon Poneman and Bruce Pavitt, co-founders of independent Sub-Pop Records. Evolving from its insular Seattle roots, grunge became a lasting multimillion-dollar phenomenon, even more successful than punk rock.

The most impressive groups in this genre included Nirvana, Pearl Jam, Soundgarden and Alice In Chains. Others in the cast of characters fitting into the grunge mold were the Thrownups, Screaming Trees, Hole, 7 Year Bitch, Fastbacks and the U-Men. The Seattle-based music industry, represented best by Sub-Pop Records, had the advantage of signing innumerable unproven bands to contract. It was not unusual for no-name groups to record an album and have it hyped as the next new thing. Grunge was immediate, spontaneous and marketable. In 1991, *Spin* included four Seattle-based groups in its "Top Best Albums of the Year." They included Nirvana's *Nevermind*, Pearl Jam's *Ten*, Soundgarden's *Badmotorfinger* and Mudhoney's *Every Good Boy Deserves Fudge*.

Grunge music launched Kurt Cobain into the ranks of leadership for his generation. Through mind-numbing coincidence and an untimely death, Kurt Cobain was anointed into martyrdom. It was his twisted, bitter-sweet genius that was celebrated as one of Generation X's finest literary accomplishments.

Born near the logging community of Aberdeen, Washington, on February 20, 1967, Kurt Cobain, at the age of seven, experienced the bitter divorce of Don and Wendy, his parents. Soon he was being shipped around from one relative to the next, uncertain of where he would be eating, sleeping, living. Diagnosed with Attention Deficit Disorder, Cobain, like so many others of his generation, was prescribed Ritalin. Wrapped in the guilt and shame of family dysfunction, Cobain's goal was merely to survive. He was passed from one household to the next, whoever had the room, the space, the time. For a while, Cobain was homeless, living under a bridge by the Wishkah River, an experience that was bitterly echoed in his song "Something in the Way."

He experienced classic states of emotional sickness: rejection, abandonment, and fear. Never able to accept this reality, Cobain fantasized about a happier existence. He created an imaginary friend he called "Boddah," a companion he reached out to even at the end as depicted in his poignant suicide note. Cobain had still other emotional problems to deal with. He soon withdrew from his immediate surroundings. He immersed himself in creating art and writing poetry. It became his therapy as he further isolated himself from a world that visited upon him only pain.

At the age of 14 Cobain received a guitar for his birthday. He taught himself to play left-handed. Over the next ten years he would practice his craft, with scattered help from musically inclined family members, until reaching the summit of his turbulent career. He quit school in 12th grade and later worked as a roadie for a local band. Buzz Osborne, guitarist for The Melvins, became a mentor to Cobain, who adapted his detuned, loud and crawling style. Osborne introduced Cobain to punk rock and to Iggy Pop, who quickly became Cobain's idol and one of his earliest musical heroes.

Cobain's musical style, with its bouncy melodies and poppy chord changes, paid tribute to the sounds of the Beatles, Monkees and surfer music of the 1960's.But those musical groups were far removed from his real passions. Later he gravitated to the heavier sounds of AC/DC, Led Zepplin and other, more progressive, acts. Bauhaus, originators of the Goth sound existed from 1979–1983. Although only producing four studio albums, Bauhaus' impact was felt by Cobain, who cited them as an early influence.

Despite his personal turmoil, Cobain was able to channel his creative energies into his music. The trio "Fecal Matter," Cobain's first band, was reflective of his languid persona and did not last long. On June 11,1988,his new band, Nirvana, released their first single "Love Buzz" for the independent label SubPop.

The band's first album, *Bleach*, was released one year later. Cobain's dark poetry became the creative force behind Nirvana. He played lead guitar and sang, or perhaps screamed, the lead vocals. From the personal angst and pain that Cobain presented in his musical vignettes, the term "grunge" was born. It was essentially a celebration of all things wrong; a recognition of the gloom and pessimism that tapped into the psyche of Generation X.

In 1991 *Nevermind*, their 2nd release was launched on Geffen Records. The first two tracks issued from the LP didn't make any waves, but on August 24, 1991, "Smells Like Teen Spirit" was released. It instantly became a teen anthem and skyrocketed the group to the top of the charts. "Smells Like Teen Spirit" was the musical embodiment of the dark, depressive and hopeless landscape of broken homes, an epidemic divorce rate and a bleak pessimism that encapsulated the mood of a generation. This atmosphere of pessimism created

"Grunge" music, which became the Rorschach test used to define this alienated demographic group.

Nevermind sold three million records in a searing four-month period, as Nirvana became the demigods of the grunge movement with Kurt Cobain as their High Priest. Some ten years later, VH1 listed the album as the second best rock album of all time. VH1 described "*Nevermind*" as "noise that articulated what it was like to come of age in darkest Nowheresville like no one since Chuck Berry."

Cobain embraced his fame in a muted, matter-of-fact manner, almost apologizing for his success. He stated in an interview: "My story is almost the same as 90 percent of everyone my age. Everyone's parents got divorced. Their kids smoked pot through high school, they grew up in an era when there was a massive Communist threat and everyone thought they were going to die from a nuclear war. And everyone's personalities are practically the same."

But if Kurt Cobain played the role of the movement's tortured star and martyr, then Pearl Jam's control artist Eddie Vedder became its self-proclaimed spokesperson.

Three of Pearl Jam's LP's were among the most successful of the decade. They released a number of songs that gained almost immediate airplay and were on regular rotation throughout the country, such as "Better Man," "Jeremy," "Corduroy," and "Alive." In 1993 their second album, *Vs.*, sold 950,000 copies in its first week of release and eventually sold 5.4 million copies. *Vitalogy* sold 877,000 in its first week and went on to sell beyond platinum status. In 1995, Pearl Jam played as the backing band on Neil Young's *Mirrorball* album and the subsequent tour. Even with their commercial success, Pearl Jam, under Vedder's direction, did everything they could to protest the forces of corporate America, and especially Ticketmaster. Among the innovations of Vedder and company was a high-tech version of the underground bootleg tapes, recorded, distributed and sold by the band itself.

Over the decades Pearl Jam has remained one of the leading proponents of grunge, but not without serious career setbacks. Andy

Wood died of a heroin overdose in 1990. Pearl Jam's celebrated European tour was cut short after nine fans were stomped and crushed to death in a hardcore moshing area at the June 30, 2000, Denmark Roskilde Festival.

A 1996 motion picture, *Hype*, was produced tracing the roots of the "Seattle scene" from 1993 to 1995 and the evolution, corporate exploitation and marketing of grunge music. The film featured interviews and music from, among others, The Gits, Mudhoney, Green River, The Fastbacks, SoundGarden and Pearl Jam. Film director Doug Pray, even as he was researching his documentary, concluded that grunge officially ended its ride in 1992. Pray reflected that: "We made this movie about something that was passé." He was wrong, as the vitality of this phenomenal musical genre continues, fueled by grunge's authenticity, its impact on American culture, and on those have refused to let the music die.

Seattle quickly became a safe refuge for those looking to escape a perceived artificial and corrupt society. It invited a hotbed of political activists and anarchists and a virtual think tank of new energies and ideals. In December 1999 thousands of protesters turned up to disrupt the meeting of the 135-nation World Trade Organization. The protesters, a strange alliance of union workers and environmentalists, argued that the WTO placed corporate profits above the rights and protections of individual workers and the environment. That maverick attitude was reflective of the entire region and helped to breathe life into the philosophy of grunge music.

Drawing on the incredible amount of talent and energy reflecting its Seattle epicenter, the grunge movement was a striking departure from the blatant commercialism of Los Angeles, San Francisco, and New York. Grunge was a reaction against the pandering excess of 80s mainstream rock. Claiming that they had sold out, grunge expressed disapproval towards the big hair bands and heavy metal groups of the era, such as Motley Crue, Iron Maiden, Judas Priest and Def Leppard. Grunge claimed to be different, unpretentious. The style of dress was unassuming: jeans, flannel shirts and *"Made in USA"* Converse All Star sneakers.

While Sub-Pop put the spin on grunge music, it was the Lollapalooza Festival, first launched in 1991, that broadcast the message of the new musical form, aptly named "alternative." Grunge became an integral part of the alternative movement, giving it emotional intensity, realism and validity.

Perry Farrell, lead singer for Jane's Addiction, organized the Lollapalooza Festival. Featuring alternative rock, rap, punk rock and techno music, the traveling music festival toured the United States and Canada. It also featured non-musical themes including the Shaolin Monks, an alternative freak show, tattooing and piercing parlors, television—smashing pits, virtual reality games and political information tables. Most concerts also had the infamous mosh pit with hordes of youngsters participating in a kind of tribal initiation rite. Moshing involved sweating human bodies being groped and slammed into one another, over and over, in a primitive dance embracing trust, intimacy and danger.

Lollapalooza was called a "cultural festival for the newly-formed 1990's counterculture." It helped promote obscure underground bands to reach the commercial mainstream, granting them immediate exposure to the masses. The original 1991 lineup was an eclectic mix reflecting the musical tastes of the day. It included Jane's Addiction, Siouxie and the Banshees, Living Color, Nine Inch Nails, Fishbone, Violent Femmes, Body Count (with Ice T), Butthole Surfers and the Rollins Band.

The symbolic end of Lollapalooza came in 1994 after the suicide of Kurt Cobain. His group, Nirvana, was scheduled to headline the 1994 festival. Courtney Love, Cobain's widow, appeared at several of the festivals that year to talk about the tragedy but the sense of magic and of community appeared to have been lost. Lollapalooza attempted to regroup in 2003, regrettably without the mass interest and support it had during its earlier years. Only two of thirty-one planned shows sold well. One Northeast date moved only 450 tickets due to, among other things, excessive ticket prices. The failure of Lollapalooza signaled the end of this grand alternative experiment just as Cobain's death validated the incidence of heroin as the unfortunate choice of grunge.

DREAMY ESTRANGEMENT

The painkilling properties of the beautiful purple and white poppy have long been known, but in 1803, after codeine was magically extracted from opium, the doors of drug perception, dreamy estrangement, opened ever so slightly. It was the first step of the journey.

In 1874 the Bayer Company of Switzerland developed the morphine derivative *diacetylmorphine*. Named *"Hero,"* after the Greek mythological character, heroin was intended to relieve symptoms of morphine addiction, yet not be addictive itself. The product was created, and then shelved. Heinrich Dresser, a chemist working for the Bayer Company of Germany, rediscovered heroin in 1898, some 24 years later. Initially marketed as a remedy for tuberculosis and laryngitis, the drug was also used for cough suppression and touted (once again) as a potential cure for morphine addiction.

Until the 1900's, heroin was sold via mail order in the United States. With inadequate controls, it was easy to obtain heroin and other opium derivatives. By 1903, heroin addiction reached alarming rates and was eventually banned. Heroin, now classified as a Schedule 1 substance, the most restrictive schedule mandated by the DEA, has no recognized medical use in the United States and has a high potential for abuse.

Heroin, a powerful substance, is potentially addictive and presents a real possibility of overdose. Traditionally, most drug users avoided the narcotic yet, despite the dangers, elite cultural groups experimented with it. This small cadre included writers of the 1950's Beat Generation, who adopted heroin as their drug of choice. They encompassed such personalities as *Junkie* author William Burroughs.

Charley "Yardbird" Parker's Be Bop musicians, replacing the Big Band phenomena, were another group seduced by the drug. Some 40 years later, after emerging from its dank cultural underbelly, the drug had arrived. A 1994 State Department report predicted that American heroin use had dramatically increased since 1990. It warned of a possible epidemic, arguing that it was a logical consequence of more than a decade of cocaine abuse. In the ebb and flow of substance abuse it is normal for a depressant like heroin to follow in the wake of stimulants such as cocaine.

Heroin arrived as a drug of choice around 1992 and immediately made its presence known. In 1994 the number of heroin ER visits rose to 64,000 cases while emergency department mentions increased nationwide 35 percent from 1995 to 2002. According to The Drug Abuse Warning Network (DAWN), a national public health surveillance system that monitors trends in drug-related emergency department visits and deaths, there was a staggering 25.7 percent increase in heroin fatalities in the United States from 1994 to 1998. That grim four-year span had 20,140 reported deaths associated with heroin or opiate use and by 1996 there were an estimated 600,000 heroin addicts in the United States.

Several factors have contributed to the resurgence of heroin including widespread availability and increased purity. The purity of heroin, seized by law enforcement officials, rose dramatically from 3.6 percent in 1980 to 37 percent in 2000, allowing for either snorting or smoking (chasing the dragon). There is a mistaken belief that snorting heroin is less dangerous than injection, due to the decreased risk of contracting HIV/AIDS or hepatitis C, associated with the use of shared needles.

Cost is another key factor and, at the wholesale level, heroin has a strong advantage over cocaine. Heroin is usually sold in small white packs or blue paper packets, each containing from .25 to 33 grams of heroin, enough for one to two hits. In Seattle the street price for heroin has remained stable with the principal unit of sale being a "$20 paper" of Mexican black tar.

Lastly, despite countless deaths, the rock culture continues to glamorize the use of heroin. This insane rationale emanates from an impressive list of junkie musicians who have amassed a stunning body of creativity and then gone public with their recovery. Among this cadre are Keith Richards (Rolling Stones), Steve Tyler (Aerosmith), Scott Weiland (Stone Temple Pilots), David Gahan (Depeche Mode), Dave Navarro (Jane's Addiction), Eric Clapton, Boy George, Ray Charles, John Lennon and Lou Reed.

New York street poet Lou Reed, then with the Velvet Underground, penned "Heroin," a stark 1967 paean to the substance. Reed's troubling lyrics spoke of his love affair with the dirty white drug: "Heroin, be the death of me/Heroin, it's my wife and it's my life ... And then I'm better off than dead." Reed's musical homage, almost 40 years ago, foretold the drug's gradual and systematic acceptance.

Heroin, leaving its portent of doom on white-collar, middle class America, has become fashionable. Marketed with an attitude of perverse commercialism, it is sold in small packets under trade names such as *Banshee, Black Tar, Grenade, Mike Tyson, Don King, Dr. Kevorkian, 357 Magnum, Self Destruction, Too Strong, X hell* and the like. *Red Rum* was the street brand that killed Jonathan Melvoin, the keyboardist and touring member of the Smashing Pumpkins. Melvoin's death on July 11, 1996, was attributed to a potent mixture of alcohol and heroin.

JUNKIE TOWN

Grunge wasn't the only game in town. More sinister forces were stalking the Pacific Northwest. The region was a thriving marketplace for heroin, and Grunge eagerly embraced this fashionable opiate. Like Seattle's Jimi Hendrix, who experimented with heroin but died in 1970 of suffocation due to " barbiturate intoxication," grunge rockers were caught up in dope's fascination.

For almost half a decade, smacked-out and trendy Seattle had a monkey on its back. Seattle and King County saw a sharp rise in opiate-related deaths from 1995-96. This upward trend spiked in 1998 with a body count of 143. Lon Friend, Editor of *RIP Magazine*, observed that the city had more heroin users per capita than any other city in the United States while *Rolling Stone Magazine*, in the late 1990's, dubbed it "junkie town". (That may not be true given the epidemic proportions of heroin use in places like Newark and Baltimore, however Seattle embraced heroin with near-religious fanaticism, placing an impressive body of musical work at the steps of the altar, as well as, sacrificing several high-profile grunge musicians.)

Of the 35 ADAM (Arrestee Drug Abuse Monitoring) sites across the country, Seattle ranked in the top six, along with New York City, Philadelphia, Chicago, and Portland, Oregon, for rates of opiate positives. In Seattle, longitudinal studies of injection heroin users show that the proportion under age 20 increased from 78 percent in 1994 to 100 percent in 1997. Community Epidemiology Work Group (CEWG) representatives reported increases in young heroin abusers, including members from Baltimore, Chicago, Denver, Detroit, Newark, and Seattle.

The number of heroin-related deaths investigated by the Medical Examiner, beginning with Kurt Cobain's 1994 suicide, triggered a public outrage. That year [1994] the number of heroin-related deaths was 89, increasing to 135 in 1996. From 1990 to 1999, opiate overdose deaths increased in King County by 134 percent, according to a July report from the Centers for Disease Control and Prevention. In 2000, 45.2 percent of all King County drug-related deaths involved heroin. Of the 99 heroin-related decedents, 81 (81.8 percent) had one or more drugs in addition to heroin in their systems at the time of death, demonstrating the danger of combining heroin with another depressant drug. In the case of Kurt Cobain there was a combination of morphine (heroin) and valium in his bloodstream while Layne Staley's autopsy revealed both morphine and cocaine.

Compared to all of the generations that have preceded them, it is arguable that Generation X has suffered the largest amount of casualties from heroin. More members of this demographic group, driven by pain and ignorance, have died from the effects of the dirty powered substance. Count among them Andrew Wood (Mother Love Bone), Kurt Cobain (Nirvana), Jonathan Melvoin (Smashing Pumpkins), Stephanie Sargeant (7 Year Bitch), Bradley Nowell (Sublime), Shannon Hoon (Blind Melon), Kristen Pfaff (Hole) and Layne Staley (Alice In Chains).

As titillating subject matter, heroin had an immediate impact on Generation X music. Two examples are "Jane Says" and "Junkhead," two dissimilar approaches to the heroin theme. "Jane Says," the song by Janes' Addiction [1988 *CD Nothing's Shocking*], is a two-chord chant, compelling in its simplistic, monotonous vocal assault. The anti-drug message in "Jane Says" is one of delusion and desperation as Jane, caught in the web of addiction, articulates the impossible dream of escaping her narcotic prison. "Jane says/She's going away to Spain/ When I get my money saved/She's gonna start tomorrow/I'm gonna kick tomorrow/Gonna kick tomorrow," she promises.

Jane's Addiction was an American rock band, named after heroin addict Jane Bainter, who was a housemate of the band. Often cited as L.A.'s version of grunge (or pre-grunge), the band formed in the late 1980s, and watched *Nothing's Shocking* spend 35 weeks on the charts, before breaking up in the 1990's.

Perry Farrell, lead singer and co-writer of the song, acknowledges that there was an actual Jane and an abusive boyfriend named Sergio: "Around 1984, I rented a big house on Wilton, near Hancock Park, right in the heart of everything good in Hollywood, but the whole neighborhood seemed deteriorated ... one of my housemates was Jane, this strangely beautiful, well-to-do girl who got caught up in the drug scene and fell in love with a dealer named Sergio. Jane was an intellectual and knew how to act aristocratic, even with a needle and a spoon on the table. I'm not sure if the song mythologized the neighborhood—St. Andrew's Place is nothing special to look at—but I do think it glamorized her life in a way ..." Eventually Jane Bainter's dream became reality. She later spent time in Spain after kicking her heroin habit and embracing her stature as one of L.A.'s "glamorized" rock icons.

"Junkhead" was dramatically different as Layne Staley, tortured lead singer of the grunge band Alice In Chains deceived himself into believing that his addictive lifestyle was superior to the "hypocrite norm" and that by contrast their life was "empty and bare." Staley boasted of his heroin use, mocking those who did not saying: "What's my drug of choice?/Well, what have you got?/I don't go broke and I do it a lot."

"Junkhead" appeared on the angry 1992 CD *Dirt*, which manifested the despondency of Generation X and the essence of grunge. The CD visited dark themes of addiction with offerings such as "Junkhead," "Godsmack" and "Angry Chair." Jerry Cantrell defended the CD, stating: "Taken as a whole, it's a really positive thing, but a lot of people will probably take it out of context." Taken as a whole, the CD provided a detailed blueprint of Staley's journey into drug use. *Spin Magazine* went even further when, in 1995, one of its writers observed: "Alice In Chains videos are elegant little travelogues of junkie life. Heroin addicts and struggling former addicts hear something in Layne's grade-school junkie poetry, a kind of siren." [Note: Layne Staley penned "Angry Chair" by himself, but co-wrote "Godsmack" and "Junkhead" with guitarist Jerry Cantrell. In all of the tunes, the heroin philosophy of misery and hopelessness is apparent.]

It is believed that Layne Staley began using heroin in the 1990's, soon descending into a noticeable physical dependency. Mudhoney's Mark Arm observed: "I remember seeing him in '95 ... he turned up and was totally green, and my stomach turned at that point—watching somebody on a track that they couldn't get off." In October 1996, Staley's former girlfriend, Demri Lara Parrott, died of bacterial endocarditis, a secondary complication of drug injection. *Dirt* producer Dave Jerden recalled that around that time Staley "weighed eighty pounds ... and was white as a ghost." His glamorous rock lifestyle was turning into a nightmare. Staley admitted during a 1996 *Rolling Stone* cover story: "If I'm staying busy, and if I'm getting my job done, and I'm doing things I think are great, then I don't have a problem with anything. I wrote about drugs and I didn't think I was being unsafe or careless by writing about them. Here's how my thinking pattern went: When I tried drugs, they were—great and they worked for me for years, and now they're turning against me—and now I'm walking through hell, and this sucks."

That hell became a self-imposed exile, a period of lost years roughly from 1999 to 2002, when he became even more depressed, reclusive and addicted.

In 2002, several months before his death, Staley was interviewed by Argentinean writer Adriana Rubio, and admitted that his existence was a personal hell. "I'm not using drugs to get high like many people think. I know I made a big mistake when I started using this shit. It's a very difficult thing to explain. My liver is not functioning and I'm throwing up all the time and shitting my pants. The pain is more than you can handle. It's the worst pain in the world. Dope sick hurts the entire body."

By slowing his breathing and stopping his heart, Layne Staley found a way to take away the pain. His tired body collapsed out of that angry chair. Slumped-over, he died alone, away from the bright lights and screaming fans who idolized him, finally embracing "serenity [so] far away."

As reported by the *Seattle Weekly's* Rick Anderson, Staley's 34-year-old lifeless body was surrounded by the drug paraphernalia of his addiction: "When police kicked in the door to Layne Staley's University District apartment on April 19, [2002], there, on a couch, lit by a flickering TV, next to several spray-paint cans on the floor, not far from a stash of cocaine, near two crack pipes on the coffee table, reposed the remains of the rock musician."

He died tragically, like Kurt Cobain, of a suspected suicide overdose, and ironically both died on April 5th.

Staley's body was not discovered until two weeks later. The autopsy report concluded that Staley died of an overdose of heroin and cocaine, the legendary "speedball" that has remorselessly snuffed out the lives of so many others.

After Staley's death, the remaining members of Alice In Chains issued a statement: "On April 19, 2002, our friend Layne Staley was found dead in his home. The official cause of death is still unknown. Yesterday, we all managed to come together in Seattle; it's good to be with friends and family as we struggle to deal with this immense loss … and try to celebrate this immense life. We are looking for all the usual things: comfort, purpose, answers, something to hold on to, a way to let him go in peace. Mostly, we are feeling heartbroken over the death of our beautiful friend. He was a sweet man with a keen sense of humor and a deep sense of humanity. He was an amazing musician and an inspiration and comfort to so many. He made great music and gifted it to the world. We are proud to have known him, to be his friend, and to create music with him. Layne struggled greatly for the past decade. We can only hope that he has at last found some peace. We love you, Layne. Dearly. And we will miss you … endlessly."

TORTURED ARTIST

Cobain was never ready for success. He remained isolated, aloof, a loner. He was the man who remained the child, described as having "tortured eyes, riveting yet fascinating." But Cobain was tortured in many other ways. According to reports he had been diagnosed with attention deficit disorder and hyper activity and medicated, like so many others of his generation, with the drug Ritalin. His ongoing stomach pain, a condition his doctors were unable to diagnose, often left him collapsed on the floor in a fetal position. Heroin, he would discover, was the only drug that had the ability to take away his horrible anguish. Cobain later explained his fascination for the drug. "I wanted to try heroin because I knew that I liked opiates." Since he enjoyed the numbing effects of the painkiller percodan, he felt that he would also like heroin. Cobain rationalized that heroin would be difficult to find in small town Aberdeen, and he would have little chance to become addicted. Cobain, at the age of 20, resorted to stealing drugs from pharmacies around Olympia, Washington, where he worked as a janitor. During an MTV interview Cobain discussed his medical problems. He said, "The pain in my stomach made me feel like a junky so if I was going to feel like a junky I might as well become one."

With his life spinning out of control and into a vortex of confusion, Cobain married singer Courtney Love of the group Hole. The marriage took place on February 24, 1992. Their only child, Frances Bean Cobain, was born on August 18, 1992, but after the Los Angeles Children's Services agency was alerted to Love's heroin use they forced the Cobains to give up their child. For a short time the child was placed into custody with Courtney's half sister, in an attempt to protect Frances from the negative influence of her drug-addicted parents. With their personal image severely damaged, the Cobains had to submit to drug testing and further public humiliation before being allowed to visit with Frances under strict supervision. After a difficult legal battle and $240,000 in legal fees they ultimately retained custody rights of their child.

Cobain had a difficult time accepting his fame and found himself unable to deal with the challenges and realities of his heroin-addicted existence. He pulled out of the high-profile Lollapalooza Tour, a tribute to alternative music, which, in retrospect, was a damaging career move for the group.

Things began to spiral downward for the troubled Cobain. On March 27, 1994, during a tour in Italy, Cobain, prone to suicide attempts, overdosed on 60 sedatives washed down with champagne. He was rushed to a hospital in Rome, where he almost died. Days later and back in the United States, Cobain entered the Exodus Recovery Center in Marina Del Ray, CA. It was March 30, 1994, and what was to be Cobain's final attempt at getting clean. He left the rehab unit against medical advice after only 48 hours and was reported missing on April 1, 1994.

DEATH BY SUICIDE

Two days later Courtney Love, who was in Los Angeles at the time, hired Seattle private detective Tom Grant to find the missing rock star. Grant was a California state licensed private investigator and former detective with the Los Angles County Sheriff's Department.

Grant and Cobain's best friend, Dylan Carlson, began to search for the missing rock star, but were unsuccessful in their attempts. On April 8, 1994, Kurt Donald Cobain was found dead, of an apparent suicide. A 12-gauge shotgun was found near his body, a mixture of valium and heroin, a popular combination among heroin addicts, in his bloodstream. Next to the body was a wooden box containing several burnt spoons, pieces of tar and needles. On a side table was Cobain's suicide note.

His body was discovered in the Green House, a loft structure built above Cobain's garage. Gary Smith, a local electrician, discovered the lifeless body. Cobain had been dead in the million-dollar home for several days and possibly died (according to forensic experts) on April 5, 1994.

CNN World News announced the death on April 9, 1994. "The music world stood still today, in disbelief, as news of the horrific death of rock star Kurt Cobain echoed around the world. The 27 year-old front man of the band Nirvana was discovered dead yesterday at his luxurious Seattle residence, after a self-inflicted gun wound to the head. Cobain's wife Courtney Love, who is currently in Paris, is said to be devastated at the news of her husband's death."

Cobain, continuously immersing himself in the warmth of addictive opiates, decided that he no longer wanted to live in a world that embraced reality. He chose, consciously, rationally and through the eyes of an addict, the inner realm of pain-free twilight sleep, a secret world where he only communicated with those make believe childlike

Buddhas. As Cobain reflected in his suicide note, "I'm too sensitive. I need to be slightly numb in order to regain the enthusiasm I once had as a child." The autopsy results indicated a significant level, 1.52 mg/ml of morphine, the chemical byproduct of heroin. Unconsciousness would have been induced in mere seconds after injection of the drug and, for Kurt Cobain; his pain would have been replaced, mercifully, with the soft blanket of eternal sleep.

A controversy ensued. Some questioned if Cobain had committed suicide or was murdered. Detective Tom Grant suspected foul play, arguing that Cobain "was worth more dead than alive." Medical Examiner Dr. Nikolas Hartshorne, one of the first to arrive at the scene, called it "a classic case of suicide" noting the "contact shotgun wound to the mouth."

Due to the high amount of heroin in Cobain's system, some theorized that it would have been impossible for Cobain to inject himself with the drug and then lift, point and accurately discharge the shotgun. Still other authorities on substance abuse argued that a person using heroin could develop "a significant individual tolerance over a period of time" that would have allowed for the actual act of suicide.

Investigator Tom Grant concluded that there was a conspiracy of sorts. He said, "Conspiracy theories often include outrageous claims requiring the involvement of large numbers of persons in order to plan and carry out the crime. There has been a cover-up in this case, primarily due to sloppy police work; however, I've never considered the event of Cobain's actual murder to be the result of a "vast" conspiracy. It did not involve a large number of persons. It did not involve the Seattle Police Department or other governmental officials." Grant later concluded that Cobain's death landed at the feet of Courtney Love and Frances Bean Cobain's nanny, whom Grant blamed for covering up the evidence that Grant felt pointed to their involvement.

On Sunday, April 10, 1994, Seattle radio stations KNDD, KISW and KNDD held a public memorial service. Courtney Love read her husband's suicide note to the mourners.

It read: "*To Boddah:*

Speaking from the tongue of an experienced simpleton who obviously would rather be an emasculated, infantile complain-ee. This note should be pretty easy to understand.

All the warnings from the punk rock 101 courses over the years, since my first introduction to the, shall we say, ethics involved with independence and the embracement of your community had proven to be very true. I haven't felt the excitement of listening to as well as creating music along with reading and writing for too many years now. I feel guilty beyond words about these things.

For example, when we're backstage and the lights go out and the manic roar of the crowds begin, it doesn't affect me the way in which it did for Freddie Mercury, who seemed to love, relish in the love and adoration from the crowd which is something I totally admire and envy. The fact is, I can't fool you, any one of you. It simply isn't fair to you or me. The worst crime I can think of would be to rip people off by faking it and pretending as if I'm having 100% fun.

Sometimes I feel as if I should have a punch-in time clock before I walk out on stage. I've tried everything within my power to appreciate it (and I do, God, believe me I do, but it's not enough). I appreciate the fact that I and we have affected and entertained a lot of people. I must be one of those narcissists who only appreciate things when they're gone. I'm too sensitive. I need to be slightly numb in order to regain the enthusiasms I once had as a child.

On our last three tours, I've had a much better appreciation for all the people I've known personally, and as fans of our music, but I still can't get over the frustration, the guilt and empathy I have for everyone. There's good in all of us and I think I simply love people too much, so much that it makes me feel too sad. The sad little, sensitive, unappreciative, Pisces,

Jesus man. Why don't you just enjoy it? I don't know!

I have a goddess of a wife who sweats ambition and empathy and a daughter who reminds me too much of what I used to be, full of love and joy, kissing every person she meets because everyone is good and will do her no harm. And that terrifies me to the point to where I can barely function. I can't stand the thought of Frances becoming the miserable, self-destructive, death rocker that I've become.

I have it good, very good, and I'm grateful, but since the age of seven, I've become hateful towards all humans in general. Only because it seems so easy for people to get along that have empathy. Only because I love and feel sorry for people too much, I guess.

Thank you all from the pit of my burning, nauseous stomach for your letters and concern during the past years. I'm too much of an erratic, moody baby! I don't have the passion anymore, and so remember, it's better to burn out than to fade away.

Peace, love, empathy,

Kurt Cobain

Frances and Courtney, I'll be at your altar. Please keep going Courtney, for Frances. For her life, which will be so much happier without me. I love you, I love you!

Curt Cobain, a high profile victim of heroin's sinister allure, was dead at the age of 27. Cobain, who combined poppy Beatlesque melodies and heavy power chords with a painful vocal delivery, screamed out for relief in a public display of contrition. Cobain's inability to accept his musical stardom and to resolve his heroin addiction had become a public issue. Cobain was quoted as saying that his use of heroin was "more for the pain, than for the fame," a reference to the stomach pains that plagued his career and the pain of withdrawal from heroin's short-lived euphoria.

"Kurt quit several times, only to start up again," according to writer Melissa Rossi. "That's the nature of heroin. Three is supposed to be the lucky number—the third time a junkie quits, legend has it, is the attempt most likely to be successful. But if it's not, if users don't quit within two years of starting, they typically stay addicted for twenty years, or so goes the junkie lore." That long-term addiction eventually led to Cobain's end game: a suicide note, a significant heroin injection and a shotgun blast to his head.

Could he have been saved? Was there anyone in his inner circle of friends and supporters capable of rescuing him from his addiction? Ron Stone, a member of Cobain's management team at Gold Mountain explained: "We constantly tried to get him help. The truth is, when he sobered up, when he made a serious attempt to get his life in order, he took a real good look at his life and he killed himself." Two years after the tragedy, Alice In Chain's lead singer Layne Staley reflected on Cobain's death: "I saw all the suffering that Kurt Cobain went through. I didn't know him real well, but I just saw this real vibrant person turn into a real shy, timid, withdrawn person who could hardly get a 'hello' out…. At the end of the day or at the end of the party, when everyone goes home, you're stuck with yourself."

But Darryl Morden, veteran music critic and radio writer-producer disagreed with that widely held premise of Cobain's legacy of suffering. He said, "Just as not every baby boomer was a hippie as a teen or in college (far from it), every Gen Xer did not exist in a world of despondent darkness. And the positioning of Cobain as a "hero" of any kind is soooo wrong-headed. Heroic? How? Popping pills? Sticking a needle in his vein? Pulling a trigger to take his life?" Mordan pondered, "we rarely toast those who are stable, have normal family lives and such, do we? Heroes should be those who strive to rise above and bring out the best in us. Despite his undeniable growing craft before his death, Cobain was no hero, however probing many of his songs." There were others who shared in that observation. Buzz Osbourne, lead guitarist of the San Francisco-based The Melvins, was Cobain's guitar mentor. After Cobain's death Osbourne was quoted as saying, "I don't have a whole lot of sympathy for rock bands that use heroin and blame it on boredom, loneliness, whatever. There are a lot of spoiled rock star brats out there using heroin."

In the aftermath, Cobain's death brought out scores of emotional responses from the close-knit grunge community. Some viewed him as a suffering artist unwillingly cast into the commercial limelight as generational spokesperson and then unfairly compared to artists such as Dylan, Kerouac and Hemingway. Cobain became a martyr to some and was equally exploited by others. The public outcry over his death emanated from some curious quarters with the most controversial being voiced by the Church of Scientology. In an article titled "Kurt Cobain Killed by psychiatry," the Citizens Commission on Human Rights Investigating and Exposing Psychiatric Human Rights Abuse, a Scientology organization, continued their unending assault against the mental health and medical community by blaming them for Cobain's death. On their CCHRIEPHRA website they described the singer's psychiatric profile as the following. "A talented and creative child, Cobain was misdiagnosed as 'hyperactive' and prescribed the cocaine-like and highly addictive Ritalin. Side effects include insomnia, nausea, abdominal pain, hallucinations and a predisposition to later cocaine use. Sedatives were prescribed to counter the insomnia. The progression to street drugs, including heroin, was a given. Compounding the Ritalin were untreated chronic medical conditions that affected him his entire life, including a 'burning, nauseous' stomach, which Cobain said heroin 'quenched.' He enrolled in a Los Angeles psychiatric drug recovery center. Thirty-six hours after admission, he bolted and ended his life with a single shotgun blast to his head. Heroin and valium were found in his blood stream."

Nirvana's final concert was in Munich, Germany. In 1994 Nirvana disbanded with their individual members branching out into other bands including Probot, Sweet 75, Eyes Adrift, the No WTO

Combo and the commercially successful Foo Fighters. A live posthumous album, *From the Muddy Banks of the Wishkah River*, a tribute to their fellow mate Cobain, was released in 1996.

4

The Culture of Goth

o o o o o o o o o o o o o o o o o o o o o o o o

"Blood of my blood ... drink and join me in eternal life."

—*Dracula*

The Goth Culture, equally fascinating, equally obscure, has been difficult, perhaps impossible, to define. Having been called New Age Zombies and "spookie kids," they reject traditional cults, gangs, and religion and espouse no single philosophy or ideology. Their quest is a personal mission to establish their uniqueness in today's society. Goth is simply Maslow's Hierarchy of Needs set into motion. After food and shelter humans seek group affiliation: a place of commonality, acceptance, and love. Defining that place is what the concept of Goth Nation connotes. Gordon A. Crews, who investigates occult themes at the School of Justice Studies at Roger Williams University in Bristol, CT, said: "It is up to the individual to define what Goth is for themselves ... The mentality is, 'I want to be left alone but I want to be seen. I want to see the shock on other peoples' faces."

Goth had its modern-day roots in the punk music that emerged in England in the 1970's. The punk movement, hard and political, was usurped and transformed into a Gothic celebration of music, attitude and fashion. This curious group embraced the dark side of life and the beauty of *Thanatos*, the Greek concept of death. According to researchers McNally and Florescu, "Belief in vampires is a poetic, imaginative way of looking at death and at life beyond death." Followers of the movement gravitated to dark and morbid themes in literature, music and fashion, some believing that Goth was a means of empowerment—a way to conquer primordial fears by embracing darkness.

Who are the travelers that have chosen to accept this strangeness? Why have they disconnected from the mainstream and an existence in a vortex of speed, stimuli overkill and long hours of nonpersonal interaction to withdraw into the Goth heart of darkness? The answers can be found in today's alien landscape, a brave new world of cyberspace and advanced technology. In this mad scenario of science fiction-turned-reality, the monster has been created and unleashed; the monster seeking refuge behind peaceful castle walls—the monster that is us.

If any one individual defined Goth culture, it was Hungarian stage-actor Bela Lugosi. At the age of 12, Bela ran away from home, motivated by the performances of a touring repertory troupe. For a time he was exploited, surviving the terrors of child labor in regional coalmines and railroad yards. He later reflected on this grim chapter of his life: "There, in the dark bowels of the earth, I did sometimes think I might go mad ... there we were sub-human men, there I learned my horror, now of the darkness ..." Those terrifying experiences helped shape his eventual craft. After arriving in New York City in 1920, he secured the title role in the 1931 film adaptation of Bram Stoker's *Dracula*. [Lugosi had previously played the role of Dracula on Broadway]. His cinematic offerings include *White Zombie* (1932), *The Black Cat* (1934), *The Raven* (1935), *The Invisible Ray* (1936), *Son of Frankenstein* (1939), *The Wolfman* (1941) and *The Black Sleep* (1956). Lugosi, a strange creation of a bygone era, brought with him an air of European elegance and chivalry that spoke of a class structure unfamiliar to most American moviegoers. With dramatic theatrical elegance Lugosi created the standard for movie vampires, combining romanticism with implied sexuality. Portraying monsters, villains and mad scientists, he personified the pain and suffering of the tragic Goth sensibility.

In 1955, Lugosi, then 73 and addicted to morphine, committed himself to the State Hospital in Norwalk, California. Over a 20-year period he had become dependent on morphine, prescribed for severe back pain and shooting pains in his legs. He later became addicted to methadone, which he administered as a cure for his first addiction. On the set he would often drink burgundy to mask his opiate abuse. According to *Answers.com* Lugosi's addiction developed over time: "Ostensibly due to injuries received during military service, Lugosi developed severe, chronic sciatica. Though at first he was treated with natural pain remedies such as asparagus juice, doctors increased the medication to opiates. The growth of his dependence on pain-killers was directly proportional to the dwindling of screen offers. He did get to recreate the role of Dracula one last time in the film *Bud Abbott and Lou Costello Meet Frankenstein* in 1948."

The actor was re-discovered by Ed Wood, an obsessed fan and amateur filmmaker later known as the "worst director in Hollywood." Wood offered Lugosi, then, according to some, living in near poverty, roles in *Glen and Glenda* (1953) and *Bride of the Monster* (1955). It is believed that Lugosi's drug treatment expenses were to be paid by proceeds from the El Capitan Theater premier of *Bride of the Monster.*

Lugosi's was a life of anguish. He sadly endured poor career choices, two bankruptcies and five failed marriages, spending the remainder of his life as a recluse: "I guess I'm pretty much of a lone wolf. I don't say I don't like people at all but, to tell you the truth I only like it then if I have a chance to look deep into their hearts and their minds" His end was as tragic as the monsters he portrayed. Although Lugosi and fellow horror actor Boris Karloff had no off-set relationship, Lugosi allegedly uttered some morphine-induced delusions that Karloff was a *boogieman* out to get him. An almost-forgotten and penniless Bela Lugosi, working in low-budget films, died of a morphine-induced heart attack in 1956. Ed Wood's script for *Final*

Curtain was curled on his lap. As requested by his son and his fifth wife, Lugosi was buried in his tuxedo, medallion and black Dracula cloak, lined in red satin. He was interred in the Holy Cross Cemetery in Culver City, California, the funeral expenses silently paid by Frank Sinatra. At the time of his death, he had only $2,900 remaining, even though he had netted more than $600,000 in all of his horror roles throughout his career.

Bela Lugosi wove an integral part of the rich Gothic tapestry. After his death, *Plan 9 From Outer Space* (1959) was released, featuring two silent minutes of Lugosi in Dracula attire. The heavy metal band White Zombie was named after the Lugosi black and white classic of the same name. Almost 40 years after his death, Martin Landau portrayed him in *Ed Wood* (1994), winning the Best Supporting Actor Oscar and rekindling interest in Lugosi's career. The English band Bauhaus recorded "Bela Lugosi's Dead," the first recognized example of the obscure Goth-rock genre. There was also a grassroots proposal appealing to the Congress of the United States "to establish now and for all time that October 20th, the birth date of Bela Lugosi, be recognized as National Gothic Horror Day." Like the undead creatures he so brilliantly played, the memory of Count Bela Lugosi, the authentic ambassador of Goth, will be remembered for all eternity.

THE GOTH NATION

The followers of Goth comprise several distinct subsets. They are the Goth Dressers, Role Players, Life Stylers and Mansonites. Wearing black clothing, weighty crosses and other symbols of a medieval past, they embrace tomes such as Anne *Rice's Vampire Chronicles* and mimic a time believed to be more sympathetic to their needs. These individuals may sleep in coffins, frequent cemeteries and shun the daylight. Superficially, Goth is a fashion statement reflecting depression and alienation. In a contrived caste system, Goth also projects an affected snobbery, that role-playing attitude of the nobleman much like the stately theatrical condescension of Bela Lugosi's Count Dracula. It is a way to identify with a time period promising to be more secure than the cold, soulless society of the New Millennium. Goth is a revolt against the slick fashions of the 1970's disco era and a protest against the colorful pastels and extravagance of the 1980's. Black hair, dark clothing and pale complexions provide the basic look of the Goth Dresser. One can paradoxically argue that the Goth look is one of deliberate overstatement as just a casual look at the heavy emphasis on dark flowing capes, ruffled cuffs, pale makeup and dyed hair demonstrate a modern-day version of late Victorian excess. Christian crosses, crucifixes and ancient Egyptian Ankh symbols are frequently part of the quasi-religious fashion.

Role players, also known as pseudo-Goths or vampire Goths, gravitated to fantasy games such as *Dungeons and Dragons* and the White Wolf Games, adapting to this virtual world for recreation and socialization. According to Religioustolerance.org: "Some Goths enjoy playing role playing games. However, RPG's are not an integral component of Goth culture. It is just that those intellectual and creative challenges that draw them to the Goth scene make them more likely to enjoy RPGs as well." Role players imitated the character of the vampire, adapting names, costumes and scenarios as provided by fantasy scenarios. Although many of the role-playing-games explored violent themes, followers have typically demonstrated an aversion towards violence. Dr David Waldron of the University of Ballarat, in Victoria, Australia, wrote: "Essentially, games like *Vampire: The Masquerade, Werewolf: The Apocalypse* and other pseudo-Gothic games are a vehicle for expressing the alienation of youth. They feature characters that are outcasts from society who must preserve their secrecy and fight against mainstream society for survival."

The Life Stylers, the more extreme subset of the genre, mimicked the *vampyre* in more excessive and complicated ways as many demonstrated a fascination for elements of black magic and satanic rites. Some had their teeth filed down, or had false teeth implanted to emulate *vampyre* fangs. Certain members of this subset had an obsession with self-mutilation, ritualistic bloodletting and blood drinking.

Within the Gothic context, blood rites fell into a finite group of categories: erotic experience, such as sexual foreplay; curiosity and experimentation; vampiric imitation, and the extremes of schizophrenics, religious cultists and fanatics. A prime example of the latter was the unfortunate case of a 17-year-old London teenager who, on November 24, 2002, killed his neighbor in a ritualistic human sacrifice and then drank her blood. Mabel Leyshon, a 90-year-old widow, was stabbed 22 times in her Llanfair home in north Wales. Her chest had been ripped open and her heart removed. Blood was drained from her legs. Prosecutors stated that the boy, obsessed with vampires, was consumed with two questions: "How do I become a vampire and how do I become immortal?"

The final group, the Mansonites or *spooky kids*, were followers of Marilyn Manson and Trent Reznor's Nine Inch Nails, (also called *ninnys*). Mansonites had been attacked from several fronts. The Crime Prevention Resource Center, an association of the Ft. Worth, Texas Chamber of Commerce's *"Code Blue Crime Prevention Project"* recommended that followers of Goth should be investigated by inspecting school lockers, tracking library books and conducting surveillance on anyone dressing in Gothic fashion or following Manson's band. Goth followers were accused of terrorism, Satanism and bloodletting on the radical Christian website www.godhatesgoths.com.

THE BLUE SPRINGS EXPERIMENT

Just how real were the dangers posed by Goth ideology and was there a valid threat to society by those delving into areas deemed "forbidden" by the mainstream culture? The leaders of Blue Springs, Missouri, a small Midwestern community of 48,000, felt endangered by perceived rampant drug abuse and self-mutilation. These, they contended, were examples of maladaptive behaviors fostered by the dangerous Goth culture: young people wearing dark clothing, defying authority and congregating around town in small threatening groups.

Responding to the threat, Congress, in 2002, earmarked $273,000 for Blue Springs, Missouri. The specific purpose of the government funding was "to combat Goth culture." U.S. Representative Sam Graves was instrumental in securing the funds for the Police Department's Youth Outreach Unit (Y.O.U.). A spokesman for Graves explained that, "It was really a community need, and they really weren't able to get the money at the local level." The monies were slated for educational training to combat the negative influence of the Goth culture. Over $118,000 of federal monies were intended for psychological interventions that would address the abnormal behaviors. These innovative approaches included assessment, case management and therapy. Plans for a number of town meetings to invite input from the community were developed. It was to be a grass-roots solution to a widespread, and perhaps dangerous, social problem.

Eric Johnson, Assistant City Administrator, anticipated a heated debate over the contentious matter and later explained that the quarter of a million dollar federal funding was not intended for peace-loving, non-criminal Goths. But it did not take long for the common sense citizens to realize that the hysteria was not the result of criminal activity, but rather the result of fear, prejudice and media overreaction. Somehow the citizens of Blue Springs allowed a negative Goth stereotype to cloud their judgment. They attacked and scapegoated a unique American group that, after all, was constitutionally entitled to demonstrate their freedom of expression and personal tastes in our precious melting pot.

In the end there was an obvious lack of interest in the YOU project as there was also the absence of a real Goth problem. Halfway through the project the goals changed, and, instead of attempting to define, address and combat Goth culture, the organization decided to investigate "counter cultures and negative influences facing children." The community of Blue Springs, Missouri returned $132,000 of the grant monies allocated to combat the Goth problem. Citizens Against Government Waste, a watchdog group exposing government pork barrel projects, revealed the Blue Springs YOU grant in its infamous

"*Pig Book.*" The Blue Springs Experiment was another unfortunate example of politically motivated individuals looking in the wrong place and at the wrong people. They should have been looking at related cultural trends such as heroin chic, the pro anorexia movement and self inflicted violence for concrete issues screaming out for solutions. To that end, the Blue Springs Experiment failed pathetically.

FANTASY GAMES

There were two incidents that helped propel Goth into the near fringes of the mainstream. One was a popular role-playing game, nipping at the heels of the *Dungeons and Dragons Fantasy Adventure Game*, while the other was a television series that refused to die a proper death.

In 1991 White Wolf Games, developed by Justin Achilli, created *"Vampire: The Masquerade."* Like *Dungeons and Dragons*, it was a role-playing game of dressing up and acting out unique characters of the genre. The predictable outcry from the religious right, inspired in part by internet renderings such as "the Lasombra's Path of Night," is based on the idea that "vampires are monsters in God's order..." *Vampire* helped give the game an element of controversy, immediately opposed by ultra-conservative Christian groups. Dr. Gary North, author of *None Dare Call It Witchcraft* and editor of the *Remnant Review,* stated: "Without any doubt in my own mind, after years of study of the history of occultism, after having researched historical research, I can say with confidence: These games are the most effective, most magnificently packaged, most profitably marked, most thoroughly researched introduction to the occult in man's recorded history, period. This is NO game."

According to White Wolf's immense website: "This new edition of *Vampire: The Masquerade* is an updated, revised version of the popular classic ... The book also contains an update on the back story of Vampires World of Darkness, as well as all thirteen clans and their

Disciplines, details on the sects, Kindred history, notes on 'the others', antagonists and all manner of other goodies …" And, in another notation, the website intones in poetic fashion: "The Midnight Dance Continues. They stalk in the shadows, moving gracefully and unseen among their prey. They are the blood-drinking fiends of whispered legends—Kindred, Cainites, and the Damned. Above all, they are vampires. Their eternal struggle, waged since the nights of Jericho and Babylon, plays itself out among the skyscrapers and nightclubs of the modern world. But the vampires' grand Masquerade is imperiled, and the night of Gehena draws ever closer. Until The End of All Things."

The Dungeons & Dragons Fantasy Adventure Game, which preceded the White Wolf Company, was created by E. Gary Gygax in 1974 as the first ever role-playing game. Dungeons and Dragons, according to its official website: "is an imaginative, social experience that engages players in a rich fantasy world filled with larger-than-life heroes, deadly monsters, and diverse settings. As a hobby game, D&D is an ongoing activity to which players might devote hours of their time—much like a weekly poker game—getting together with friends on a regular basis for weeks, months, or even years." But not everyone shared that view of the role-playing game and Dungeons and Dragons became the focal point of much dispute. In his thesis *Satanism: The World of the Occult,* by Russ Wise (1994), the writer warned against influences promoting occultism: "We have been discussing the problems of satanic involvement. Whether we become deceived by use of the Ouija Board, music, divination or by Dungeons and Dragons, the end result is the same occult bondage."

There were troubling signs that something terrible was about to happen. Irving "Bink" Pulling, a disturbed follower of Adolf Hitler, was depressed at his Richmond, Virginia school, had trouble fitting in, and had displayed "Lycanthropic tendencies" according to his mother. Several weeks prior to his death, a house cat and nineteen pet rabbits were found gutted and disemboweled. After returning home from school on June 9th, 1982, a troubled "Bink" Pulling committed suicide with his mother's revolver. He left no suicide note but had scrawled, "Life is a joke" on his school blackboard as his final statement.

His mother, Patricia Pulling, quickly blamed the suicide on a Dungeons and Dragons session that occurred when Bink's character allegedly received a curse from his teacher. Although her lawsuit was eventually tossed out, Pulling did file suit against the school district and principal Robert A. Bracey, Ill. TSR, Inc., publishers of Dungeons and Dragons, was also listed in the lawsuit. In the aftermath, Pulling, founded Bothered About Dungeons & Dragons (BADD), creating a "Trophy List" of RPG (Role Playing Game) players who, like her son, had committed suicide. For a short time she toured the country as an anti-occult campaigner speaking against the suicidal, homicidal and satanic influences of RPG's. Describing the evils of Dungeons and Dragons, Pulling called the game "a fantasy role-playing game which uses demonology, witchcraft, voodoo, murder, rape, blasphemy, suicide, assassination, insanity, sexual perversion, homosexuality, prostitution, satanic type rituals, gambling, barbarism, cannibalism, sadism, desecration, demon summoning, necromantics, divination and other teachings." She wrote *Interviewing Techniques For Adolescents*, an elementary textbook for law enforcement officers dealing with crimes associated with role-playing games and in 1989 published *The Devil's Web: Who Is Stalking Your Children For Satan?* She petitioned the Consumer Product Safety Commission to place warning labels on role-playing games claiming that the game had caused a number of suicides and murders. After review, the Safety Commission decided that Dungeons and Dragons was not a danger to the U.S. public and summarily dismissed the petition. According to researcher Jeff Freeman: "No study yet has revealed any sort of danger to playing fantasy role-playing games. Instead, researchers discovered that gamers as a group have fewer criminal tendencies than average, no psychological abnormalities, and a slight increase in creativity among long-time players and a greater sense of self-worth."

Michael A. Stackpole, a designer and recognized authority on role-playing games was assigned by the Game Manufacturers' Association to investigate the claims. In *The Pulling Report* (1990) he concluded: "There is no causal link between games and suicide any more than there is a link between breathing and suicide. Suicide is a desperate act of a very sick individual and to trivialize their condition by suggesting a game could push them over edge is cruel and unfeeling. To suggest a game could change an otherwise normal child into a suicidal or homicidal maniac asks us to believe that a normal individual cannot distinguish between fantasy and reality. It also vests an incredible amount of power in a game, and allows people to put their responsibility and guilt off onto an inanimate object." A further review of Pulling's poorly substantiated "Trophy List" revealed that gamers had a suicide rate some ten times below the national average. Pulling died of cancer in 1997; her research data against RPG's largely discredited due to questionable research methodology and a basic lack of knowledge. As one blatant example Pulling treated *The Necronomicon* as an authentic and legitimate occult publication that poisoned the minds of its readers. Horror fans, however, were quick to point out that the fabled book was a fictitious invention of writer H.P. Lovecraft and cited extensively in the author's numerous fantasy tales.

DARK SHADOWS

Followers of Goth have utilized the classic Gothic literature of Bram Stoker, Oscar Wilde, Mary Shelly, H.P. Lovecraft and Anne Rice to gain inspiration, mood and atmosphere. Other period influences, which helped lay the foundation, were Dante, Byron and Tolstoy. But it was another, more contemporary, cultural event that added to Goth's revival. This was the NBC re-release of *Dark Shadows*. The television series, a fantasy soap opera, was short-lived, possibly due to the immediacy of the Gulf War and the dark and somber attitude of the series. The extravagant soap, which was a more sinister incarnation of the original, aired briefly on NBC from January 13, 1991 to March 22 1991.

The original *Dark Shadows* was a minimalist black and white soap opera. It was created and produced by Dan Curtis, and was extremely popular. It premiered on ABC June 27, 1966, and aired 1225 episodes until April 2,1971. Based on *The House*, by Art Wallace, it depicted the story of dreary Collinwood Manor and its inhabitants, notably, Victoria Winters, Elizabeth Collins Stoddard and a vampire anti-hero named Barnabas Collins. It was Barnabas Collins who fascinated us with his lonely and painful existence. The success of *Dark Shadows* demonstrated that there was much potential profit in Goth themes. Two feature length motion pictures were released during the late 1960's and early 1970's including *House of Dark Shadows* (1970), in which vampire Barnabas Collins was destroyed, and *Night of Dark Shadows* (1971.)

In 1975 the series was resurrected and aired in syndication on stations, including PBS. It lasted for 15 years, until 1990.The Sci-Fi Channel debuted in 1992 with *Dark Shadows* being the initial TV series purchased. It was the first time since its initial broadcast that the popular series catalog was available for mass viewing.

It took almost a decade for Hollywood to realize the commercial potential of Goth-related product. Although slow to realize the commercial potential, Hollywood eventually provided the movie version of *Dungeons and Dragons*. In December 8, 2000, this cinematic depiction, that starred Jeremy Irons, Marlon Wayans and Thora Birch, proved to be an unrecognized effort that met with little popular acclaim amongst the masses. Shamelessly, it attempted to blend Shakespearian drama with cartoonish Hollywood special effects that did little to advance the philosophy of Goth.

The cinematic versions of *Dracula* and other lesser-known vampires have long been a staple of horror fans. The original, based on Bram Stoker's horror tale, starred Bela Lugosi in the 1931 film adaptation. The actual genesis of the genre, however, was filmed some nine years earlier as the silent *Nosferatu,* starring Max Schreck as the hideous and gnome-like vampyre.

In the 1960's Hammer Films of Great Britain turned the vampire lore into a major industry. They contributed a rash of films, many featuring Christopher Lee as the infamous count. Among their bloody catalog were the titles *The Horror of Dracula* (1958), *Brides of Dracula* (1960), *Kiss of the Vampire* (1963), *Dracula Has Risen From the Grave* (1968), *Taste the Blood of Dracula* (1970), *Dracula-Prince of Darkness* (1971), *Lust for a Vampire* (1971), *Countess Dracula* (1971), *Captain Kronos, Vampire Hunter* (1972), *Dracula A.D-1972* (1972), *Vampire Circus* (1972),*The Satanic Rites of Dracula* (1973) and *Legend of the Seven Golden Vampires* (1974).

Helping to slake the thirst for the genre were numerous contributions adding to the Hammer legacy. They included *Count Yorga, Vampire* (1970), *The Return of Count Yorga* (1971), *The Vampire Lovers* (1971), *Nosferatu the Vampyre* (1979) and *Steven King's Salem's Lot—the Miniseries* (1979). The comedy *Once Bitten* (1985) featured Lauren Hutton as a vampire countess.

Anne Rice's skillful *Interview With the Vampire* presented Brad Pitt and Tom Cruise in the initial offering of Rice's Vampire Chronicles (1994). Anne Rice's *Queen of the Damned,* with (deceased) popstar Aaliyah, Stuart Townsend, Lena Olin and Vincent Perez, blended vampire mythology with the overwhelming Goth-rock music of Korn's Jonathan Davis.

In *Wes Craven Presents: Dracula 2000,* the Count, in this updated version, undergoes a mod transformation and featured Gerard Butler, Jonny Lee Miller and Christopher Plummer. The 1922 German cult classic *Nosferatu* was the inspiration for *Shadow of the Vampire* (2001) and starred Willem Dafoe as Max Schreck, real-life German stage and film actor in the role of Count Orlok and John Malkovich as Director F.W. Murnau. The fictionalized account of the making of the original horror film was re-scored by rock band Type O Negative.

All told, Hollywood's depiction of the vampire legend has tapped into a subliminal thirst that is buried within. *The Vampire Mythos* was a bloody page ripped from the damned *Book of the Occult*, a quasi religion with striking parallels to Christianity. To the faithful, Vampirism offered blood as the sacrament and promised life after death. It also granted sexual fulfillment and hedonistic pleasures, a stark departure from Christian tenets of abstinence, suffering and sacrifice. Just as the Christian gains everlasting life through the sacrament of Communion, the vampire sought to achieve immortality through another's blood. That immortality was, for the vampire, the state of being "undead," and, according to *In Search of Dracula*: "Behind the vampire is the Oriental concept of eternal return, in which nothing is ever really destroyed but comes back in endless recreations and reincarnations. The vampire takes blood from the living, but should she mix her blood with that of her victim, that person in turn becomes an undead, having survived mortal death."

Eating blood was a central part of pagan rituals believing that the animal's blood would provide the blood eater with the animal's courage, strength and cunning. That example of pagan transformation went counter to The Word, as God's people relied upon Him alone for their strength. Communion, central to Christianity, accepts Jesus Christ as Lord and Savior, as explained in John 6:53-58: "I tell you the truth, unless you eat the flesh of the Son of Man and drink his blood, you have no life in you. Whoever eats my flesh and drinks my blood has eternal life, and I will raise him up at the last day. For my flesh is real food and my blood is real drink. Whoever eats my flesh and drinks my blood remains in me, and I in him. Just as the living Father sent me and I live because of the Father, so the one who feeds on me will live because of me. This is the bread that came down from heaven. Your forefathers ate manna and died, but he who feeds on this bread will live forever."

Early Christians were forbidden to eat blood as it represented life, considered sacred to God. It was also symbolic of the animal sacrifice made by the sinner and to eat the blood would destroy the symbolism of that sacrificial act. In Deuteronomy 12:23, we find the proscription: "But be sure you do not eat the blood, because the blood is the life, and you must not eat the life with the meat. You must not eat the blood; pour it out on the ground like water."

Although modern day interest in *The Vampire Mythos* began with the 15th Century Dracula, Vlad Tepes, known as "Vlad the Impailer," vampirism remained an established, universal myth, having been documented in ancient Babylonian and Assyrian artifacts thousands of years before Christ. Vampirism remained with us, an interesting yet outdated folklore that could be viewed on a strict political level. It could be explained as an allegory, a veiled political statement against an omnipotent church-state that exerted total control over the fear struck masses. Some historians felt that *The Vampire Mythos* was a dangerous and provocative desecration of God's Word as it symbolically represented the evil opposite of Jesus Christ. In his cinema persona Dracula promised an unholy communion to Jonathan Harker's wife Mina: "I give you life eternal. Everlasting love. The power of the storm. And the beasts of the earth. Walk with me ... to be my loving wife ... forever ... I condemn you to living death. To eternal hunger for living blood."

According to cult expert Marcos Quinones of Cult Solutions: "There is increased targeting of teenagers by satanic and vampire cults. The risk of cult terrorism has never been greater. Recent publicity of the Columbine High School shootings should be a wake-up call to law enforcement, parents, mental health professionals and clergy. More and more teens are becoming involved in cult and cult terrorist activities. Mental health professionals often misdiagnose these children as harmless dabblers of Satanism or vampirism. There is a fine line between harmless dabbling and a serious interest in these dark activities. It is heartbreaking to meet the family of a teen suicide victim involved in these cults. The parents often blame themselves for not recognizing the severity of their children's behavior. We hope to give parents the awareness they need."

Apart from the controversy and vast library of vampire films and books, the genre created a movement that brought the realm of literary fantasy into the domain of real-life role-playing. Vampirism was unique in this respect with few others in that number, as it embraced the beauty and danger of Goth, in a pragmatic manner.

GOTH ROCK

The Goth Movement spawned a strange and eerie musical expression that was christened Dark Wave or Dark Psychedelia. It had also been labeled Doom Rock or Death Rock. Collectively, it represented a musical form that celebrated the atmosphere of the "undead." The music was dark, depressing, atmospheric and moody, with the most commercial brand being the violent "death metal."

The earliest indication of Goth Music can be traced to another era. Goth Music had its dark roots in a musical form some 30 years earlier. The genre of suicide rock was an obscure form of music stemming from the 1950's fascination with sudden death and suicide. The sound immortalized young pop stars that died in their prime, forever young. It included such icons as James Dean, Eddie Cochran, Ritchie Valens and Buddy Holly. It was a fascination that continued over six decades later with the addition of Janis Joplin, Jimi Hendrix, Jim Morrison, Kurt Cobain and Layne Staley.

Pearl Jam's "Last Kiss," a curious choice for these grunge rockers, was a cover of a J. Frank Wilson and the Cavaliers 1960 original. Other tunes that paid homage to this morbid death fascination included Jody Reynold's haunting "Endless Sleep" (1958), Thomas Wayne's "Tragedy" (1959), Ray Peterson's "Tell Laura I Love Her" (1960), Johnny Preston's "Running Bear," (1960) Dickey Lee's "Patches" (1962) and "Laurie (Strange Things Happen in This World)" (1965), Mark Dinning's "Teen Angel " (1960) and Jan and Dean's "Dead Man's Curve" (1964). After Eddie Cochran's 1960 death in a London taxicab accident, his song "Three Steps to Heaven" (1960) was released as a haunting tribute to the fallen teen idol and his girlfriend.

The precise moment that begat Goth Rock can be traced to Great Britain and the bands Bauhaus and Joy Division. The volatile 1970's was a time of radical cultural change from the commercialism of the sixties, represented by the British Invasion, mod fashion and James Bondism. All that was about to shift into something dramatically different as Goth slowly evolved from the politically charged punk movement. During the early 1980's, all the varied elements of Goth fused together. The Batcave, a trendy London nightclub, helped define Goth in terms of attitude, fashion and musical presentation. Bauhaus contributed the initial example of Goth rock. Bauhaus, who sang the song "Bela Lugosi's Dead" (1979), had their tune featured in the 1982 vampire film *The Hunger*. That musical expression, dramatized by effortless execution and a haunting primal minimalism, is believed to have launched the atmospheric Goth genre: "Bela Lugosi's dead/The bats have left the bell tower/The victims have been bled/Red velvet lines the black box." Although they lasted for only five years, (1979–1983) the English band Bauhaus, initially criticized for being another David Bowie clone, begot a host of copycat groups such as Siouxsie and the Banshees, The Sisters of Mercy and Dead Can Dance. Other musical groups associated with the movement include London After Midnight, Unto Ashes, Faith and Amuse, Inkubus Sukkubus, Switchblade Symphony, Prodigy, Nosferatu and Love is Colder Than Death. Although popular with members of the Goth subset, this atmospheric musical expression (as of this writing) had yet to find a widespread audience and appeal with the exception of The Cure, The Damned and Evanescence.

Joy Division was the first band to proclaim the gospel of Goth, influencing groups like U2, Nine Inch Nails, The Smashing Pumpkins and Nirvana. Taking their name from a cluster of Nazi concentration camp brothels, the Manchester, England, band attracted a following in the 1970's. During an interview on BBC TV, Joy Division manager Anthony H. Wilson described his band's music as being "gothic, and not pop mainstream." Their sound was a post-punk explosion of synthesizers and personalized doom. Just one day before their 1980 debut American tour, lead singer and songwriter Ian Curtis, 23, committed suicide by hanging himself. Iggy Pop's "The Idiot" was found on the turntable and a note screamed: "At this very moment, I wish I were dead. I just can't cope anymore." Curtis' body was found by his estranged wife, Deborah. Curtis had been hospitalized numerous times and suffered from epileptic seizures, extreme mood swings and bouts of depression. His dark, brooding lyrics embraced themes of violence, death, alienation and emotional anguish. A prime example of his skill at uncovering the humanness behind the misery was "Atrocity Exhibition: … asylums with doors open wide/Where people had paid to see inside/For entertainment they watch his body twist/Behind his eyes he says 'I still exist.'" In 1995, his widow, Deborah Curtis, wrote the biography *Touching From a Distance: Ian Curtis & Joy Division*, hinting at the possibility that Curtis, emulating his heroes, wanted to die young.

MARILYN MANSON

The individual who would go on to assume the mantle of the Goth Movement remains a confused and indefinable persona. Critics of the iconoclastic Marilyn Manson claimed that the shock—rocker was nothing more than a commercial, self-promoting, con artist. They likened him to a cheap imitation of other theatrical acts such as Screaming Jay Hawkins, Alice Cooper, Wendy O. Williams and the Plasmatics, Black Sabbath and Rob Zombie. Despite the flak, this Generation X group immediately carved out its niche to become one of the most notorious bands in history.

Manson was not the originator of the genre but was simply picking up where the Master of Shock Rock, Alice Cooper, left off. Cooper (a.k.a. Vincent Furnier) was born in Detroit, the son of a Baptist minister. In 1969, right at the height of psychedelia, Cooper launched his successful stage career: "We were into fun, sex, death and money when everybody was into peace and love. We wanted to see what was next. It turned out we were next, and we drove a stake through the heart of the Love Generation." Legally changing his name to "*Alice Cooper*" he wore jet-black hair, thick eye makeup and outrageous clothing. Musically his performance was a loud, acerbic music framing intelligent lyrics with musical prowess. His stage presentation was a combination of hard rock and lavish theatrics, what he described as " a classic morality play—the bad guy always gets it."

Cooper began his visual assault by entering the stage with a boa constrictor wrapped around his neck. His extravagant tours utilized multi-level stage sets and theatrical devices such as a guillotine, an electric chair and a gallows. Cooper's outrageous antics, with fake blood dripping everywhere, included decapitating babies and killing Santa Claus. He would go on to sell over 50 million albums that included such teenage-rebellion anthems as "School's Out," "Eighteen," and "No More Mr. Nice Guy." Alice Cooper's unique rock-burlesque was actually a morality play injected with heavy doses of deadpan satire. In the end, Cooper, the self-acknowledged bad guy, would always get it. He had the perfect formula of controversy, cool and commercial hit records. But he also dabbled into the darker side singing songs of necrophilia, transvestism, doom and murder with cult favorites including "Killer," "Halo of Flies," "Ballad of Dwight Frye," "Sick Things" and, from 1973's *Billion Dollar Babies*, "I Love the Dead": "I love the dead before they're cold/They're bluing flesh for me to hold/Cadaver eyes upon me see nothing/I love the dead before they rise." Cooper's sway did not diminish as he continued to address contemporary social issues like Columbine. His 2000 CD *Brutal Planet* included a song called "Wicked Young Man" about a hate-filled skinhead who warns: "I never ever sleep, I just lay in my bed/dreamin' of the day when everyone is dead." But Cooper was quick to explain that "It's not the games that I play/the movies I see/the music I dig/I'm just a wicked young man."

Another purveyor of the genre, Ozzy Osbourne was a founding member of Black Sabbath, one of the definitive heavy metal bands noted for their dark lyrics embracing the occult. Since their inception, Black Sabbath had sold over 70 million albums, with songs such as "Mr. Crowley," "Crazy Train," "War Pigs," "Paranoid" and "Iron Man" netting regular radio airplay. VH1's *100 Greatest Artists of Hard*

Rock ranked them second, behind Led Zeppelin. In 1978, the charismatic Osbourne, "the Godfather of heavy metal," was fired from Black Sabbath due to his drug use and erratic behavior.

At an early age he dealt with learning disabilities and was diagnosed with bipolar disorder. Continued abuse of alcohol and cocaine and a divorce from his first wife, Thelma, led to a further series of bizarre antics, statements and behaviors. Osbourne's addictive lifestyle during the 1980's was becoming legendary. "I am a raging alcoholic and a raging addict," he confessed. "Somebody said to me this morning, 'To what do you attribute your longevity?' I don't know. I mean, I couldn't have planned my life out better. By all accounts I should be dead! The abuse I put my body through: the drugs, the alcohol, the lifestyle I've lived the last 30 years!" And in a quintessential moment of self promotion, Osbourne gained legendary notoriety after allegedly biting off a bat's head at a 1982 Des Moines, Iowa, concert. As a result the show was cancelled, as the singer had to receive a series of rabies vaccination injections as a preventative measure, but his reputation as "madman" was forever assured. In 2005, Osbourne was diagnosed with Parkinsonian Syndrome, a non-progressive genetic condition, similar to Parkinson's disease, and yet another phase in his life of struggle and controversy.

The lyrics to "Suicide Solution" created the biggest controversy that Osbourne would experience. On the evening of October 26, 1984, nineteen-year-old John McCollum shot himself in the head with a .22-caliber handgun. McCollum, who suffered from alcohol abuse and emotional instability, had been listening to *Diary of a Madman, Blizzard of Ozz* and *Speak of the Devil* prior to his suicide. His parents sued Osbourne and CBS Records claiming that the song "Suicide Solution," from the LP *Blizzard of Ozz,* and the music's pounding rhythm encouraged self-destructive behavior: "Suicide is slow with liquor/Where to hide, suicide is the only way out/Don't you know what it's really about?"

The U.S. Lawsuit alleged that McCollum's death was triggered by "subliminal lyrics" not listed on the album jacket but contained within a 28 second instrumental break: "You really know where it's at/You got it/Why try, why try/Get the gun and try it/Shoot, shoot, shoot." The California civil court's verdict supported Osbourne, contending that he could not be held responsible for a listener's actions and that the song was clearly about alcohol abuse. Further, the California Court of Appeals affirmed the lower court decision, stating: "Musical lyrics and poetry cannot be construed to contain the requisite 'call to action' for the elementary reason they simply are not intended to be and should not be read literally ... Reasonable persons understand musical lyrics and poetic conventions as the figurative expressions which they are." In essence Osbourne was protected by the First Amendment to the United States Constitution and had the right to express his views, regardless of how controversial they might be, via music lyrics.

Osbourne's "Suicide Solution" would eventually find itself in strange company with another song, this one called "Night Prowler." Serial killer Richard Ramirez, known to the news media as the Los Angeles Night Stalker, had a weird relationship with heavy-metal groups who promoted satanic themes. Besides Ozzy Osbourne's musical offerings, Ramirez had an affinity for AC/DC and their 1979 LP *Highway to Hell*. Ramirez was especially drawn to the song "Night Prowler," believed to have been his favorite, as law enforcement officials later theorized "that the style of the brutal rapes and thirteen murders Ramirez committed resembled the lyrics of the song." "Night Prowler" contained the lyrics, "Was that a noise outside your window?/What's that shadow on the blind?/As you lie there naked like a body in a tomb/suspended animation as I slip into your room." (Note: Six months after the release of *Highway to Hell*, the band's first million selling LP, AC/DC lead singer Bon Scott would be found dead in the back of a friend's car. The official cause of death was listed as "acute alcohol poisoning" and "death by misadventure".)

Ramirez began his wanton bloodletting in 1984, striking only during nighttime, and created an atmosphere of widespread fear in Los Angeles County. He was convicted in 1989 on 43 counts including thirteen gruesome murders, five attempted murders, eleven sexual assaults and fourteen burglaries. Ramirez was a chronic user of marijuana and also used cocaine and PCP, drugs that promoted paranoia, depression, psychosis and aggression. He believed that Satan made him invincible and had frequently drawn the five-point pentagram, the symbol of the devil, on his own body. At his murder trial a disruptive Ramirez shouted out "Hail Satan" during the court proceedings, similar to the calculated courtroom theatrics of Charles Manson, back in 1969.

And yet, just like "Suicide Solution," it is not easy to deduce that the pounding lyrics of "Night Prowler" and the fog of marijuana, would turn a misdirected youth, a member of the self-empowered Baby Boomer generation, into "one of the most heinous serial rapists and murderers in modern history." Whatever the reason for the carnage, perhaps we need to collectively look beyond the words of a provocative song or possibly at the final words of a crazed serial killer.

Before he received sentencing at his trial, and before he began his incarceration on San Quinton's Death Row, Ramirez ranted, "It's nothing you'd understand, but I do have something to say. In fact, I have a lot to say, but now is not the time or place. I don't know why I'm wasting my time or breath. But what the hell? As for what is said of my life, there have been lies in the past and there will be lies in the future. I don't believe in the hypocritical, moralistic dogma of this so-called civilized society. I need not look beyond this room to see all the liars, haters, the killers, the crooks, the paranoid cowards—truly trematodes of the Earth, each one in his own legal profession. You maggots make me sick—hypocrites one and all. And no one knows that better than those who kill for policy, clandestinely or openly, as do the governments of the world, which kill in the name of God and country or for whatever reason they deem appropriate. I don't need to hear all of society's rationalizations, I've heard them all before and the fact remains that what is, is. You don't understand me. You are not expected to. You are not capable of it. I am beyond your experience. I am beyond good and evil, Legions of the night—night breed—repeat not the errors of the Night Prowler and show no mercy. I will be avenged. Lucifer dwells within us all. That's it."

Continuing to reinvent itself, rock borrowed on themes that had worked in previous decades. Nine Inch Nails, formed by Trent Reznor in 1988, gained a huge underground following as they blazed new musical trails dealing with despondent themes that incorporated "sex, death, pigs and God." NIN proved to be one of the most innovative bands since Nirvana, propelling punk and heavy metal to another echelon, soon mislabeled "industrial rock." In 1997 *Time Magazine* listed Reznor as one of the twenty-five most influential people, while NIN was recognized as one of the *100 Greatest Artists of All Time* by *Rolling Stone Magazine*. NIN's musical approach, with traces of techno and shock rock, proved difficult to easily classify, while their videos were more immediate and visceral.

Thus far the band's most controversial chapter was the "almost universally banned" sadomasochistic "Happiness Is Slavery" video, from the 1992 CD *Broken*. In this disturbing snuff film, performance artist Bob Flanagan is symbolically tortured, raped and dismembered in a mechanical dungeon. The entire video had never been aired on MTV and was called "unplayable." Trent Reznor explained that the project was more about artistic control and having the freedom to produce a video, forgetting about "standards and censorship." The cryptic meaning of the video, he explained, was about surrendering control, one of Reznor's recurring themes. The harsh lyrics intoned: "I have found you can find happiness in slavery/Slave screams he spends his life learning conformity/Slave screams he claims he has his own identity."

After the Columbine massacre, NIN was again forced on the defensive as some charged that the group's provocative wordplay played a part in the high school bloodletting. On November 17, 1998, Columbine killer Eric Harris wrote in detail about his desire to have violent, animalistic sex with a woman and taste human flesh. Quoting a line from NIN's song "Closer To God," Harris rants: "Who can I trick into my room first? I can sweep someone off their feet, tell them what they want to hear, be all nice and sweet, and then 'fuck them like an animal, feel them from the inside' as [Trent] Reznor said, oh, that's something else ... that one. NIN video I saw, ... the one where the guy is kidnapped and tortured like hell—actual hell—I want to do that too. I want to tear a throat out with my own teeth like a pop can. I want to gut someone with my hand, to tear a head off and rip out the heart and lungs from the neck ..." The actual "Closer To God" sex-charged lyrics, called "supernegative and superhateful" by Reznor, screamed out its salacious content: "You let me violate you/you let me desecrate you/You let me penetrate you/You let me complicate you/Help me."

The crude and shocking authenticity of NIN evolved into the commercial and mainstream offerings of Marilyn Manson. *The Long Hard Road Out of Hell* was the title of Manson's 1998 best selling autobiography about his band and his music. Co-written by *Rolling Stone Magazine's* Neil Strauss, it explored the rocker's life of sex, drugs and twisted relationships. Christened Brian Warner, Marilyn Manson was born in Canton, Ohio, on January 5, 1969, forming his group Marilyn Manson and the Spooky Kids at the beginning of the decade. The band wrapped themselves around the persona of serial killers coupled with teen queens. One by one the band evolved, taking names of Daisy Berkowitz, Gidget Gein, Madonna Wayne—Gacy, Sara Lee Lucas and Marilyn Manson. "I picked that as the fakest stage name of all to say that this is what show business is, fake," Manson explained of his stage persona. The group got their big break in 1993 when Trent Reznor offered them a contract on his *Nothing Records* label and invited them to tour with NIN the following year.

Manson, as the world was soon to discover, pushed the limits of free speech and acceptable standards, often baiting organized religion in the process. Manson began calling himself the "*Antichrist Superstar*" and was bestowed the title of "*Reverend*" by Anton Szandor LaVey, [late] founder of the Church of Satan. He frequently performed quasi-sexual acts on stage, while desecrating the American flag and symbols of Christianity. And, along with the expected publicity, somewhere during that warped journey, he became labeled as a spokesperson for Goth. Although there are no active role models promoting the philosophies of Goth, Marilyn Manson, because he touched on many of the Goth elements, including themes of darkness, violence, suicide and death, had been mistakenly promoted as Goth's Ambassador. The public erroneously linked Goth with Manson and Satanism. [NOTE: The high profile Manson was musically more steeped in the tradition of Heavy Metal or Death Metal and not Goth Rock, but because the nebulous Goth movement lacked high-visibility spokespersons, Manson has mistakenly been labeled the ambassador of Goth by an uninformed media. It was a mistake that Manson has been able to successfully exploit.]

Early on Manson was propelled into the heated debate of free speech vs. censorship. Well prepared for the fight, he lashed out against organized religion: "The people who want to crucify me for my so-called violent views should sit down and read the Bible. They should examine the virtues of wonderful 'Christian' stories of disease, murder, adultery, suicide and child sacrifice. In comparison to the stories in the Old Testament, I'm surprised that they don't find my songs far too tame and boring for their liking." In a 1999 *Rolling Stone* interview, Manson stated: "Whether you interpret the Bible as literature or as the final word of whatever God may be, Christianity has given us an image of death and sexuality that we have based our culture around. A half-naked dead man hangs in most homes and around our necks, and we have just taken that for granted all of our lives ... is it a symbol of hope or hopelessness?" Describing the death of Christ as history's "most famous murder-suicide," Manson identifies the event as "the birth of the death icon."

Anthony DeCurtis, writer for *beliefnet*, said: "Perhaps no figure in modern culture is as famous or reviled for his use of religious imagery as Marilyn Manson." During a concert in Salt Lake City, Manson ripped a copy of the Book of Mormon apart, throwing the pages at the audience. Tearing pages from the Bible and tossing them to the screaming fans became a staple of Manson's show. As a result of his antics, the shock rocker received death threats and was attacked by, among others, website activists, religious organizations and People For the Ethical Treatment of Animals. Several ultra-right conservative groups called for boycotts of Manson concerts, organizing prayer meetings and demonstrations against him. The Citizens for Peace and Respect said that Manson: "glorifies death and human destruction." On its website CPR warned: "HATE is coming to town. What are YOU going to do about it?" Taking the bait, Manson reacted prior to a scheduled 2001 concert: "In response to their protests, I will provide a show where I balance my songs with a wholesome Bible reading. This way, fans will not only hear my so-called 'violent' point of view, but we can also examine the virtues of wonderful 'Christian' stories of disease, murder, adultery, suicide and child sacrifice. Now that seems like 'entertainment' to me."

Through his lyrics Manson continued to push the limits of crassness, controversy and debate. Critics identified the line "One shot and the world gets smaller" as a message promoting suicide. Another, "We're all stars now in the Dope Show" intones "I don't like the drugs but the drugs like me." And in "Lunchbox" Manson takes on school bullies with the lines "I've got my lunchbox and I'm armed real well .../Next motherfucker gonna get my metal .../next motherfucker/pow pow pow, pow pow pow, pow pow pow, pow pow pow/I wanna grow up so no one fucks with me."

Looking for scapegoats, it was easy for the media to blame the Goth culture, violent video games and individuals like Manson and Trent Reznor for the April 20,1999, Columbine High School tragedy. Manson, had been around for less than three years before the carnage in Littleton, Colorado, yet initial reports linked him to the murders, alleging that Dylan Klebold and Eric Harris were fans of the shock rocker (although later accounts refuted the claim.) Manson denied responsibility for the killings and denounced them. Said Manson: "It's tragic and disgusting anytime young peoples' lives are taken in an act of senseless violence. My condolences go out to the students and families." He cancelled the last five of his 1999 *"Rock Is Dead"* tour, after pressure from Denver Mayor Wellington Webb "out of respect for the victims" and turned down countless requests for radio and TV appearances. Manson's most visible response was appearing in Michael Moore's documentary *Bowling for Columbine* (2002), in which he discussed possible influences including his lyrics. Manson, being interviewed before a concert in Littleton, was asked what he would say if he could talk to Harris and Klebold. He responded, "I wouldn't say a thing. I would listen to what they had to say, and that's what nobody did."

Interviewed by the *Denver Post*, Manson said: "The way the national news media dove on [the Columbine tragedy] and made it into something worse than it even started out being annoyed and disgusted me. And it didn't surprise me at all. For them to blame me was sadly ironic ... The media takes violence, makes it into entertainment, and the killer becomes the star." In 2000 Manson went on the offensive, releasing *Holy Wood (In the Shadow of the Valley of Death)*. Major outlets including Walmart and Best Buy subsequently banned the cover artwork, featuring a mutilated Manson in a crucifix-like pose. In the CD he explored the Columbine High School massacre, specifically in "The Fight Song," "The Nobodies," and "Disposable Teens," looking at society's mindless obsession with the glorification of guns, violence and death. On his website Manson wrote: "I am truly amazed that after all this time, religious groups still need to attack entertainment and use these tragedies as a pitiful excuse for their own self-serving publicity." Still, this CD, along with his others, reflected a savvy marketer most adept at baiting hyper-vigilant Christian groups and disenfranchised youth with a boorish formula and fraudulent Goth persona.

Like a rabid hound the specter of Columbine stalked Manson back to the mountains of Denver. The 2001 Ozzfest featured festival headliners Black Sabbath, Slipknot, Papa Roach and Crazy Town but not Marilyn Manson, the tour's major attraction. Manson, after allegedly receiving numerous death threats, cancelled his appearance in the throes of anti-Columbine hysteria. "We're against him because he promotes six things," Jason Janz of the South Sheridan Baptist Church told *Rolling Stone*: "We believe he promotes hate, violence, death, suicide, drug use, and the attitudes and actions of the Columbine killers." The concert would have been Manson's first in the area since the April 1999 shootings at Columbine High School

In July 2005, a 36-year-old Marilyn Manson informed *Rolling Stone Magazine* that he was shifting his concentration to filmmaking: "I just don't think the world is worth putting music into right now. I no longer want to make art that other people—particularly record companies—are turning into a product. I just want to make art." But Manson's course correction, once again, followed in the wake of others. Rob Zombie, former singer/leader of White Zombie, had already charted a new and exciting direction as screenwriter and film director. Among Zombie's credits were the horror films *Halloween* (2007), *The Devil's Rejects* (2005) and *House of 1000 Corpses* (2003.)

Manson's foray into that realm and his well-articulated logic spoke more to the shock-rockers' inability to develop new themes, as music critics have bashed him for tiresome and redundant musical offerings. Manson's boorish lyrics never caught up to his exciting stage persona, as he continued to re-work the same pedestrian materials of violence, vulgarity, God-bashing, and nihilism. Manson's legacy became that of a clownish muckraker, shallow and insignificant, sulking in the shadow of Alice Cooper and others much more important.

5

River Jude Phoenix

o o o o o o o o o o o o o o o o o o o o o

"I would rather quit while I was ahead. There's no need to overstay your welcome."

—River Phoenix

THE BRAT PACK

The original Hollywood Brat Pack, an interesting semantic variation of Frank Sinatra's earlier Rat Pack, was introduced to the world via an article in *New York* magazine. Born on the cusp between Baby Boomer idealism and Generation X melancholia, Brat Packers inherited the passion and nonconformist zeal of their Woodstock-era parents and jointly helped influence the mindset of Generation X as many of their Silent Generation counterparts did to sway the idealistic Boomers. Brat Pack members counted among their ilk an assortment of energetic personalities who frequently appeared in films together. This cadre of actors were represented by members of both the Baby Boomer [Judd Nelson (b. 1959), Mare Willingham (1959), Sean Penn (1960), James Spader (1960), Demi Moore (1962), Ally Sheedy (1962), Andrew McCarthy (1962), Emilio Estevez (1962), Matt Dillon (1964) and Rob Lowe (1964)] and Generation X [Robert Downey Jr. (1965), Charlie Sheen (1965), John Cusack (1966) and Molly Ringwald (1968)] groups.

The Brat Pack acted in a youth-oriented collection of films released in the 1980's that protested the status quo, social conformity and excessive materialism of the times. The commercially successful films, with a significant contribution from director John Hughes, also attempted to define what it was like to be a teenager during this era. Among this body of work were *Risky Business* (1983), *Sixteen Candles* (1984), *St. Elmo's Fire* (1985), *The Breakfast Club* (1985), *The Sure Thing* (1985), *Pretty in Pink* (1986) and *Ferris Bueller's Day Off* (1986). It was easy for some to dismiss these films as examples of banal teenage angst or rite of passage rebellion, but offstage, and during their private moments, there was a darker, more sinister side to the collective twenty-something Brat Pack.

Heartthrob Rob Lowe was a founding member of this Hollywood inner circle. After he teamed with Demi Moore, Emilio Estevez, Ally Sheedy and Judd Nelson in *St. Elmo's Fire*, the clique inherited the title of "Brat Pack." Lowe rapidly picked up choice roles in *The Hotel New Hampshire* (1984), *Oxford Blues* (1984) and *About Last Night* (1986). He was about to break it wide open.

But Lowe was no stranger to controversy and seemingly thrived on it. His most infamous episode gave the term "sexual politics" an updated twist. While attending the 1988 Democratic National Convention in Atlanta, Lowe videotaped a sexual encounter with two females, one of them underage. The teenager's mother sued. The tabloids had a field day with the 24-year-old actor .To many he became Public Enemy Number One. The following year Lowe was penalized with a token 20 hours of public service and the resulting negative publicity. Lowe later entered into treatment for alcohol abuse and sex addiction. Years later the controversy continued as Lowe's homemade video was discovered among the porno collection of Paul Reubens, a.k.a. Pee-Wee Herman. Reubens, booked on November 15, 2002, on suspicion of possessing child—porn material, pleaded innocent to the misdemeanor charge.

Lowe's acting career, which had taken a turn for the worse, was presented with the proverbial "second chance." Practically unseen until the mid 90's, he emerged as a TV regular on TV's White House drama *The West Wing* and later in the 2004 adaptation of Stephen King's *Salem's Lot*. The passage of time and Lowe's onscreen maturity resulted in an enthusiastic public acceptance and forgiveness. Fellow actor Mike Myers, who signed the actor to co-star in a string of successful comedies, including *Wayne's World* and *Austin Powers*, also helped resurrect Lowe's career. In 2006 Lowe accepted the role of Senator Robert McCallester on ABC Tv's *Brothers & Sisters*.

Robert Downey Jr., another Brat Pack alumnus, assumed the cloak of the pathetic, wild-eyed poster child of Hollywood excess. The talented actor, son of underground filmmaker Robert Downey Sr., landed a spot on TV's *Saturday Night Live* at the tender age of 20. He later earned Golden Globe and Oscar nominations for Best Actor in Sir Richard Attenborough's film *Chaplin* (1992) and was nominated for an Outstanding Supporting Actor Emmy Award for his role in the comedy series *Ally Mc Beal* (2001). But none of those accolades provided him the freedom and inner peace he so desperately sought. For years Downey struggled against the shackles of a highly publicized addiction and a precarious, almost unattainable, rehabilitation. Since the age of 31 he had been arrested on drug-related charges numerous times. Attempts to kick the habit and Downey's failed drug rehab programs have all been a matter of public record.

Arrested in Malibu in June 1996 for driving while under the influence, Downey was in possession of a concealed .357 Magnum handgun. He also had crack cocaine, powdered cocaine, and Mexican black-tar heroin on his person. In 1999 an introspective yet fatalistic Downey told a judge, "It's like I have a loaded gun in my mouth and my finger's on the trigger. And I like the taste of the gunmetal." Downey was released in August 2000 after a year-long, drug-related stint in prison and then re-arrested twice for cocaine possession.

During one of these incidents Downey was arrested in Palm Springs, CA, for violating terms of his parole, including possession of cocaine and methamphetamine. He had unsuccessfully attempted to clean up his life, to leave the drugs behind and had openly admitted his addiction in candid interviews in *Vanity Fair* and other media publications. But Downey's quasi-secret life came into full public view after *Time Magazine* profiled his active addiction in an expose entitled "Downey's Downfall" (December 2000). The article referred to the extreme "Jekyll and Hyde" personas and detailed Downey's separation from his wife and son and his prison incarcerations. There was nowhere left to hide. Robert Downey Jr. did not have the advantage of dealing with his addiction in confidential solitude. His painful ordeal, open and raw, was one that had become public knowledge.

The Singing Detective (2003), his first film after a three-year period, may have been a turning point for him. "You can make miraculous recoveries from seemingly hopeless situations if you put your mind to it and you have enough support. I think it's about the process of maturing," Downey, then age 38, said in 2003 of his drug addiction.

Winona Ryder, a member of yet another, albeit younger, Brat Pack incarnation, was raised in Northern California on a ranch commune without electricity. The liberal-thinking Ryder family were close friends of Beat poet Allen Ginsberg, and the elfish Winona was goddaughter of LSD guru Timothy Leary. She was an aspiring Academy Award nominated actress. Among her films were *Beetlejuice* (1988), *Reality Bites* (1994), *Alien: Resurrection* (1997) and *Girl Interrupted* (1999).

But it was Ryder's off-stage antics that placed her in the harsh glare of public condemnation. On December 12, 2001, Ryder was arrested for theft and vandalism after a $5,560.40 shoplifting spree in a Beverly Hills Saks Fifth Avenue. A witness watched as Ryder used scissors to cut off large anti-theft sensors from the high-fashion merchandise. In her defense, Ryder explained to store workers that she was researching a role for a film called *Shopgirl* but later told police that the movie was actually called *White Jazz*. Moreover, the out-of-control actress was found carrying illegal pharmaceutical drugs without a prescription. A 2002 probation report showed that Ryder used numerous aliases to secure prescription drugs. The practice, known as "doctor shopping," netted Ryder 37 prescriptions written by 20 physicians over a three-year period. "It's not uncommon for a high-profile person to get a prescription filled under an alias. It happens with great frequency," explained Ryder's attorney Mark Geragos.

In the sensational People v. Ryder two-day trial, criminal defense attorney Mark Geragos represented Ryder. (Geragos continues to receive widespread media attention as he defends clients in sensational cases, such as Michael Jackson, Gary Condit and Scott Peterson. In 2006 Geragos represented Greg Anderson, personal trainer of suspected steroid-user Barry Bonds.) Even with the expertise of Geragos, Ryder was found guilty of felony grand theft and vandalism. The jury took two days and 5 1/2 hours of intense deliberations. Ryder was cleared of burglary charges. Still, like Lowe, the actress was court-ordered to perform community service. Ryder was ordered to complete 480 hours of community service and sentenced to three years probation. She was also instructed to pay $3700 in fines and $6355 in restitution and was further sentenced to three years probation and ordered to undergo psychological and drug counseling for her bizarre behavior.

PSYCHEDELIC HAZE

The impulsive, blonde haired and childlike River Phoenix (b. 1970) was an alumnus of the second wave of Tinsel town Brat Packers. Among his peers were youthful motion picture actors such as Johnny Depp (1960), Keanu Reeves (1964), Martha Plimpton (1970) and the aforementioned Winona Ryder (1971). It is impossible to determine with any clarity the winners and losers in this bunch. Only time will reveal the answer as we review their body of work and levels of success. From all indications River Phoenix had the talent, charisma and drive to have been among the best. His tragic public death deprived us of the promise of those wonderful gifts.

◆ ◆ ◆

The sequence of events leading to the birth of River Jude Phoenix transpired after America, in an undeclared war, marched into the steamy jungles of Southeast Asia. For most Americans the rationale for our involvement in Vietnam appeared to be honorable. Draped in vestiges of patriotism, freedom and liberty, America sent her young men into Southeast Asia to stem the evil red tide. Our political and military analysts called this concept the "Domino Theory." Their philosophy, later proved to be a gross miscalculation, postulated that the communists would take over one country after the other, much like a pile of falling dominoes. It would begin in North Vietnam with fanatical leader Ho Chi Minh and systematically march into South Vietnam, Cambodia, Laos and all the rest.

On January 30, 1968, on the eve of the lunar New Year celebrations, four-star General Vo Nguyen Giap launched a surprise offensive against American and South Vietnamese troops. Throughout war-torn South Vietnam, provincial capitals were attacked in guerilla-style hit-and-run blitzes. During this bloody Tet Offensive the U.S. Embassy in Saigon, believed to have been secure from attack, was overrun. The suicidal battle gambit, although costing a staggering amount of North Vietnamese lives, proved to be the turning point of the war. Although the Communists were beaten back, Tet was viewed as a major setback for the United States and its South Vietnam allies. For President Lyndon Johnson's White House the Tet Offensive represented a media disaster as it further destroyed morale through endless televised newsreels of flag-draped body bags and perceived American ineptitude.

The blood that was spilled in the name of the Vietnam War came from patriotic soldiers who fought on the battlefield as well as from patriotic students who protested at Kent State. America staggered, drunk in the spirits of war and peace, of protest, confrontation, and change. Revolution was in the air. During the Summer of 1968, the anti-war and peace and love movements mixed, blended and swirled until the world revolved in a vortex of marijuana smoke and psychedelic haze. Arlyn Dunetz, then a 23-year-old New York secretary, hated her job and her banal existence. Packing her memories, she left a husband and family, escaping the concrete Bronx landscape for the California Promised Land. With expectations of a more fulfilling life, she smiled and began to hitchhike west.

Fate stepped in after gardener/handyman John Bottom picked up the young runaway along the Pacific-swept Santa Monica Boulevard. Bottom and Arlyn Dunetz were members of the counter-culture movement of the 1960's, hippies who yearned for the adventure of the road and freedom from social conformity. Like latter-day characters from Kerouac's *On the Road*, John Bottoms and Arlyn Dunetz shared parallel universes with Sal Paradise and his Mexican girlfriend Terry. Bottom and Dunetz were not "sad and wild" beatniks but were wide-eyed hippies who sought shelter, searched for work and attempted to make sense of the changing times. After traveling from one commune to another, employed as itinerant fruit pickers, they fell in love and were married in a festive hippie ceremony in 1969.

In the summer of 1970, the Bottoms migrated north from California to the outskirts of scenic Metolius, Oregon. Taking up residence at the Nance Farm, the clan resided in a log cabin and helped harvest the local mint crop. Arlyn was already pregnant when they arrived at the commune. Into this peaceful Utopia River Jude Bottom was born. On August 23, 1970 he entered the world at 12:10 p.m. as a Virgo. Much creativity went into his name, which alluded to the River of Life, from Hermann Hesse's spiritual novel *Siddhartha*, and to the Beatles' song "Hey Jude".

After an extremely complicated natural birth that lasted several days and Arlyn's difficult recovery, the family found themselves facing a cold, hard Oregon winter. Following the ordeal, Arlyn remained ill for several months. The next year John Bottom moved his new family back to California, where he embraced the warmer temperatures and the seductive message of David Berg.

CHILDREN OF GOD

Evangelist David Berg was the leader of the Jesus People, a group of middle-class hippies spreading the Gospel to the counterculture. Berg claimed that he spoke to God. In 1969, while preaching in Huntington Beach, he claimed to receive a revelation that California would be devastated by an earthquake, causing part of the Golden State to fall into the ocean. For eight months Berg led his flock, wearing sackcloths and carrying staffs, into the Southwest. They were looking for a sign. After coming out of the desert Berg changed his name to Moses David and the name of his group (initially called the Light Club) to The Children of God.

The Children of God preached that all governments and societies were evil. Group members were instructed to turn over their possessions to the group, to sever contact from their family of origin and to become full time evangelists. Children of God members assumed a life of poverty, communal living and free love. Moses David encouraged female members to engage in "flirty fishing" and seduce potential group members through sex. In a 1979 annual report, David announced that Flirty Fishers had witnessed "to over a quarter of a million souls, loved over 25,000 of them and won about 19,000 to the Lord."

Moses David believed that he was the "End Time Prophet" and would play an important role during the Second Coming of Christ. Among David's revelations was the doomsday prophecy announcing the total destruction of the United States by a comet. David encouraged his flock to participate in a "Great Escape," leaving the United States and settling in Europe, South America, India and Australia.

John Bottom needed a safe haven. To escape the ongoing hostility they encountered on the road and the criticism of their hippie lifestyles, the Bottom Family decided to join the Children of God. In 1974 John Bottom moved his family to Crockett, Texas, which was the main commune for the cult. It was here that Rain Joan of Arc was born. After demonstrating their allegiance to the group, John and Arlyn became missionaries and, later, Bottom was designated as Archbishop of Venezuela and the Caribbean. For almost two years the Bottom family lived in San Juan, Puerto Rico, before heading south to Caracas, Venezuela. The family, at this time, spoke fluent Spanish. River and Rain sang, preached and panhandled for food as they handed out Children of God literature to anyone who would accept it.

Life for the newly-appointed Archbishop of Venezuela and the Caribbean and his family was not a glamorous tropical vacation. The Bottom clan lived in poverty. They slept in a shack with no toilet. The tropical paradise that surrounded them was a rat-infested slum. The paradise found was soon to be the paradise lost.

At the time of River's seventh birthday, the family had moved to the outskirts of the city, living in a dirty beach hut. Arlyn, disillusioned by the ultra-liberal sexual attitudes of the Children of God, later recollected, "The group was being distorted by a leader who was getting very full of power and wealth. He sought to attract rich disciples through sex. No way." They eventually escaped from their jungle prison after being smuggled back to the United States by a Catholic priest. They arrived in Englewood, Florida, on a toy-laden ocean freighter.

In a whirlwind odyssey lasting from 1972 to 1978, the Bottom family lived in Colorado, Texas, Mexico, Puerto Rico, Venezuela and Florida, before eventually arriving at their final destination: Hollywood.

The events leading to the hills of Hollywood were simplistic in their beauty and design. Mother Arlyn had written a letter to a Hollywood studio, requesting them to consider using her son River in one of its pictures. Soon after she received a form letter, a standard generic response, from Paramount Studios. Arlyn interpreted the letter as a cryptic invitation to return to California and Hollywood's promised land.

In 1977 the family drove their station wagon across the country to Los Angeles. They changed their name from Bottom to Phoenix and encouraged their talented children to pursue Hollywood careers. The clan included River Jude Phoenix, Joaquin Rafael Phoenix (who had his name changed to Leaf at age four), Summer Joy Phoenix, Rain Joan of Arc Phoenix and Libertad Mariposa (Liberty Butterfly) Phoenix. Arlyn would later change her name to Heart Phoenix.

River Phoenix took to acting without effort. He had spent years as a street musician, pan handling for money and preaching the word of The Children of God. Acting, he found, became a painless exercise to elicit approval from his audience. He was a natural, saving his best for the lights and the camera. By age 10 he was a professional TV actor, thanks to the energies of Hollywood's leading children's agent, Iris Burton.

Burton secured several small stints on the children's TV programs *Real Kids* and *Fantasy* for both River and his sister Rain. Later Burton was able to get him a number of television commercials. "River was the most beautiful child you've ever seen-like a little Elvis," she later recollected. From 1982 to 1983 he was featured in the CBS television series *Seven Brides for Seven Brothers*. At age 12 Phoenix played the youngest son but, although the program gave him an opportunity to showcase his talents, the series was cancelled after 22 episodes.

Still, there was something innately magical about the talent of River Phoenix. At the age of 13 he starred in a 1984 after-school TV special entitled *Backwards: The Riddle of Dyslexia*. The special was about a hidden reading impairment and featured a tortured and silent River Phoenix.

STAND BY ME

Phoenix made his motion picture debut in the 1985 science-fiction film *Explorers*. The next year, at 16, he acted in *Stand By Me*, a male-bonding suspense tale based on the Steven King short story "The Body." It was directed by Rob Reiner, who became one of his strongest supporters and who attended River's memorial service after his untimely death. But even with his newfound stardom, there were rumors that Phoenix had begun to experiment with drugs around this time.

The Mosquito Coast, starring Harrison Ford, seemed to parallel Phoenix's real life adventure of living in Mexico, Puerto Rico and Venezuela. Directed by Peter Weir, it was also shot in 1986. Phoenix would work in another Harrison Ford film later, as young Indiana Jones, in *Indiana Jones and the Last Crusade* (1989).

Phoenix was Oscar-nominated for Best Supporting Actor in the film *Running on Empty* (1988) and also garnered the National Board of Review's Best Supporting Actor Award. Featured as the mysterious Danny Pope, Phoenix' character was a gentle and vulnerable individual whose family of 60's radicals were on the run from the law. Phoenix shared the screen with Martha Plimpton, who became his real-life girlfriend as he was coming into his own as a talented actor. Sidney Lumet directed the film, which included Christine Lahti and Judd Hirsch. Phoenix lost the Oscar for Best Supporting Actor to Kevin Kline, who won for his role in *A Fish Called Wanda*.

Phoenix, at the age of 21, was teamed with independent director Gus Van Sant. Playing the part of a drugged-out narcoleptic street hustler in *My Own Private Idaho* (1991), his cinema persona discovered that his brother was actually his father. He won the National Society of Film Critics Best-Actor award at the 1992 Venice Film Festival. The real life project, an abstract Freudian road movie combining elements of Shakespeare's Henry IV, was filmed in Portland, OR, close to the Seattle epicenter of grunge, despondency and Mexican black tar heroin. There were rumors that an ever-curious River Phoenix began to associate with local heroin users during the shoot. After his death, there were speculations that he may have experimented with the opiate.

He had also experimented with music. Having learned to play guitar as a child, and while living in Gainesville, Florida, River formed the band "Aleka's Attic" with sister Rain. River Phoenix sang, played guitar and wrote songs for the group. A friend, Sasa Raphael, played bass. Their song "Across The Way" was included on the PETA (People for the Ethical Treatment of Animals) album called *Tame Yourself* with the proceeds used to fight animal abuse. A six-week tour of the East Coast in 1989 resulted in rioting mobs of young girls, all eager to worship at the altar of River Phoenix.

During the hot summer months prior to his death, Phoenix recorded an album entitled *Never Odd or Even*. It has never been released officially; however, Sasa Raphael attempted to make the album available for free download in 2000, on the anniversary of what would have been Phoenix's 30th birthday. The River Phoenix Estate sued for copyright infringement.

THE VIPER ROOM

It was Halloween morning, October 31,1993, sometime around 1:30 a.m. when the 911 call was made.

It came from the Viper Room, one of the Hollywood in-spots noted for hip celebrities, tabloid sensationalism and illegal substances. Owned at the time by actor Johnny Depp, the private nightclub was located at 8852 Sunset Boulevard in West Hollywood. Only a few blocks from Rodeo Drive, the Viper Room is just west of Spago and in the neighborhood of Hollywood and Vine, the Kodak Theatre and the Motion Picture Walk of Fame. It is surrounded by headquarters for Scientology, *Hustler Magazine* and Frederick's of Hollywood and is a frequent haunt for the LA *paparazzi* stalking their prey.

The Viper Room had always been mired in front-page controversy combining music with Hollywood-style personalities. In the 1940's it was called "The Melody Room," with gangster Bugsy Siegel as a regular. Los Angeles rock luminaries Arthur Lee and Love and Jim Morrison and The Doors played there in the late 1960's.

In 1993 the Viper Room was a windowless black hole with subtle green lights. It featured a total of five black vinyl booths reserved for hip luminaries looking to escape predatory paparazzi and the lusting public eye. One sported a bronze plaque warning "Don't f*** with it", reserved for Johnny Depp's agent. The Viper Room had long been a favorite haunt of young Hollywood types and rock stars, including River Phoenix.

River Phoenix spent Saturday, October 30, 1993 on a Hollywood sound stage shooting interior scenes for the horror film *Dark Blood*. Around 7:00 p.m. he returned to the Hotel Nikko. His girlfriend, actress Samantha Mathis, and Joaquin and Rain Phoenix met him. Later, members of the Red Hot Chili Peppers (Flea), Butthole Surfers (Gibby Haynes) and Ministry (Al J.) joined the entourage. The group drove from the Hotel Nikko to the Viper Room and arrived around 10:00 p.m. at the Hollywood nightclub.

The Viper Room was a favorite venue for groups that walked the perilous fault line between commercial success and cult status. They included Green Day, Oasis, Matchbox 20, Run-D.M.C., Sheryl Crow, Billy Idol, The Go-Go's, The Black Crowes, Iggy Pop, Lenny Kravitz and the Stone Temple Pilots. Flea, Al J. and Gibby Haynes were all scheduled to perform on the night of Phoenix's death.

According to reports, after several hours, Phoenix was observed sweating, and later vomiting, in the men's room. He was confused and gasping for breath. Just past midnight Mathis and Joaquin carried him outside into the night air. The actor began to convulse as he collapsed on the cold, hard concrete, bathed in reflections of neon. Minutes later Rain Phoenix rushed to her brother's side and lay on his convulsing body.

Patrons came outside and stared, some hysterical and crying, but most dulled and anesthetized from hours of alcohol and drug use. Later, a celebrity photographer related that Joaquin was yelling at the others to leave River alone, convinced that he would be all right. After about 25 minutes, Joaquin ran to a pay phone and frantically dialed 911, screaming to emergency personnel, "You must get here, please, because he's dying."

An Internet website dedicated to his life reported that River Phoenix spoke his last words to a reporter attempting to help the drugged actor. His final request, spoken under the Viper Room's purple awning was for "no *paparazzi*, I want anonymity." Honoring his wishes, the reporter took no photographs, silently watching as the young star's breathing slowed.

When the paramedics arrived, River Phoenix had no signs of pulse or blood pressure. He had gone into cardiac arrest. With only a short period of time that can pass between cardiac arrest and life saving treatment, Joaquin's anguished 911 call may have already been too late. River had stopped breathing, his skin a sickly blue color, even as they lifted his corpse onto the stretcher.

The ambulance transported his lifeless body to Cedars-Sinai Medical Center. Flea (a.k.a. Michael Balzary), bass player for the Red Hot Chili Peppers and Phoenix's good friend, sat in the front seat. Los Angles County Fire Captain Ray Ribar was also in the vehicle. They arrived at the hospital at 1:34 a.m. Emergency room surgeons worked on him for 20 minutes, attempting to revive the actor. It was all in vain. River Phoenix was pronounced dead at about 1:54 a.m.

Listed in the L.A. coroner's case as No. 93-10011, his belongings included a pair of medium long brown pants with dark stripes, a pair of All Star black and white high-topped tennis sneakers and a pair of socks. That was how his end came: simple, unassuming, final. He had so much promise, so many possibilities to realize before his unfulfilled life ended at 23 years of age.

Immediately after his death, the media postulated that Phoenix had died from either an epileptic seizure or a stroke. Joaquin admitted that his brother had taken the sedative Valium, which only fueled the morbid public debate as to what had caused his death.

A coroner's spokesman reported that Phoenix died from a lethal combination of cocaine and heroin, the same deadly speedball that had claimed the life of comedian John Belushi (1949-1982) in the '80's and the same drug concoction that, according to at least one credible source, was used by the Beatles during the recording of Sgt. *Pepper's Lonely Heart's Club Band*. Among the toxic flotsam found in Phoenix's blood stream were traces of marijuana, the prescription sedative Valium and an over-the-counter cold medication.

GHB

As word spread that River had taken GHB that night, it became the classic urban legend. In November 1993, the *Los Angeles Times* featured an expose on GHB, dubbing it "the newest designer drug to fuel the Hollywood fast lane." The article speculated that River Phoenix's death was linked to GHB, that his multi drug cocktail was certain to have had GHB included in its mix. The well publicized seizure and hospitalization of punk rocker Billy Idol outside Tatou, another trendy Beverly Hills nightclub and restaurant, was mentioned in the same piece as a further example of GHB's deadly popularity.

In 1990, before the release of his *Charmed Life* album, the hard charging Idol almost lost a leg in a near-tragic motorcycle accident. Billy Idol would later sing the praises of GHB in his pro-drug song "Then The Night Comes." "I take some GHB/I feel love, joy and wonderful tingling music." Years later, during an MTV interview, Idol seemed to denounce GHB and stated that it would have been sad to have died on the streets of Hollywood from an overdose.

The GHB connection wasn't anything new. This sedative had been around since the 1980's, usually drunk with an orange juice or alcohol chaser. Gamma-Hydroxybutyrate was known on the streets as Easy Lay, Liquid X, Georgia Home Boy, Grievous Bodily Harm, Scoop and Somatomax. And in the New York City club scene a mixture of GHB and methamphetamine was called a "Max Cocktail." The drug, sometimes called "Salty Water," was odorless but had a salty taste. GHB increased euphoria, relaxation and produced deep REM sleep. It reduced inhibitions and triggered the libido. It combined all the elements of a recreational club drug and predatory rape drug, with the added element of danger. When mixed with alcohol and benzodiazepines, the mix could lead to central nervous system and respiratory depression and acute gastro intestinal poisoning. In higher doses GHB could cause seizure activity, coma and death.

After Phoenix's death, the incidence of GHB abuse in nightclubs and raves increased. Due to the unrelenting *paparazzi* hysteria and in the wake of River's death and Idol's two overdoses, GHB overdoses took a steady climb. It was a bizarre but not uncommon response to celebrity death and near death publicity. At the time of Phoenix's death, GHB was popular in the club scene, was not illegal and was virtually unknown to medical and law enforcement professions. GHB is difficult to detect and leaves the system rapidly with a half-life of about 20 minutes. GHB clears from blood in about 4 or 5 hours and is in urine only about 12 hours. Because of this rapid half-life and the lack of adequate testing (the Los Angeles Coroners Office had no ability to test for GHB at this time), it was impossible to determine if River Phoenix had ingested GHB at the time of his fatal drug overdose.

BACKGROUND

In Europe during the 1960's GHB had been used as a general anesthetic on a limited basis. It was also prescribed for insomnia, narcolepsy and childbirth. There were reports of successful treatment for alcoholism and alcohol withdrawal with this substance, although it is now known that GHB in itself is addictive with a withdrawal syndrome even more prolonged and severe than that of alcohol.

The sedative made its way to America where, in the 1980's, it was sold over the counter in health food stores and was a popular product with bodybuilders and among steroid abusers. A 1977 Japanese study (which was incorrect in its explanation of how GHB worked) claimed that GHB increased the production of human growth hormone. The study further claimed that GHB could increase lean muscle mass and decrease stored body fat.

The drug remained mired in myth and fantasy as extensive studies on humans, possible benefits of the substance, and abuse potential had all contributed to a morass of confusing data. In November 1990, after several deaths, the Food and Drug Administration banned over-the-counter sales of GHB. In early 2000, the DEA listed more than 5,700 reported overdoses of GHB and at least 58 deaths since 1990. Reported overdoses on GHB had dropped after it was banned.

Georgia and Rhode Island were the first states to recognize the dangers of GHB, and declared it a controlled substance. Responding to a nationwide epidemic of sexual assault via chemicals, including GHB, Congress passed the Drug-Induced Rape Prevention and Punishment Act of 1996. This federal law provided for up to 20 years in prison for anyone convicted of using a controlled substance such as GHB or GBL to commit sexual assault or other violent crimes.

Three years later a sensational date rape trial captured the attention of America. Samantha Reid, a 15 year-old girl from Grosse Ile, Michigan, died on January 17,1999; her soft drink had been laced with GHB. Her death resulted in convictions of three young men who secretly gave her the drug. Found guilty of involuntary manslaughter and poisoning charges were Joshua Cloie, 19, Daniel Brayman, 18 and Nicholas Holtschlag, 18. Erick Limmer, the fourth defendant, was convicted of a lesser charge. Narrowly sidestepping a more-serious manslaughter charge, Limmer was convicted of one count each of being an accessory to manslaughter, poisoning, delivery of marijuana and possession of gamma-hydroxybutyrate. (All four individuals are members of the Generation Y demographic cluster, a group this author believes to be one of the most violent.)

GHB, being marketed as Xyrem, is currently a DEA Schedule lll controlled substance, but if diverted for abuse, it is handled as a Schedule l drug for sentencing. Xyrem has been approved for the treatment of narcolepsy and cataplexy. Because of its abuse as a predatory drug, GHB and its analogs became Schedule l federally in March 2000.

Unfortunately, the mystery of River Phoenix' possible GHB ingestion will never be solved. By the time the Los Angeles Coroner was capable of testing for GHB (several years later), his toxicology samples had already been destroyed. But to Trinka Porrata, retired LAPD narcotics detective and President of Project GHB (a nonprofit website dedicated to education, prevention, research and treatment related to GHB abuse issues), it all makes sense. "River wasn't trying to commit suicide. So why would he take so much of so many drugs? GHB is a dissociative anesthetic. It can cause separation of mind from body. If he did take GHB at some point and hit that dissociative state, he may not have "felt" the other drugs and just kept piling them on, not realizing the quantity that would then take its toll. In any case, the belief that he did take GHB sadly has added to its spread as a drug of abuse."

Despite the FDA ban, GHB is also sold openly over the Internet. Numerous recipes for making homemade GHB are available from a variety of sources, including bodybuilding publications such as Dan Duchaine's infamous *Underground Steroid Handbook for Men and Women*.

HOLLYWOOD DRUG USE

Drug use among the trendy Hollywood rock crowd is nothing new. It goes with the territory, the artificial mantra of the jet set, the insane yin-yang of art imitating life and life imitating art. Sixties alumni such as Jim Morrison (1943-1971), Jimi Hendrix (1942-1970) and Janis Joplin (1943-1970) have all seen their stars shine ever so brightly only to be snuffed out in their prime. And then cult leader Jerry Garcia (1942–1995), Woodstock guru and quasi-religious icon, reaped what he had sown, his heart giving out, unable to maintain a system weakened by heroin and cocaine and marijuana and LSD. In a perverse sense, River Phoenix was only following the patterns set out before him, only emulating the roles played out by so many others preceding him.

In a prepared statement, River Phoenix's publicist Susan Patricola said, "Hopefully, it's a wake up call to the world. It leaves you to question why are young people compelled to do this?" A memorial service was held on November 19, 1993 on the Paramount lot in Hollywood. In attendance were Sidney Poitier, John Boorman and Rob Reiner.

Phoenix espoused the credo of keeping his temple holy. He personified one who abstained from, and abhorred, illegal substances.

His innocent Hollywood image evoked the vision of a healthy individual in sync with Mother Earth and all things pure. River Phoenix was an animal rights activist and environmentalist. He had purchased hundreds of acres of rain forest in Costa Rica and Brazil to prevent them from being commercially developed. As a strict vegan he refused to eat meat, fish, eggs or dairy products. He refused to wear leather. The irony of River Phoenix's unexpected, yet predictable, death is that his public persona was a lie, wrapped around the false dogma of someone that he wanted to be.

In Leonard Maltin's 1994 *Movie Encyclopedia*, Phoenix's Biography read in part, "His all-American looks and pensive manner made him appealing to teenage fans, but his dedication to the craft of acting set him apart from other youthful heartthrobs." For those who knew him, or knew of him, he was the gentle, soft-spoken, drug free conscience of his generation. He was the 90's version of *Rebel Without a Cause* James Dean, some 40 years before.

But, like Dean, both cloaked their dark side beneath a smoldering, brooding and troubled persona.

He died too soon, frozen in our collective psyches as that youthful and carefree beautiful boy. In the end, it was River Phoenix's gentle vulnerability, his ageless angelic innocence that lost its appeal to an audience looking for the next new thing. His last films, such as 1992's *The Thing Called Love*, made little impact on the marketplace and foretold what would be his tragic ending. In the thirteen films he made, he successfully portrayed the vulnerability, the sensitivity, the alienation of Generation X. But even that beautiful and personal softness became a curse, as he began to lose important roles and be upstaged by other youthful male actors with a darker, harder edge, peers such as Brad Pitt, Johnny Deep, Keanu Reeves and Christian Slater.

But even that persona was about to change as Phoenix began to transform, abandoning his childlike innocence for the darker side. At the time of his death he was in production on a desert horror flick called *Dark Blood*, playing the part of "Boy." Along with Judy Davis and Jonathan Pryce he was spending grueling 12-hour days, shooting the film in Utah. *Dark Blood,* directed by George Slier, was never finished, as there were too many unfilled scenes, crucial to the plot, that would need to be reshot with another actor.

Phoenix was also scheduled to begin production on the film version of Anne Rice's book *Interview With the Vampire: The Vampire Chronicles,* the following year. Phoenix had been cast as reporter Daniel Malloy, a part that went to actor Christian Slater after Phoenix' drug overdose.

When word of his overdose got out, the reality of River Phoenix and his plunge into the netherworld of substance abuse became clear. Agent Iris Burton felt that Phoenix had been using drugs for a long time. She said, "I'm in the same amount of pain no matter how he died. We're all really in enough pain that he passed away."

Not everyone showed compassion for his tragic death. The *Houston Post* noted, "Every person who abuses drugs is directly responsible for the death and destruction caused by those drugs. It matters little whether his is a casual or serious use."

Director John Boorman, who attended Phoenix's memorial tribute at the Paramount Studio lot, recalled what Heart Phoenix had said. His mother said that she'd been in labor with River for 48 hours and that she was convinced he hadn't really wanted to be born. Heart thought River had struck some sort of deal so that he wouldn't have to stay very long on this earth.

"People were invited to say things ... so I got up and said, 'Why did he have to take all those drugs?' ... His girlfriend (Samantha Mathis) stood up and said that she thought he could feel people's pain: the pain of the world. And he had to find a way to dull that pain. He simply couldn't deal with it," Boorman said.

His star had dimmed much too soon, too early in the game. His potential, the promise of what could have been, underscored the tragic loss as reflected by tributes from so many of his peers.

The media's immediate and critical impact on our culture and on our cultural icons is of particular interest to singer-songwriter Natalie

Merchant. In "River," a song from the 1995 CD *Tigerlily*, Merchant defends Phoenix as she castigates the media for systematically dissecting the child actor after his death. Much of their emphasis was on Phoenix' suspected drug using lifestyle. In her haunting song Merchant screams out " Why don't you let him be/Give his mother and father peace," as she rails against the media vultures hovering over his cold body, picking away at the remains. Merchant's anger is later replaced with quiet reflection, asking, "It was such a nightmare raving, 'How could we save him from himself?'"

Natalie Merchant's "River" was one of many tributes that expressed the love and respect of his peers. "Transcending," by the Red Hot Chile Peppers, from their CD *One Hot Minute*, was dedicated to Phoenix. Other tributes came from Belinda Carlisle and Rufus Wainwright. Director Gus Van Sant's film *Even Cowgirls Get the Blues* (1993) offered a dedication "For River" in the opening credits. Van Sant later published the novel *Pink* (1997), which was "a thinly veiled exploration of his grief over River Phoenix's 1993 death," according to Rebecca Flint's *All Movie Guide*.

Monster, the 1994 R.E.M. CD, contains in the liner notes the dedication "for River." Calling Phoenix's death "The most shattering experience of my life," R.E.M. lead singer Michael Stipe was quoted as saying, "He was my brother and I loved him a great deal. It was just an awful, awful mistake. We fed off each other and learned a lot from each other."

River Phoenix had been listed as one of twelve "Promising New Actors of 1986" in John Willis' *Screen World*, Vol. 38. He was ranked #86 in the 1997 *Empire* Magazine's (UK) "The Top 100 Movie Stars of All Time" listing and #69 on "100 Greatest Movie Stars" on the UK's Channel 4.

Mother Heart Phoenix had her son dressed in beads and necklaces, wearing his Aleka's Attic T-shirt. She placed a single pink carnation in the coffin. The body of River Phoenix was cremated, his ashes scattered at the family's Florida ranch. In keeping with his wishes, the Phoenix family requested that all donations made in his name should go to his favorite charities: Earth Trust in Malibu and Earth Save in Santa Cruz. Christian Slater, who replaced Phoenix in the part of reporter Daniel Malloy in *Interview With the Vampire*, donated all of his salary to Earth Trust.

The day prior to the cremation a *paparazzo* broke into the funeral parlor and rearranged the lifeless body. He took at least one ghoulish photograph. That illegally—obtained photo was sold to the National Enquirer for $5000.00 in a final act of degradation to one of Generation X's most promising talents.

6

Hollywood on Dope

Reflected in 1950's pulp fiction, heroin's Golden Age navigated the dark alleyways of opiate abuse through a strange collection of motion pictures, magazine articles and books. Nelson Algren's 1949 novel, *The Man With The Golden Arm,* uniquely portrayed heroin as a serious literary topic that rejected the standard "dope fiend" approach of the time. *The Man With The Golden Arm*, a gritty 1955 black and white film adaptation, was the first of its kind to tackle the marginalized issue of illicit drug use. A youthful Frank Sinatra, lean and intense, played the role of heroin-addicted card shark "Johnny Machine" and received an Oscar nomination for Best Actor. But because it dealt with the subject of "narcotics," Hollywood's Production Code refused to grant a seal of approval for the film, which was considered taboo.

Other motion pictures taking a retro look at the era included *Lady Sings The Blues, Ray* and *Bird*, tracing the tortured lives of artists Billie Holiday, Ray Charles and Charlie Parker. Addicted to heroin, these musicians were representative of the deadly relationship between the opiate and the black music community. According to the Chicago *Tribune's* Mark Caro, "Jazz's age of heroin peaked in the 1950s with Charlie Parker, the alto saxophone genius whose addiction led uncounted jazz artists to emulate him in the hope that they, too, might play at his level. Parker, who was ashamed of his addiction, implored his followers not to turn to heroin, but artists as formidable as the young Miles Davis, Sonny Rollins, Red Rodney and numerous others took up the habit."

Directed by Clint Eastwood, *Bird* had been called "the most personal" of Eastwood's films. On his website the documentary is described as "a biography of Charlie Parker, the self-taught, self-destructive musician making his way up out of rural poverty to play his revolutionary music in the jazz clubs during the '40s and '50s ... It pays full tribute to the man's genius and the sweetness of his spirit, yet offers no easy excuses or sentimental explanations for his suicidal behavior. *Bird* is ultimately, as Clint sees it, a tragedy about a man refusing to take responsibility for himself and his gifts ..."

Due to his own unique set of circumstances Charlie Parker became addicted to the illegal drug. It is important to note that after the Harrison Narcotics Act of 1914, heroin became the drug of choice for many black urban males, with Charlie "Bird" Parker being a prime example of that cadre. Prior to that, the individual most likely to be a narcotics addict in the nineteenth century was a middle-class Southern female abusing morphine. Lowry's 1956 study of the Lexington, KY Federal Hospital demonstrated how heroin impacted on the black community in a disproportionate manner. Of 1,000 admissions in 1936 20% were white males while only 8.9% were African-Americans. In 1956, white male prisoners (abusing morphine) comprised 60% of all admissions while African-Americans comprised 52%. In a nineteen year span, the profile of the Lexington addict changed from a 38-year-old white male prisoner to a twenty-something African-American male prisoner (abusing heroin.)

Ray, starring Jamie Foxx, is a survival epic about a man who faced incredible odds. Haunted by inner demons, including the accidental drowning death of his brother George, Ray Charles, later billed as "the blind Ray Charles," ended up as a backup musician bussed around the Florida Chitlin Circuit, isolated and, at times, not even knowing the town he was in. "Everyday I have the blues," the musician, blind since the age of seven, related. In his *Encyclopedia of Jazz in the Sixties*, Leonard Feather noted "The tragedies of his personal life … lent a poignancy to his blues interpretations that had no equal in the jazz of the late 1950s and early 1960s."

Directed by Taylor Hackford, this 2005 film explained how Charles created his music, a mix of rhythm and blues, gospel, jazz and country. As he blended diverse musical forms, Charles outraged many in his community with his music. "You're making money off the Lord," one critic scolded him. Ray Charles was later inducted into the inaugural Rock & Roll Hall of Fame in 1986 and awarded twelve Grammys for his "devil music."

In the film *Ray* there are numerous scenes that reflected Charles' 17-year heroin addiction, such as his introduction to the narcotic by band mate David "Fathead" Newman: "This is boy. This boy will make your ass null and void." Ray responded, "My life is already null and void." But in his 1978 autobiography, *Brother Ray*, Charles assumes full responsibility for his addiction. He explained that curiosity led to his eventual habit and that it had nothing to do with his poverty, blindness or blackness. He also emphasized that no one approached him to do the drugs, but rather he approached them. One telling moment had Charles singing in the Atlantic Records recording booth, as an engineer observed, "Look at him. He's got that junkie itch." And soon after as another sarcastic voice cautioned, "You can never trust a junkie." During an interview with CBS's Ed Bradley, Charles explored his music-heroin connection: "Some of the biggest records that I've ever had is during the time when I was using drugs. You see, but that ain't to say that it was the drugs that created the big records." And when asked if heroin made him play better, Charles responded, "I never did think that. I used them because I enjoy, I mean, I enjoyed what I was doing."

Brother Ray appeared to sidestep the issue of heroin-induced creativity, perhaps unwilling to credit the drug for his artistry and vast body of work. But some felt that the opiate helped channel the imaginative juices and pointed to the collection of work by such individuals as Chet Baker, Kurt Cobain, Eric Clapton, Miles Davis, Billie Holiday, Janis Joplin, John Lennon, Charlie Parker, Jim Morrison, Gram

Parsons, Lou Reed, Steven Tyler, and countless others as evidence of the drug-music connection. Author Stanley Booth wrote that during the recording of 1972's *Exile On Main Street* lead guitarist and heroin addict Keith Richards was "strung out during this peak of genius." Throughout history there have been numerous inspired individuals who have used or been addicted to the opiates, including such luminaries as Charles Baudelaire, Aleister Crowley, Thomas De Quincey, Edgar Allan Poe and Oscar Wilde. In 1797 Samuel Taylor Coleridge, under the influence of laudanum, wrote the poem *Kubla Khan, Or A Vision In A Dream. A Fragment*. Still, the extent to which drugs affect literary creativity is subjective and debatable. Not everyone agreed that heroin triggered or enhanced the creative process. The Sex Pistols front man, John (a.k.a. Johnny Rotten) Lydon called heroin "the drug of self-pity" and described it as "the only drug that cancels out all forms of creativity."

One school of thought is that creativity is genetically determined with input from environment and individual experience. Drug use, such as with heroin, produces highs and lows, extreme emotions and altered perceptions. It also lowers inhibitions and allows for a more instinctual and emotive response rather than one focused on content, specificity and process. In the musical realm that precise drug experience may lend itself to a free-flowing and improvisational creative process such as with experimental be-bop, jazz or techno, but, then again, drug use could also allow for a redundant and repetitive work that is boring and uninteresting in its scope.

In 1964, while in Boston, Charles was arrested for possession of heroin and marijuana. It was his third offence and, along with a five-year suspended sentence, he was offered a last chance. Charles was determined to kick his habit rather that be incarcerated. "When you're blind, you don't have that many choices," he later remarked. Hospitalized in Lynwood, California, at the St. Francis Rehabilitation Clinic, Charles was introduced to Dr. Frederick J. Hacker. Hacker, a Viennese psychiatrist with successful clinics in Austria and Beverly Hills, helped Charles withdraw from heroin. Charles' decision was to go through "cold turkey" withdrawal without methadone replacement therapy. Charles later felt that the physical aspects of his four-day withdrawal were easier to deal with than the psychological aspects, but in the film, the scene where Ray kicks the habit is possibly one of the most intense withdrawal scenes ever filmed.

Ray Charles, *"The Genius,"* died on June 10, 2004 of cancer. He died in Los Angeles, "The place where the Negro comes to spread his wings," Charles explained in the film portrayal of his life.

ACTUAL DRUG INJECTION

In this fixed genre, there were two heroin-centered films that explored the relationships of addicted lovers. *The Panic In Needle Park*, photographed in a moving *cinema verte* style, depicted a tender story of two young lovers (Al Pacino and Kitty Winn) trapped in heroin's ironclad grip. The movie trailers cried, "God help Bobby and Helen. They're in love in Needle Park." The film's reality-like aura, shot in 1971 with fuzzy, unfocused techniques, inspired future documentaries *Black Tar Heroin: The Dark End of the Street, Shooting Up In San Francisco* and HBO's *The Corner*, the latter investigating the plight of addicts who lived around West Baltimore's open-air drug markets. *Panic* is believed to have been the first mainstream film to portray, in graphic close-ups, actual drug injection from the needle into the vein.

Sid and Nancy was the 1986 biography of Sid Vicious (Gary Oldman) and his American girlfriend, ex-prostitute and heroin addict, Nancy Spungen (Chloe Webb). Essentially it told an explosive love story, originally titled *Love Kills* that proved the maxim "true love never runs smooth." Vicious, whose real name was John Simon Richie, was bass player with the outrageous, albeit legendary, British punk group the Sex Pistols. Vicious, in the throes of a heroin addiction and a volatile, mutually destructive relationship with Spungen, attempted a solo career when the Sex Pistols broke up after their disastrous 1978 U.S. tour. Vicious, the punk figurehead described as "a lost and bewildered man-child," was deemed to be interesting and bankable. The final chapter came one morning, after Spungen was found stabbed to death and Vicious, covered in blood and in a heroin daze, was arrested for second-degree homicide. The film materialized during a time of renewed interest in the period of punk rock, heroin addiction and specifically the life of Sid Vicious. Director Alex Cox told the *New Musical Express*: "We wanted to make the film not just about Sid Vicious and punk, but as an anti-drug statement, to show the degradation caused to various people is not at all glamorous."

Roger Ebert gave *Sid and Nancy* a four-star review for The Chicago *Sun Times*, writing that Cox and his staff "pull off the neat trick of creating a movie full of noise and fury, and telling a meticulous story right in the middle of it." In a subsequent article about actor Gary Oldman, Ebert referred to the movie's ostensible couple as "Punk Rock's *Romeo and Juliet*." Somewhat paradoxically, Courtney Love was later compared to Nancy Spungen, in relevance to her relationship with Nirvana's Kurt Cobain. And in his book *Sid Vicious: Rock N' Roll Star*, Malcolm Butt described Webb's performance as Nancy as "intense, powerful, and most important of all, believable." Leslie Halliwell, in contrast, had no praise for the movie stating, "Some have said stimulating, most have preferred revolting. Consensus, an example of the dregs to which cinema has been reduced."

And in his 1994 autobiography, *Rotten: No Irish, No Blacks, No Dogs*, John Lyndon (a.k.a. Johnny Rotten) equally criticized the movie: "I cannot understand why anyone would want to put out a movie like *Sid and Nancy* and not bother to speak to me; Alex Cox, the director, didn't. He used as his point of reference—of all the people on this earth—Joe Strummer! That guttural singer from The Clash? What the fuck did he know about Sid and Nancy? That's probably all he could find, which was really scraping the bottom of the barrel ... The only time Alex Cox made any approach toward me was when he sent the chap who was playing me over to New York where I was." Lyndon continued, "To me this movie is the lowest form of life. I honestly believe that it celebrates heroin addiction. It definitely glorifies it at the end when that stupid taxi drives off into the sky. That's such nonsense," explained the former punk-god Johnny Rotten.

Critics debated the "pro" and "anti-drug" stance of the film, with many invoking the standard argument about the "glorification" of drug use. The movie ended with a bizarre fantasy sequence where Sid rejoined Nancy in the back seat of a New York taxi and they drove off, happily in love, into the never-never land of their private opiate sunset. But that tender scene of lovers reunited was far from the harsh reality. The final ride for The Sex Pistol's bass player was not in the back of a New York City cab but inside of a plastic body bag. The truth about the death of Sid Vicious is that, after his release from Rikers Island on $50,000 bail from Virgin Records, he shot heroin, collapsed, seizured and died in his Greenwich Village apartment. His mother, Anne Beverley, who provided him the heroin, said: "He knew the smack was pure and strong and took a lot less than usual." (Studies have indicated that two weeks after prison is the most dangerous time period for an addict. Thirteen percent report their last overdose shortly after release from incarceration.) An autopsy confirmed that Vicious died from an accumulation of fluid in the lungs that was consistent with heroin overdose. A syringe, spoon and heroin residue was discovered by police officers near the lifeless body.

At the end of the *Sid and Nancy* taxi dream sequence the following script appeared against a black backdrop. It read:

Sid Vicious died of a heroin overdose on February 2nd, 1979.
R.I.P. Nancy and Sid

STATE DEPARTMENT REPORT

In the mid-1990's, heroin, once shunned like a medieval plague, was embraced with possibility and open, track-scarred arms. All indicators pointed to the theory that heroin was destined to be the new drug of the decade and an integral part of the drug sub-culture. Following a decade of rampant cocaine abuse in the 1980's the U.S. Government anticipated heroin's arrival and warned of a "possible" heroin epidemic. They cited aggressive Columbian drug cartels and cheaper production costs as evidence for the shift in drug use patterns.

"In the past five years, there has been a steady increase in the flow and purity of heroin to the U.S., suggesting that the taste for the drug is growing," warned a State Department report in 1994. The report further stated, "With the likelihood that heroin will be to the 1990's what cocaine was to the 1980's, Latin American trafficking organizations are poised to cash in on a heroin epidemic." After more than a decade of widespread cocaine abuse, heroin quickly emerged as the newest trend in American recreational drug use.

In 1994 the DEA estimated that 20 tons of heroin were being shipped into the United States, an alarming increase of from four to six tons in the early 1980's. It was not long before our cultish fascination with diacetylmorphine exploded into mass appeal and heroin arrived as "the" fashionable recreational drug of the 1990's. The number of Americans who had tried heroin rose from between 400 and 750 thousand to roughly 1.5 million citizens. According to Join Together, a drug education organization, the overall number of estimated heroin users rose from 68,0000 in 1993 to 325,000 in 1997. There was also an alarming 100% increase in heroin use by 12th graders from 1990 to 1997.

The 1990's, for some a decade of despondency, isolation and hopelessness, begat a trend towards heroin use quietly embraced by Generation X grunge rockers. The drug had evolved from a cultural phenomena, a party drug that could be smoked or snorted, to that of a savage wrecking machine. Heroin became a major problem in the Pacific Northwest as it claimed the lives of Generation X musicians in "epidemic" proportions. No other cluster of heroin addicts would suffer more than this unfortunate group. The deaths of Nirvana's Kurt Cobain, Alice in Chain's Layne Staley and the Smashing Pumpkin's Jonathan Melvoin illustrated the perils associated with the dirty powdered substance and its toxic relationship with the Seattle music scene.

During this period the film industry contributed to the heroin frenzy. *Gia* was a 1998 Emmy-winning HBO movie that unveiled the dark side of the fashion industry and starred an unknown Angelina Jolie as drug-addicted model Gia Carangi. The documentary, with the tag line "Too wild to live. Too beautiful to die," followed the rise of America's first supermodel from a Philadelphia lunch counter to the international walkways of the high fashion industry. Unfortunately, Gia's meteoric rise to fame was short lived. Within a two-year period she had become addicted to heroin and frequented the hardcore shooting galleries of Manhattan's Lower East Side, the bowels of the city. For her performance Jolie won a Golden Globe for Best Actress and another Emmy Nomination—as she had already previously won for the TV movie *George Wallace*. Overall, Gia received six Emmy nominations and won two Golden Globe Awards including Outstanding Motion Picture For Television, as well as both the Writers Guild and the Directors Guild Awards. The film featured Faye Dunaway and Mercedes Ruehl and was directed by Michael Cristofer.

The idea behind *Gia* came from an excerpt of the book *Thing of Beauty: The Tragedy of Supermodel Gia* that appeared in *Vanity Fair*. The book had been written by Stephen Fried (1993) but was under option to Paramount, according to *Gia's* Executive Producer Illene Power-Kahn, who had to seek out other sources for her film.

Gia remained a person of fascination and mystery, her tragic story told and retold for those who hungered to learn more about the model. Several two-hour, primetime programs were developed about the late supermodel's life and were later featured on ABC's *Vanished* series and E!s *True Hollywood Stories*.

Her death resulted from a combination of emotional uncertainty, heroin addiction and the AIDS virus. "Gia was a beautiful junkie who was completely undone by the beauty business and her mother leaving her," said Power-Kahn of the star. And in their far-reaching review, *TV Guide* noted, "The tragic, true-life story of Gia Carangi contains so many highs and lows (mostly the latter) that it was merely a matter of time before it served as the source material for a movie.

This small-screen production does justice to the cautionary tale of her rise and fall in fashion circles, emphasizing a lifestyle of sex, drugs, and indulgence that seemingly had to end in death ...

"Indeed, the film poses some difficult questions about the underside of glamour, and makes a very strong argument against the 'heroin chic' phenomenon."

Another cluster of motion pictures glamorized the gritty lifestyle of opiate addiction to a mainstream audience and included *Pulp Fiction* (1994), *The Basketball Diaries* (1995) and *Trainspotting* (1996). The success of these films revealed that the heroin culture, although dark and forbidden, was equally fascinating. It demonstrated that the American public hungered for glimpses into heroin's dark and mysterious culture. It was also commercially viable. Quintin Tarantino's *Pulp Fiction,* an independent film made on a shoestring budget of only eight million dollars, grossed over 107 million dollars in box office revenue. *Pulp Fiction* set the standard with its mix of drugs and violence cleverly interspaced with music and humor. The experiment in chemistry paid off as *Pulp Fiction* was nominated for seven Academy Awards. The film portrayed Samuel L. Jackson as a Bible-quoting assassin and helped resurrect the career of John Travolta, portraying him as a sympathetic, likable hit man. *Pulp Fiction* was ranked at # 280 on the all time list of films grossing over 100 million dollars in ticket sales according to All Time USA Box Office.

The quintessential heroin—related film, *Traffic*, came in at # 211 on the list and netted $124,107,476 in box-office ticket sales. *Traffic* (2000) became the most commercially successful heroin film of all time as it effectively intertwined four graphic stories that surrounded the illegal drug trade. Winner of four Academy Awards, *Traffic* earned Benicio Del Toro an Oscar as Best Supporting Actor.

Director Danny Boyle's *Trainspotting,* an adaptation of Irvine Welsh's best-selling novel, took a hard yet curious look at Scotland's violent junkie subculture. The film explored the use of smack via protagonist Mark Renton, who attempted to kick his habit throughout the film. It blended some gripping, uncomfortable scenes with a straight out declaration of the glories and authenticity of heroin. Said a reflective Mark Renton: "Life's boring and futile. We fill up our lives with shit, things like careers and relationships that delude ourselves that it isn't all totally pointless. Smack's an honest drug, because it strips away these delusions. With smack, when you feel good, you feel immortal. When you feel bad, it intensifies the shit that's already there. It's the only real honest drug. It doesn't alter your consciousness. It just gives you a hit and a sense of well-being. After that, you see the misery in the world as it is, and you cannot anesthetize yourself against it."

Critics immediately charged that the film, and others like it, somehow glamorized the use of heroin. Two months after *Trainspotting's* 1996 U.S. release, US Presidential candidate Bob Dole publicly condemned the film, as well as *Pulp Fiction*, in an attack on Hollywood's portrayal of drug use. Dole later admitted, under media pressure, that he had not actually seen either film. What these films did accomplish—besides providing politicians with inflammatory and contemporary social issues, was to introduce us to a nether world seldom before seen. *Trainspotting, Pulp Fiction, The Basketball Diaries* and *Traffic* did acknowledge the pleasures of heroin use and the fascinating sub-cultures that surrounded the drug's use. But these motion pictures also depicted the horrors of substance abuse including addiction, depravity and death. Although the excitement and dark humor of the heroin experience in *Trainspotting* are evident, there is also a chilling image of Renton (actor Ewan McGregor) as he experiences a violent withdrawal. Above him, crawling spider-like on the ceiling, is the dead baby of his junkie neighbor, a macabre reminder of his haunted past.

The Basketball Diaries, directed by Scott Kalvert, was a more accessible version of the Beat Generation's *Naked Lunch*, and a more stylized version of both *Man With the Golden Arm* and *Panic in Needle Park*. All of these films worked the same side of the street; a decaying neighborhood reeking of isolation and despondency. And violence. *The Basketball Diaries,* billed as "The true story of the death of innocence and the birth of an artist," detailed the rite of passage of Jim Carroll (actor Leonardo DiCaprio). Carroll, a promising high school basketball player, became caught up in the fight against boredom and the quest for cheap thrills. In the process he also became addicted. The film, heavy on dramatic content, dabbled in outlaw behaviors, homosexuality, prostitution and the inevitable conflict with family and social values.

Exploring the dark heroin culture, these drug-themed motion pictures were accepted by the public with interest and fascination. And even as they portrayed an angry needle piercing hungry flesh and the inevitable withdrawal, all of these cinematic offerings shared commonality in the message that life may not be so bad after addiction. In *Trainspotting*, Lou Reed's "Perfect Day" is softly played in the background: Oh It's Such A Perfect Day/I'm Glad I Spent It With You adding to the dreamy ambience of the opiate high. And in an ironic twist there emerged a strange cult of celebrity comprised of former-heroin addicts who were able to beat the drug and somehow capitalize on this status. *The Basketball Diaries*' author Jim Carroll, after beating his sundry demons, arrived as a celebrated poet—playwright with his own rock band. Carroll's victory over heroin won him the title of "survivor" which translated into "street-wise, authentic and real." And Motley Crue's bassist Nikki Sixx watched as his tell-all *The Heroin Diaries: A Year in the Life of a Shattered Rock Star* landed on the *New York Times* best-seller list. Note, too, that author Irvine Welsh, on the other side of that warped and twisted coin, had been forced to defend accusations that he was never addicted to heroin, thus his text was somewhat less valid, less authentic, because he wasn't a user of the drug.

The Columbine slaughter at the end of the decade found an easy connection to many of these aforementioned films. The media frenzy began as critics quickly pointed fingers in every direction looking for answers. Every symbolic, cultural oddity was suspect. After the horrific bloodshed, *The Basketball Diaries* was examined as being a possible causal factor for Columbine. Eric Harris and Dylan Klebold called themselves "The Trenchcoat Mafia," imitating the black leather trench coat worn by DiCaprio in the film's "dream sequence." The "dream sequence," featuring revenge—seeking Carroll, showed him silently killing six of his classmates. DiCaprio swaggered dramatically through the scene, rapid-fire shotgun swinging seductively as Graeme Revell's eerie "Dream Massacre" followed the slow motion slaughter. This symbolic vignette, although only lasting a few minutes, was believed by some to have inspired the Paducah, KY, and the Columbine school shootings.

The 1997 Heath High School tragedy in Paducah, KY, had preceded Columbine by two years. It was one of numerous school shootings that set the stage for Columbine. Michael Carneal, 14, admitted that *The Basketball Diaries* influenced him. The parents of three students who were slaughtered by Carneal sued the film's makers and distributors for $130 million on April 12, 1999. They charged that Internet pornography, violent computer games and the film *The Basketball Diaries* all added to Carneal's murderous rampage. Attorney Jack Thompson threatened, "We intend to hurt Hollywood. We intend to hurt the video game industry. We intend to hurt the sex porn sites." Thompson did acknowledge that Jim Carroll was not responsible and that his 1977 novel did not contain the infamous "dream sequence." Thompson blamed the film producers for including the violent scene "for the sole purpose of hyping the movie and increasing its appeal to young audiences. This had the effect of harmfully influencing impressionable minors such as Michael Carneal and causing the shootings."

Twenty-five years after the publication of *The Basketball Diaries*, a ten-minute wanton killing spree would upstage the Columbine drama. Dressed completely in black, including tight gloves and cap, Robert Steinhaeuser, an expert marksman and gun enthusiast, shot and killed 17 persons at the Johann Gutenberg Gymnasium in Erfurt, Germany. Among the dead were 13 teachers, two girls, a school secretary and a policeman. The carnage occurred on Friday, April 26, 2002. It was the deadliest school shooting since the Littleton, CO, incident and matched the carnage of the 1966 shooting in Dunblane, Scotland, where 16 children, a teacher and a policeman were murdered at an elementary school.

Unlike America, Germany has tight gun control laws, even though there were millions of legal firearms used for hunting and sports and stored by gun collectors. Steinhaeuser, 19, was upset because he had been expelled from his school for forging a doctor's note. He reportedly told another student "One day I want everyone to know my name and I want to be famous." Investigators discovered 500 unspent rounds of ammunition next to the killer. Another 500 rounds were found at his home. Steinhaeuser killed himself as German commandos stormed the facility.

Where do we begin to look as we attempt to explain the process of repressed anger that has spiraled into deadly rage? All we can do is remain vigilant, remain connected and wait. It may be impossible to uncover the true motivation, the layers of human anguish hiding behind such wanton killings as those at Erfurt and Columbine, and those awaiting us in the distant future. We need to take responsibility for things that occur in our communities,

Author Jim Carroll was one of numerous artists blamed for the Columbine shootings. Others were Marilyn Manson, Nine Inch Nails and the motion picture and porn industries, including the cult movie *The Matrix*. Carroll defended the original theme of his 1977 novel: "The ridiculous thing is that, in fact, books like mine and others have made a lot of kids feel less isolated, less alone, relieved to know that someone else out there understood how they feel. I mean, if you deal with negative feelings and emotions in your writing or whatever medium you work in, it's always possible it will be interpreted in ways you never intended. But ultimately, that doesn't make you responsible. Being associated with a tragedy like this merely because of some vague similarities written in a book more than twenty years ago is very troublesome to me."

Life imitates art as art imitates life. Many of these films, in subtle degrees, promoted the varied themes of recovery from heroin. In several of the films *(The Man With The Golden Arm, Drugstore Cowboy, The Basketball Dairies, Ray, Killing Zoe)* the protagonist, burned by the fires of substance abuse and addiction, continued with an active recovery. In four of them, (*Lady Sings the Blues, Bird, Sid and Nancy, Gia*) the protagonist dies and in another four of the films(*Panic in Needle Park, Trainspotting, Pulp Fiction, Traffic*) the ending is left open-ended, a work in progress much like the real-life, one-day-at-a-time struggle of addiction, recovery and survival.

7

Heroin Chic

Heroin chic evolved as a perverse and twisted fashion trend that attempted to influence and exploit vulnerable young minds. Synonymous with the decadence of the 1990's, heroin chic's roots sprang from two unique decades of exciting London culture. The first was the London fashion scene of the 1960's. London was the birthplace of numerous cultural trends that reflected the incredible energies of Beatlemania, the resulting English Invasion, the James Bond craze and Carnaby Street fashion. London-based designers, artists, singers and models created trends, such as Dr. Martens and Mary Quant designs, that resonated around the globe.

Twiggy, working as a shampoo girl, walked out of that microcosm and embraced global celebrity. It only took one photograph in the *London Daily News* with the caption "This is the face of 1966" to revolutionize the international concept of female beauty. Standing at 5', 6 ½" with a 91-pound pubescent figure, Lesley Hornsby, aka Twiggy, was recognized as the world's first supermodel. The seventeen-year-old Twiggy exemplified the mod look, androgynous, anorexic and hip, that would set the dubious standard that continues to this day. She alone altered the ideal of beauty to that of an irrational image that bordered on dangerous near-starvation levels. A 1967 article in *Newsweek* entitled "Twiggy: Click! Click!" called her "the 17 year old Cockney sprig from Northwest London" and noted: "Whatever her ultimate influence on fashion, Twiggy is a radical departure from the past."

That departure from the past helped catapult the stick-thin model, with a sickly body mass index of 14.7, to the head of the class. Twiggy was the first in a line of emaciated models who promoted the extreme look that would eventually degrade into heroin chic. Three decades later Kate Moss would be dubbed the "Twiggy of the '90's," and in May 2005, everything came full circle as Twiggy was signed to the UPN reality series *America's Next Top Model*, as a replacement for Janice Dickinson.

Heroin chic also mimicked the punk fashion that developed in the waning days of the late 1970's. The look echoed the hard street culture of the drugged-out London underground with oversized leather jackets, metal studs, Mohawk haircuts, safety-pin piercings and political expression. Groups such as the Sex Pistols attempted to give voice to the British working class as they expressed themes of rage, anger and rebellion. In their "God Save the Queen" (1977) the Pistols promoted blue-collar values and then attacked the monarchy, who celebrated the Queen's Jubilee Day, where much of Britain came together for tens of thousands of wild street parties. Lead singer Johnny Rotten noted that "God Save The Queen" "wasn't written specifically for the Queen's Jubilee. We weren't aware of it at the time. It wasn't a contrived effort to go out and shock everyone." Rotten further explained that, "You don't write a song like 'God Save the Queen' because you hate the English race. You write a song like that because you love them, and you're sick of seeing them mistreated."

Things were slightly different across the pond. In America, heroin chic, associated with the look of lifeless and empty drug addicts, was a cultural anomaly lasting for roughly six years. It was the next new thing, the next new "in look," and a look that reflected evil and death. Thin white-skinned models, with either black or pale lipstick, stared vacantly into nothingness. Their exaggerated red eyes were fixed, highlighted with green and hyper blue shadows to emphasize the blank, hollow stare of the junkie.

The look, promoting emaciated features and androgyny, was a marketing strategy, an attempt by the fashion industry to uncover the next new look, that attracted teenagers and young women in their twenties ever so closer to the flame. A ghoulish "heroin addict look" developed. Called the "dead look," the "waif look," and later "junkie chic," it became known more properly as the sophisticated "heroin chic." For a segment of Generation X it became the "in" look. It was a fashion statement, a bizarre alternative that stood in direct contradiction to the healthy and vibrant look of models such as Christy Brinkley, Cindy Crawford, Claudia Schiffer and Heidi Klum. Heroin was a likely choice for the fashion industry as the morphine-derivative suppressed the appetite and allowed models enough euphoria and energy to work long strenuous hours under the lights and in front of the cameras. But it was equally dangerous and raised scattered voices of concern. In 1996 an article in the Los Angeles Times charged that the fashion industry had "a nihilistic vision of beauty" that was reflective of drug addiction, and U.S. News and World Report called the movement a "cynical trend."

It was never about beauty. It was always about those who controlled the reins of power and exercised the art of exploitation. It was about the objectification and devaluing of physically beautiful human beings by others. Marge Piercy's "Barbie Doll" was a poem written about a young woman who committed suicide because she was confined to the rigid expectations, standards and images imposed by men in a patriarchal society. Striving to attain an unattainable body image, promoted through innumerable media images, has become the impossible quest for today's woman.

Heroin chic was the basis of a 1993 Calvin Klein advertising campaign that featured Kate Moss and actor-film director Vincent Gallo. Later, in 1997, Calvin Klein released a notorious set of print ads that used a number of junkie-like models to hype his new perfume cKbe. Some of the sickly models appeared to be in the throes of withdrawal. All were young, drastically underweight, and conveyed that lost, spaced out look.

Robert Triefus, Calvin Klein spokesman, denied the allegations, stating that the ad campaign for cKbe was about "being yourself, being independent and being real." He continued, "We obviously refute any suggestion that our advertising relates to drug taking at all." The following year, in a *New York Times* article, Calvin Klein reflected, "Clearly people were upset by heroin chic, and people accused me of it. We thought it was creative, but it was perceived as drug-related and messy. People don't want that now," he explained. Although Calvin Klein was the most obvious of the corporate exploiters, he was not alone. Gucci, Guess, Miu Miu and Jil Sander also exploited the heroin look and its close cousin the earthy grunge look.

The grunge look came out of the youthful energies that emerged from the Pacific Northwest during the early 1990's. Fashion expert Pauline Weston Thomas explained that "The key to the look was that nothing matched, nothing was coordinated and an item was preferable if old and worn. The point was to look tousled, uncombed and unkempt, as if not too much effort had been made." In an article entitled "40 Years of Rock Style," *Rolling Stone Magazine* described the look through one of its icons: "(Kurt) Cobain managed to make unwashed look hot. He wore dirty torn jeans, ragged flannel shirts layered over dingy tees and, for added effect, dresses and pajamas. His hair was stringy and his stubble a perennial ten o'clock shadow."

Still, even that pedestrian look had the potential to make money such as with the Hard Candy product line of nail polish colors called Pimp and Porno. Alternative rock act Garbage marketed a bright-orange Garbage Nail polish, packaged in a miniature garbage pail. The San Francisco-based Urban Decay, in a slick marketing maneuver, began selling its cosmetic line in upscale boutiques including Urban Outfitters, Rolo, Nordstrom and Villains. Superstars Madonna, Dennis Rodman, Drew Barrymore and Julia Roberts raised the look's profile as they used and promoted the vogue products. Jenny Shimuza and Stella Tennant were other so-called "grunge models." Many consumers thought the look was pointless, overpriced and ugly. Actresses like Julia Roberts, who adopted the grunge dress, were heavily criticized for their lack of glamour. In 1997 Urban Decay initiated a legal action against Revlon's Street Wear line of grunge cosmetics and argued that Revlon had imitated Urban Decay grunge products that included Frostbite and Pallor. (The upscale Urban Decay was founded in 1995 by Sandy Lerner and David Soward, almost one year before Revlon launched their Street Wear line, sold at Walgreen and other mass outlets.) Among the shades that were used by the competing companies were product names Roach, Rust, Bruise, Salmonella, Acid Rain, Oil Slick and Plague. Although grunge died after a year, perhaps a victim of its despondent themes, the fashion term remained and is now used "to describe unattractive fashion features or unkempt individuals."

Called the "Guru of Grunge" by *Women's Wear Daily*, Marc Jacobs, former fashion student at New York's acclaimed Parsons School of Design, created a Seattle-inspired collection for the fashion runway while working for Perry Ellis. Jacobs explained that he wanted to visually translate the musical sounds of grunge artists, such as Pearl Jam and Nirvana, into pattern and color. The collection, described by Jacobs as his "best ever," blended floral dresses with combat boots and oversized plaid shirts and received substantial media attention, including the cover of *Mademoiselle*. Jacob's inspiration, regrettably, was one of the most critically slammed collections in fashion history. In 1992 after presenting his grunge-inspired collection, perceived in some circles as too radical for the average American woman, Jacobs and business partner Robert Duffy were immediately fired by Perry Ellis. Paradoxically the Council of Fashion Designers of America awarded Jacobs the Women's Designer of the Year Award that same year, and in 1997 Jacobs become the creative director of Louis Vuitton, the world-renowned fashion empire.

That empire turned out to be one built of sand. Jacobs had struggled with heroin and alcohol dependence in the past and successfully combated a heroin addiction in 1999 after going into rehab. He reportedly had been clean for seven years before his 2007 relapse and was working on Louis Vuitton's latest collection that appeared at

Paris Fashion Week. The hip designer attempted to explain his rationale for using drugs during an interview with Australia's TheAge.com: "I felt taller, I felt sexier, I felt funnier, I felt less insecure. All those things were magic potions—and then they stopped working. But then, they weren't ever really magic potions. I dunno, maybe I just wanted to fit in." And during his 2007 stay at Passages Addiction Care Center in Malibu, Jacobs submitted to *CNN Showbiz Tonight* anchor Brooke Anderson a possible reason for his addiction problems: "I didn't have the ideal family. I was teased and sort of made fun of by my peers, and I had no one to go to and talk to. I was too full of shame to really approach someone to talk to. I was always looking over my shoulder saying, he's better, she's better, they're better."

GIA CARANGI

In the late 1970's Philadelphia-born Gia Carangi became one of the most successful of the supermodels; her arrival was both immediate and profound. Gia went from taking lunch orders at her father's Hoagie City to sipping Crystal at New York night spots Studio 54 and the Mudd Club. She was described as being "about melancholy and darkness, and that made great pictures." New York's Wilhelmina Models signed her at the age of 18 and her first major modeling job was with Gianni Versace. During her initial years in the industry she appeared on the covers of *Vogue* and *Cosmopolitan* magazines and made over one hundred thousand dollars a year. She was expected to continue her success and earn over five hundred thousand dollars in 1980.

Gia Carangi's amazing physical beauty had brought her fame, $10,000-a-day fashion shoots and international recognition, but, in the end, even that was ripped away. It was 10:00 on the morning of November 18, 1986 when 26-year-old Gia Carangi died. She would be remembered as one of the first women in the United States, and certainly the most recognizable, to have died of complications from the AIDS virus, which she may have contracted from a contaminated needle.

The use of drugs within the glamorous world of high fashion had a long and secret past. Even before the term "heroin chic" was coined, model Gia, the bisexual drug addicted supermodel, began to unravel in a public display of self-destruction. Thrown into a frenetic, high-pressured environment, she developed a heroin habit within her first two years of working the New York catwalks. Her reputation, work ethic and health suffered. She changed agencies twice, was arrested for driving erratically under the influence of a narcotic, and agreed to enter a rehab program in 1984. It only got worse after Wilhelmina Cooper, the person most responsible for having launched Gia's career, and her surrogate mother, died in 1980. Gia began to frequent the infamous shooting galleries of New York's Lower East Side. Blackballed by an unforgiving industry, her downward spiral threw her onto the mean streets of New York and Atlantic City before she ended up a drugged-out hospital welfare case waiting to die.

Her biography was the subject of Stephen Fried's 1993 book, *Thing of Beauty: The Tragedy of Supermodel Gia*, and was later made into the 1998 Emmy-winning HBO motion picture *Gia* ("Too beautiful to die. Too wild to live") starring a then unknown Angelina Jolie. It was a sad and tragic conclusion to what could have been a career of endless potential, but it was an ending that pointed to earlier tribulations. When she was five Gia was sexually abused by an unknown man and, as a child, forced to endure ongoing verbal abuse and physical violence between her parents. The worst trauma occurred after Kathleen Carangi abandoned her husband, Joe, and her children for another man. That loss of the most important person in Gia's life, her mother, would always remain as a cruel reminder of a cold and heartless world.

In the end Gia Carangi became the industry's most blatant, and most public, example of substance abuse excess. In his tell-all narrative, *Model: The Ugly Business of Beautiful Women*, author Michael Gross explained: "The model business remains, as it has always been, a seething morass of beauty and money, grace and envy, sensuality and lust, yearning and backstabbing, glamour, greed, and glory beyond measure." Still, even in Gross' 500—plus page *Model* the life of Gia Carangi warranted only a few select mentions with much emphasis placed on the fact that she was a "drug-addicted bisexual."

How interesting, too, to observe within the fashion industry the ebb and flow of drug use as it shifted from cocaine to heroin and then returned back to the more accepted and fashionable cocaine once again.

New faces would soon follow. At the age of 16, Amy Wesson, one of the youngest of the Generation X group, emerged from a Tupelo, Mississippi, trailer park to become one of the top ranked fashion models in the world. She was discovered while working at a shopping mall clothing store and ultimately landed twice on the cover of *Italian Vogue* and on the cover of *W*. The model worked for such prestigious agencies as Why Not, Modelwerk and Marilyn. Wesson was later recognized as the cover girl for The Smashing Pumpkins' 1998 *Adore* studio album. But behind the hot studio lights and celebrity she battled a drug addiction that, in full public view, began to destroy her career. Wesson missed modeling assignments, was frequently late and "had to be propped up at fashion shoots." In 1997 Company Management sued Wesson in Manhattan Supreme Court in New York for five million dollars alleging a "breach of contract." The marketing agency alleged that Wesson's drug addiction, including cocaine and other drugs, prevented her from working and violated the terms of her contract. Vogue and Neiman Marcus both cancelled assignments with the model, who had just turned nineteen. Michael Flutie, head of Company Management and the individual who had represented Wesson, reflected on her ongoing drug use, "Everyone knew it but they closed their eyes to it" he said.

It was Zoe Fleischauer, with sunken cheeks and dark circles under her eyes, who revealed the industry's "dirty little secret." Fleischauer candidly admitted her heroin addiction in a 1996 *Allure Magazine* interview and confessed, "There are a lot of junkies in the industry.

It's very hush-hush. They wanted models that looked like junkies. The more skinny and fucked up you look, the more everybody thinks you're fabulous." Fleischauer began using heroin in 1993, around the beginning of her modeling career, and was representative of so many others.

Discovered at age 14, Kate Moss, from Croydon south London, encountered almost immediate media condemnation when fashion critics compared her "slight figure" unfavorably to that of Twiggy. Moss became synonymous with the gaunt androgynous look that defined the 1990's and was blamed for helping to create the blank image of the heroin look, even though the "boyishly thin" Moss was only nineteen when the term "heroin chic" was coined. Model-turned grunge photographer Corinne Day had discovered Moss, and it was Day who, feathering a sad-looking Kate Moss without makeup and in underwear, created the "waif" look. Day was also held responsible for "encouraging anorexia, drugs, even pedophilia," and promoting her own brand of heroin chic in British fashion. Accused of an "anti-glamour snobbery," she forcefully defended her style and stated, "Photography is getting as close as you can to real life, showing us things we don't normally see. These are peoples' most intimate moments, and sometimes intimacy is sad."

A member of both Alcoholics Anonymous and Narcotics Anonymous, supermodel Moss had publicly admitted that she had never been sober during her turns on the fashion catwalk "even at ten in the morning" and, regrettably, her drug abuse continued to be a significant aspect of her portfolio. Moss, like many British luminaries, was often stalked by fierce and relentless paparazzi. In September 2005 the *London Daily Mirror* published photographs of Moss, then 31, allegedly snorting cocaine with Pete Doherty, at a London recording studio. Doherty, Moss' boyfriend and front man for the British rock act Babyshambles, was then dealing with a public heroin addiction. "Ms. Moss was never the poster child for healthy living," observed Lauren Mechling, writing in The New York *Sun*. "She was an English teenager with a boyish figure and vacant, slightly amoral expression who rose from obscurity to infamy in the early 1990's when she started dating—and trashing hotel rooms with—actor Johnny Depp. Feminists took umbrage at the glamorization of an emaciated waif-child and blamed her for anorexia among teenage girls …"

There were speculations that Moss' career was, after the cocaine incident, finished, but Kate Moss continued to be the bankable darling of the industry and a prime example of public forgiveness. The December 2005 issue of *French Vogue* devoted an issue to Moss with the cover tag line reading "Scandalous Beauty," and while the model landed two other major covers she also fittingly continued to promote Yves Saint Laurent's "Opium" perfume.

Michael Flutie felt that the Kate Moss scandal marked a transition for the industry as certain issues, such as widespread drug use, were being addressed in an honest manner. "We're making tremendous progress by the mere fact we're no longer living in denial," he said. "I think we've come a long way because five years ago the world was in denial, and now we get Kate Moss getting caught and she says, 'Mea culpa. I'm sorry.' We live in a world in which we forgive and we grow. I'm acknowledging her heroism because I think it's fantastic she stood up and said, 'Yes, I did it.'"

Even though the Kate Moss's of the industry have survived, others have not fared as well. Dutch model Karen Mulder watched as her stellar career dissipated into nothingness due to drug use and emotional instability. The European fashion model, who had battled chronic depression for years, experienced a mental breakdown and, in the throes of desperation and hopelessness, attempted suicide. The 34-year-old blonde beauty was found, passed out and in a coma, on the floor of her apartment on Paris's exclusive Avenue Montaigne. Officials stated that in her comatose state she was one hour away from death. She had ingested a large amount of sleeping pills, an unfortunate chapter in her life that was far removed from the radiant 17-year-old who entered the Elite model agency's talent-spotting contest and won the Look of the Year Award with her stunning beauty.

Known as "the blonde with class," she retired in 2000 and in 2002 spent three months under sedation at the Villa Montsouris Clinic after suffering a breakdown and drug-induced suicide attempt. "She was ruined by cocaine and the knowledge that her life as a model was over," stated her father. " She's broken, emotionally and physically. When I visited her, I saw notebooks full of her mad ideas. She's accused everyone and everything. It's awful."

Mulder's father, Ben, was a main focal point of Karen's "mad ideas," but he was not alone. On October 31, 2001, during a taping of the French channel *Tout le Monde en Parle* (Everyone is Talking About It), she alleged that numerous persons sexually abused her throughout her career. Among the individuals whom the troubled model implicated were her father and Prince Albert of Monaco and unnamed "fashion predators." She also claimed that she and other models were used as sex slaves by members of the police and the French government. Later, reflecting on her emotional state during that time, she said: "It seemed everyone was against me. People told me I was fantasizing, that my psychoanalysis was wrong. So in order to be heard, I exaggerated. And I went overboard."

Everyone seemed to take his or her turn at promoting the dark look of the addict. Jil Sander, who founded her label in 1973 only to leave in 2000 after Prada bought the brand, was known as the queen of German fashion. Sander capitalized on the extreme look and took the genre a step further. Sander, during the media persecution, was criticized for showing a wasted looking model waiting for her fix. The model's sleeve was pushed up, leaving very little to the imagination in this blending of the culture of fashion with the culture of addiction.

The heroin chic marketing blitz had its calculated and desired effect. Young women admired these high fashion models with sunken faces and high cheekbones and strived to emulate them. The pressure to be thin, and even anorexic, was the obvious result of seductive ad campaigns promoting heroin chic as fashionable, glamorous and acceptable. Along with Hollywood, MTV and VH1, the fashion industry did its part to portray heroin use as hip and trendy, swaying the perception of the drug from highly dangerous to highly desirable.

The end for heroin chic came as a result of the very public overdose death of 20-year-old fashion photographer Davide Sorrenti. A promising member of Generation X, Sorrenti was known for his photographs of seemingly strung-out models in stupor-like poses that, some felt, emulated the blank look of the heroin addict and glamorized drug use. Based on reports from the BBC's *Online*, Sorrenti fell in love with teenage model James King, herself a heroin addict, and Sorrenti quickly stepped into the void of substance abuse. Vulnerable due to a lifelong blood disorder and a lethal injection "not normally considered unusual," Sorrenti was dead within six months. Sorrenti died in the winter of 1997. He drew his final breath on his dealer's couch, posed like an empty, lifeless rag, much like his real-life models.

James King, from Omaha, Nebraska, was only 14 when she landed her first modeling job. The following year Jamie, a.k.a. James King, had worked for scores of the major fashion magazines, including *Vogue, Allure, Mademoiselle*, and *Seventeen*. She later appeared in Filter's 1999 "Take a Picture" video, in a soft and melodic presentation of industrial rock. Unknown to the public, her personal and confidential resume revealed that, since the age of sixteen, she had been a "former heroin addict and recovering alcoholic." King entered rehab at the age of nineteen, another casualty, albeit an acknowledged survivor, of the high-pressured and demanding fashion industry. Her boyfriend, Davide Sorrenti, had not been as fortunate.

Davide Sorrenti's death drew attention to the incidence of heroin abuse within the fashion industry and resonated in high political circles. After a revealing *New York Times* article on Sorrenti's fatal overdose, President Bill Clinton accused the fashion industry of portraying heroin use as a glamorous, fashionable drug of choice and as a means of promoting clothing lines.

On May 21, 1997, in an address organized by the United States Conference of Mayors, Clinton addressed a group of 35 mayors at the White House. The meeting was intended to discuss issues of drug control in major American cities, but Clinton took the opportunity to attack the destructive "heroin chic." He stated, " In the press in recent days, we've seen reports that many of our fashion leaders are now admitting—and I honor them for doing this—they're admitting flat—out that images projected in fashion photos in the last few years have made heroin addiction seem glamorous and sexy and cool. And as some of those people in those images start to die now, it has become obvious that this is not true. You do not need to glamorize addiction to sell clothes.

"American fashion has been an enormous source of creativity and beauty and art, and frankly, economic prosperity for the United States, and we should respect that. But the glorification of heroin is not creative, it's destructive. It's not beautiful, it is ugly. And this is not about art; it's about life and death. And glorifying death is not good for any society. Society can't take a tough attitude toward illegal drugs and on the other hand send a very different message every time there might be a little money to be made out of it."

Reflecting on his youth, Clinton added that heroin had, for many, always been associated with fear and dread. "There were these horrible images associated with it ... strung-out junkies lying on street corners in decidedly unglamorous ways." Clinton's concern about the drug was apparent. "We now see in college campuses and neighborhoods heroin becoming increasingly the drug of choice," he said.

Ultimately the facts revealed that heroin was not a popular drug of choice, especially when measured against substances such as marijuana, cocaine and methamphetamine. For example, the 1995 National Household Survey on Drug Abuse cited a mere 0.1 percent of respondents who reported using heroin in the previous month. A similar study conducted in 1994 for the Department of Health and Human Services determined roughly the same amount of heroin use among 19 to 28-year-olds. Alcohol was the most popular of all substances, and marijuana was about 140 times as common as heroin. Clearly, Clinton had allowed his anti-drug passions to get in the way of the facts. All major studies indicated that heroin was not a "major" problem compared with other substances of abuse. Some charged that it was Clinton who, seeking political advantage, had publicized "heroin chic" at the expense of more serious drug and social problems. Still, Clinton's political theatre and calculated assault on "heroin chic" demonstrated several fascinating variables. First, despite the controversy surrounding heroin's popularity and usage, the drug was being promoted as a tool of enticement for fashion via the so-called "heroin look." And too, the relentless media hype and attention, including that emanating from the President, all began to shift perception of the drug's importance as a recreational substance. Many were convinced that there was a significant outbreak surrounding the drug's use, based in part on a State Department study that anticipated "a possible U.S. heroin epidemic." That harbinger helped evoke the perception that heroin was more widespread, and ostensibly more safer, that it actually was.

Still, there was reason for concern. As was indicated, there were ominous signs that heroin had become more prevalent and increasingly accessible in the country. Although alcohol and marijuana were the prominent drugs of abuse on campus, heroin was gaining widespread acceptance among select demographic groups including white middle-class youth and sectors of the fashion industry. According to Join Together, a group that, since 1991, "has supported community-based efforts to advance effective alcohol and drug policy, prevention, and treatment," the overall number of estimated heroin users rose from 68,000 in 1993 to 325,000 in 1997, and those numbers were indeed troubling. The Uniform Crime Reporting Program (UCR) of the Federal Bureau of Investigation (FBI) reported that in 1997, 5.1% of the 15,837 homicides in which circumstances were known were narcotics related. (For these statistics murders that occurred specifically during a narcotics felony, such as drug trafficking or manufacturing, are considered drug related.)

Fern Mallis, the executive director of the Council of Fashion Designers of America argued that "heroin chic" was never pervasive in the industry and was only done by a certain group of individuals. "It is unfair that the whole industry should be blamed for heroin abuses," she said. "The fashion industry should not be the easy target to blame for society's woes." Mallis further explained that her organization was "going to take another very serious look at this issue. Drugs are not fashionable and we want to make sure that nobody in the fashion industry thinks that it's the case."

The Clinton Administration wasn't the only group who rallied against the promotion of the drug's romanticized image. Patrick McCarthy, editorial director of *W Magazine*, agreed, "The President's right. There is a problem, and responsible editors and fashion designers are doing something about it. He has stated the obvious, but when the President of the United States states it, he states it even louder. It will have an effect. This is going to be everywhere tonight and tomorrow and you'd have to be crazy not to listen."

Two days after Clinton's verbal assault against the industry, Jacob Sullum responded in the article "Victims of Everything." He rationalized, "there is no reason to expect that people attracted to the look promoted by Calvin Klein and other advertisers—a cynical, sanitized vision of drug use that pretends to reflect a gritty reality—will also be attracted to heroin, any more than suburban teen-agers who wear baggy pants and backward caps will end up shooting people from moving cars."

Others had listened and responded in kind. Later that year, the London-based Designers Against Addictions signed a statement publicly condemning heroin chic. A total of thirteen designers signed the document, perhaps in response to widespread public pressure, but certainly an indication that the trend had played itself out as the darkness and gloom of the 1990's came to a close.

Within the hip artistic community, not all went along with the junkie chic movement and not everyone thought that it was cool to be skinny or that being skinny was being sexy. Contained in Pearl Jam's *Vitalogy* CD was the garage-rock song "Satan's Bed," with Eddie Vedder screaming out: "Who made ... up the myth/That we were born to be covered in bliss?/Who set the standard, born to be rich?/Such fine examples, skinny little bitch/Model, role model, roll some models in blood/Get some flesh to stick, so they look like us." In the song Vedder expressed his anger at seductive anorexic women and protested their role model status, brought about only by their lack of flesh. *Vitalogy*, compared by some to the Beatles' *White Album*, followed in the wake of the classic *Ten* and *Vs.* but was unique in Vedder's expressed outrage as he threatened to "roll some models in blood."

Not far removed from the look of heroin chic was a further trend that provided yet another risky temptation for vulnerable young girls. A group of radical women had embraced the concept that anorexia was a positive lifestyle choice and their philosophies promoted anorexia via such "underground" web sites as *The Proanasanctuary Club* and *Proanorexia*. Women, encouraged to find ways to diet and lose weight, perceived their personal accomplishments as a means of positive self-control. They viewed their weight—loss efforts as a means of cleansing and purifying their bodies, a means of attaining a sense of freedom. It fit conveniently into the Gothic imagery that promoted the extreme gaunt look with its pale, frightening look of deathlike starvation. The current movement is unique because women suffering from anorexia are now banding together in support, not of recovery from their addiction, but as a means of embracing and celebrating this lifestyle choice.

Regrettably, the role models who are worshipped and idolized by young women in the early 2000's are represented by the likes of Hilary Duff, Paris Hilton, Mary Kate and Ashley Olsen, and Nicole Richie, all falling into the realm of "seriously underweight" or "anorexic." In 2006 the CDC's National Eating Disorders Association compared the average American woman, at 5'4", 163 pounds, BMX 28, with that of the average American fashion model, at 5'11", 117 pounds, BMX 16.3. According to *Women's Health Weekly*, over three-fourths of professional models have body weights that are below normal, and a quarter of these women meet the weight criteria for anorexia nervosa. Anorexia is a serious disorder that has caused young girls to starve themselves. There are an estimated five million individuals, the majority of them teenage girls, who have suffered from this life-threatening condition. Over one out of every ten individuals diagnosed with anorexia die and at least 1,000 individuals diagnosed with anorexia expire each year. Half of them die from medical complications such as organ failure, but the other half, depressed over their fatal quest to be stick-thin, die of suicide, never able to attain their ideal body image.

In her poem "Barbie Doll," Marge Piercy, American poet and social activist, addressed this state of hopelessness and despair. It is the ultimate price that some women pay when forced to conform to standards of physical beauty, strict standards imposed by those in authority. In "Barbie Doll:" "[Barbie] was advised to play coy,/exhorted to come on hearty,/exercise, diet, smile and wheedle./Her good nature wore out like a fan belt./So she cut off her nose and her legs/and offered them up." They asked, "Doesn't she look pretty," as they viewed the lifeless woman, a victim of suicide and social convention, in the satin casket "with the undertaker's cosmetics painted on" and with "a turned-up putty nose?"

So sad that often times, the dream becomes an impossible quest of absolute melancholy and hopelessness. Hot Chocolate's 1974 song, "Emma," evoked the heartbreaking tale of Emily, who "could be anything" because she had a "face like an angel." Emma began her life with great promise and optimism, "a star in everyone's eye" and was destined to become "the biggest star the world had ever seen." Like so many other nameless models and aspiring actresses Emma spent her days introducing herself, knocking on doors and "searching for that play that never, ever came her way." And "on a cold and dark December night" her lover found her lifeless body "lying still and cold on the bed" with the suicide note lamenting "I just can't keep on living on dreams no more."

Is there ever a moment when society stands up and says "no" to such outrage? Perhaps the tipping point occurred after the terrible deaths of two Latin American models who starved themselves to death. On August 2, 2006, Luisel Ramos died soon after stepping off the Montevideo, Uruguay, Fashion Week runway. Ramos a 22-year-old Uruguayan model, fainted on the way to her dressing room and suffered "heart failure caused by anorexia nervosa." Medical personnel were unable to revive her. According to her father, the model had gone "several days" without eating and, for a three-month-period, had existed on a starvation diet of salads, greens and Diet Coke. At the time of her death she stood 5', 9" and weighed 98 pounds. Her BMI was only 14.5. (The body mass index [BMI] is a measurement of body fat that doctors typically apply to study obesity. It is based on height and weight and calculated for both adult men and women. Any reading under 18.5 is considered to be underweight, and a reading under 15 is considered "grossly underweight." United Nations health experts had recommended a BMI of between 18.5 and about 25 for healthy individuals.)

The 21-year-old Brazilian model Ana Carolina Reston, who worked for Giorgio Armani, had been in the business since the age of thirteen. She had been hospitalized on October 25, 2006, for kidney malfunction due to anorexia and bulimia nervosa. Her condition became more serious and deteriorated into generalized infection that led to her death. At the end of her life, in order to maintain a lowered body weight, she ate only tomatoes and apples. Reston died on November 14, 2006, at a hospital in San Paulo. At the time of her passing Reston weighed only 88 pounds and stood 5' 8". Her BMI was a shocking 13.4.

One immediate consequence of Reston's condition (and eventual death) came from the Spanish Association of Fashion Designers, who banned underweight models on the basis of their BMI. As of September 18, 2006, rail-thin models with a BMI of fewer than 18 were rejected from the Madrid catwalks and offered medical treatment for their anorexia. The Madrid group explained that it wanted to promote a more positive and healthy aesthetic of feminine beauty for teenagers to follow. That mindset was not lost on Spain's Association in Defense of Attention for Anorexia and Bulimia, which threatened to have the government legislate to ban stick-thin models if designers refused to cooperate with the voluntary restrictions.

Italy's fashion industry followed in December 2006 as it, too, implemented a code of conduct to battle anorexia. The self-regulatory code was intended to ban models younger than sixteen and called for fashion collections to add larger sizes. The code, drawn up in cooperation with the Italian government, also required models to provide medical proof that they did not suffer from eating disorders. It has been estimated that about three million individuals suffer from eating disorders in Italy. The Italian fashion code aimed to redefine feminine beauty and to promote "a healthy, sunny, generous Mediterranean model of beauty."

Yet despite the controversy, the outrage and the deaths, there were some in the industry who definitely were not swayed. In the spring of 2006 the Banana Republic introduced "sub-zero" sized fashions for American women. The Nicole Miller group was expected to introduce their "sub-zero" collection the following year.

Why have we allowed Twiggy, if we are to acknowledge her as the beginning of this sickly trend, with a skeletal BMI of 14.7, to have established a pathological standard of beauty that mimics starvation? The Food and Agricultural Organization of the United Nations has defined starvation as a "severe reduction in vitamin, nutrient and energy intake," and is the most extreme form of malnutrition. In humans, prolonged starvation (in excess of one to two months) causes permanent organ damage and will eventually result in death. As a fashion concept it has no rational basis and is difficult for a majority of us to comprehend.

Even then, at the beginning, there were voices of protest against the unrealistic expectations that were being imposed on young women, voices such as that of Gillian Bobkoff, a British model in the sixties, calling out against the movement: "It was dreadful. [Twiggy] started a trend, and you had to be just the same. I had my hair cut and started killing myself, taking a million slimming pills. I had bulimia. It was a nightmare, trying to keep up." And from Anna Greer, editor of the feminist *Wo! Magazine*, charging that "Eating disorders are a huge problem for especially teenage girls, and I think the impossible body ideals imposed on them by the fashion industry and media and pop culture is obviously a huge contributor to this."

Why would anyone consider anorexia and starvation as a deliberate lifestyle choice and as an ideal of beauty? What began with "the Twiggy look" was generally ignored for the next three decades, but then, that deliberate look of death, that celebration of addiction, found a home in the 1990's. It became yet another example of a purposeful and deliberate act of self-destruction that defined this group of individuals.

Young women need a dramatic alternative, a paradigm shift, away from the images that are being bombarded at them. Paradigms cannot shift by simply amassing numerical lists of deceased beautiful people consumed by their ineffable realities. We must proceed beyond the emotional shock. What is needed is a palpable exploration that includes an ethical framework of change. As a caring and protective society we must provide our children with positive role models who project positive values and body images. The carnage visited upon Generation X, reflected in "heroin chic," has endured long enough, both on and off the catwalk.

8

Woodstock Burning

○ ○
Violence is the last refuge of the incompetent.

—*Isaac Asimov*

The Woodstock festivals happened in 1969 in Bethel, New York, in 1994 in Saugerties, New York, and again in 1999 in Rome, New York. The 1999 Woodstock, like the others, was intended to promote peace and harmony but, 30 years after the original celebration, and, like Alice tumbling down a crazy time-warped rabbit hole, it was the twisted reality of a new breed of citizen-youth, and not peace and love that were uncovered.

As avid observers of Generations X and Y, many Baby Boomers keenly followed the much-anticipated rite of passage and gathering of the tribes at Woodstock 1994 and 1999. The concept of masses of young people getting together for three days of fun, music and fellowship was a surreal experiment of sorts. It was a high-profile litmus test; a unique way of examining that generation's social interactions and an opportunity to observe and evaluate the primitive essence of the tribe while at play.

I had the good fortune of being at the original Woodstock Nation, billed as "Three days of peace and music," in 1969. With precious time on my hands before entering St. Gregory's College I eagerly drove up to Bethel, New York, and to Max Yasgur's dairy farm, along with 400,000 other wanderlust travelers. My sole motivation was to see several bands that had not performed at the Atlantic City Pop Festival, held several weeks earlier. These included The Who, Jimi Hendrix and the cult-like Grateful Dead. And, like so many others, I had no conception that the festival would significantly transform into something so big, so significant and, in retrospect, so much larger than life.

The original Woodstock Music and Art Fair: An Aquarian Exposition, held in Bethel, NY, featured 30-some acts: Joan Baez, the Band, Blood, Sweat & Tears, the Paul Butterfield Blues Band, Canned Heat, Joe Cocker, Country Joe McDonald and the Fish, Creedence Clearwater Revival, Crosby, Stills and Nash, the Grateful Dead, Arlo Guthrie, Tim Hardin, the Keef Hartley Band, Richie Havens, Jimi Hendrix, the Incredible String Band, Jefferson Airplane, Janis Joplin, Melanie, Mountain, Quill, Santana, John Sebastian, Sha-Na-na, Ravi Shankar, Sly & the Family Stone, Bert Sommer, Sweetwater, Ten Years After, the Who and Johnny Winter.

Dairy farmer Max Yasgur, who rented his 600-acre farm to the Woodstock promoters, praised the concertgoers at the end of the event. "I think you have proven something to the world—that a half a million kids can get together and have three days of fun and music and have nothing but fun and music. And I God-bless you for it," Yasgur said of the defining cultural moment. As scripted by Joni Mitchell, we were trying "to get back to the garden." In 1969 the collective dream was to make the world a better place and to eradicate the disease of racism. Members of Woodstock Nation felt empowered by the sheer masses, by the seemingly unstoppable movement of social consciousness. Remember Jim Morrison's "They got the guns but we got the numbers?" Many felt that the power and authority to rage and protest against an unjust government and an unjust war was already in their hands. At Woodstock '69 there was anger, frustration and teenage angst, but it was a controlled rebellion, a proper and correct social protest. As citizens mobilized and attempted to end the

Vietnam War (the government termed it a "conflict") life, at least for a nebulous and magical two-year period, was a psychedelic, rose-colored, drug induced vision of life's possibilities. The 1969 festival was a spontaneous explosion of colors and musical synergy and the largest rock festival up until that time. (In 1973 Bill Graham produced The Watkins Glen rock festival that featured the Allman Brothers, the Band, and the Grateful Dead. Graham's concert drew 650,000 people, the single largest paying crowd in concert history.)

It was peaceful and simple and gentle, and then it ended. The Woodstock gestalt was centered after 1967's Summer of Love and before the Altamont violence and Manson Family murders. Even as it foretold the end of the counterculture's idealism and search for its lost Eden, Woodstock somehow became frozen in time to become an integral part of our national cultural myth. In observation of the 20th anniversary Grateful Dead drummer Mickey Hart reflected: "Society took a drastic turn in the years following Woodstock. Heroin, speed and cocaine came in. People weren't seeking a higher consciousness, but a lower. They started getting twisted. These are paranoid drugs; the motives for doing them are destructive." Much of the destructive energy was fueled by the promise of music, sex, rebellion and drugs. In a ten-month period Janis Joplin, Jimi Hendrix and Jim Morrison, three important spokespersons of the counterculture, died from drug-related causes. At some point reality set in as people began to quickly die and others became addicted and died more slowly. Heroin and methamphetamine emerged as players on the scene as organized crime, biker gangs and Jamaican posses realized the equation between drugs and money. Suddenly America was confronted with a drug problem that would consume our society like some mythological monster, not just in the 1960's but also far beyond the 1990's. This, along with our sacred music, was the legacy that we beget Generation X. It was Crosby, Stills, Nash and Young who instructed us to "Teach your children well," but this message fell on deaf ears.

SAUGERTIES

Saugerties, the 25th anniversary of the original Woodstock, was the mega-concert geared towards Generation X. Costing $30 million to produce, the 1994 event that began on Friday, August 12th, was promoted as only a two-day festival.

Woodstock '94, promoted as the largest festival since Live Aid had a lineup that included Aerosmith, The Allman Brothers, Arrested Development, the Band, Blues Traveller, Candlebox, Johnny Cash, Joe Cocker, Crosby, Stills and Nash, Cyprus Hill, Bob Dylan, Melissa Etheridge, Peter Gabriel, Green Day, Metallica, Nine Inch Nails, Porno For Pyros, Red Hot Chili Peppers, the Henry Rollins Band, Salt 'N' Pepa, Santana, the Spin Doctors and the Violent Femmes. There had also been rumors circulated that grunge super bands Soundgarden and Pearl Jam would make a surprise appearance.

Saugerties, the smallest of the three Woodstocks, drew an estimated 203,000 fans that paid $135.00 to pass through metal detectors in order to attend the event. (Note, too, that tickets had to be purchased in blocks of four for fans arriving by car.) Held on the Winston Farm, an 840-acre site two hours north of New York City, it contained austere clusters of over 900 concession stands and more than a thousand security guards. Two hospitals, including an X-ray lab, were also constructed. Other features integrated a "Surreal Field" containing interactive games and an "Eco-Village" featuring political activist and environmental informational booths. Saugerties also featured mist machines, mosh pits, shuttle buses, Porta Potties, ATM machines and bad acid. There was one death, an individual who died due to a heart attack. Some critics argued that the festival was akin to a "rock and roll prison" that lacked a musical lineup with significant star power. In retrospect, Saugerties, the concert designed for the youth of Generation X, suffered from a negative vibe and the unfortunate perception that the festival was a "commercial corporate rip-off." Corporate sponsorships from Polygram and Pepsi and the anticipated $49.95 pay-per-view broadcast all added to the critical point of view.

THE NIGHT THE MUSIC DIED

"Painted, pierced and ready to rock" was the advertising slogan used to entice fans to the most recent version of Woodstock Nation. The Woodstock that ran from July 23 to the 25th was strikingly different. *Woodstuck '99,* as it was derisively termed, was devoid of the purist and altruistic qualities that were the foundation of the legendary concert some 30 years before. The bombastic music of Woodstock '99 (with few exceptions such as Willy Nelson and James Brown) was an assault of heavy metal and hip-hop. The pile-driving percussion and angry lyrics only served to underscore the belligerent anti-social attitude that society had embraced. But according to writer Brian McCollum, Woodstock '99 had more musical might than the original lineup: "While 14 artists at the original event never enjoyed top ten albums, 29 artists scheduled (in 1999) already have achieved that feat. Woodstock may have had the magic; Woodstock lll has the muscle," he observed.

The '99 lineup consisted of over 50 acts including James Brown, Buckcherry, Bush, the Chemical Brothers, George Clinton, Collective Soul, Bootsy Collins, Elvis Costello, Counting Crows, Creed, Sheryl Crow, DMX, John Entwistle, Everclear, Everlast, Fatboy Slim, G Love and Special Sauce, Godsmack, Al Green, Guster, Mickey Hart-Planet Drum, the Bruce Hornsby Group, Ice Cube, Insane Clown Posse, Jamiroquai, Wycief Jean & the Refugee Allstars, Jewel, Kid Rock, Korn, Limp Bizkit, Lit, Live, Los Lobos, Dave Matthews, Megadeth, Metallica, Moby, moe, Alanis Morissette, Willie Nelson, Mike Ness, The Offspring, Oleander, Our Lady of Peace, Parliament/Funkadelic, Rage Against the Machine, Sugar Ray, Red Hot Chili Peppers, the Roots, Rusted Root, Brian Setzer Orchestra, The Tragically Hip and the Umbilical Brothers.

The event brought together 225,000 individuals who congregated at the abandoned 3,552-acre former Strategic Air Command (SAC) Griffiss Air Force Base. In the murky background stood Goth like hangars that, in another time, housed lethal B-52 bombers. Patrons each paid $157 dollars for the 72-hour experience that included three days of music, 90-degree heat and the availability of an assortment of pharmaceutical and street drugs. It was fitting, perhaps, that this concert was held inside the confines of a prison-like fortress with 6 to 8 foot fencing topped with razor-sharp cyclone wire. An additional three-miles of twelve-foot-high plywood fence, backed with steel scaffolding, guaranteed that non-ticket holders would be left outside the perimeter.

What will be remembered about this festival was the widespread pyromania, evidenced by numerous arson fires raging in the night, rampant vandalism, rapes, disrespect of women and mindless violence. Tragic scenes of half naked, drunken women, surfing across a sea of people on plywood slabs, bodies being pawed, clothes torn, as they gravitated toward the mosh pit, where they were, once again, sexually assaulted. Factor in, too, those twelve tractor-trailers engulfed in flames after a deliberate propane tank explosion and a five-hour riot that brought in 500 angry cops.

We could debate the root cause of this mob anarchy but the graphic symbols, as viewed on the evening news, said it all. In retrospect, many blamed the high costs of $4 bottled water and $12 pizza and other staples as being the smoldering fuse that eventually exploded into an angry expression of anarchy and violence. Moreover, unlike the 1994 concert, which attempted to keep the festival alcohol-free, Woodstock '99 allowed beer to be sold on the grounds. It was about commercialism, consumerism and capitalism. The Woodstock of Generation Y was peppered with ATM's located more conveniently than the Port-A-Pots and Job-Johnnys that were equally in demand.

On Saturday night Fred Durst, lead singer of Limp Bizkit encouraged the audience to "smash stuff." And like a horde of crazed army ants, a mob of some 200 needed little encouragement to deface whatever lay in their path. The worst was yet to come on Sunday night after The Red Hot Chili Peppers ended the festival. Bass player Flea had performed in the nude while the Chilis closed their set with a version of Jimi Hendrix' "Fire." Rioting exploded at the conclusion of the Chili's set as a sound tower was torn down and set afire. Soon the hordes, in a vicious, feral wilding, began looting tractor-trailers, ripping open ATM machines, destroying Port-A-Pots and setting fire to anything that could be burned. Twelve tractor-trailers were engulfed in flames from a deliberate propane explosion.

As hundreds of New York State Police in riot gear, helmets and batons, marched onto the battlefield, Woodstock burned. There were 1,200 emergency medical personnel who were unprepared to deal with overturned cars, a toppled lighting tower, and the closing of the Cyber café due to hordes of fans urinating in the area. Just before daybreak on Monday the authorities regained control of the battleground. The New York State Police investigated eight allegations of rapes and made 37 arrests. Two individuals died during the concert. Financial damages caused by the rioting were estimated at $400,000 to $600,000. Organizers of the festival released a statement in the violent aftermath: "We're shocked and dismayed by the allegations of sexual abuse, and we're doing everything we can do to help the investigation. If the alleged perpetrators are caught, we hope that they will be prosecuted to the fullest extent of the law." And noted, too, by reporter Steve Corbett, in a pointed opinion piece, "Pyres marking the end of the millennium darkened the heavens as vandals and looters pillaged forever the memory of a festival that somehow gave birth to this madness."

These were cynical times, times not about brotherhood and caring but about self. The angry vandals who attended Woodstock '99 found a way to disconnect themselves from the peace and harmony of an earlier generation. Writing for *The Patriot-News*, Tina Moore observed, "If peace, social activism, Vietnam protests and marijuana were hallmarks of the 1960's, then the first Woodstock was a culmination of that decade. If the 1990's have been about commercialism, instant diversions, teen violence and drugs, then last weekend's festival epitomized this decade." The times could not have been more different. On July 20, 1969 astronaut Buzz Aldrin planted an American flag on the airless surface of the moon. By combining rock, rebellion and patriotism, Jimi Hendrix, on the morning of Sunday, August 17, 1969, at 10:30 a.m., performed the "Star Spangled Banner." But at the 1999 event, Rage Against the Machine took to the stage and then burned the American flag in a profane symbol of sacrilege. Woodstock '99 wasn't about going back to the garden. It was about the desecration and attempted destruction of that sacred place. But according to Woodstock's Mel Lawrence, it was more complicated than that. " Since I was the Director of Operations at the original Woodstock in '69, I think that any comparison between the two events is ludicrous," explained Lawrence. "The times were different, the kids were different and most of all the "peace not war " theme was not as urgent to the festival goers because there was no "draft" ... Of course, there was a certain naivety about music festivals in the sixties that made each experience something new ... I think that "newness" has been lost and the expectations of a Woodstock Festival in '99 couldn't be met ... Woodstock '69 was a miracle that can't be re-created ..."

Over the decades Woodstock, the tribal feast later described as a cultural revolution, remained a topic that has continued to elicit passion and controversy. In 1969, then Governor Nelson Rockefeller declared the region surrounding the festival a "disaster area." Woodstock Nation had swelled to become the third largest city in New York State. Bumper-to-bumper traffic jammed up Route 17-B for over 11 miles as total gridlock prevented people from getting in or out. The New York *Times* published a searing editorial entitled "Nightmare in the Catskills."

Yet, some 38 years later, presidential candidate John McCain blasted Sen. Hillary Clinton at a GOP presidential debate held on October 21, 2007 in Orlando, Florida. During one of his responses McCain stated: "In case you missed it, a few days ago, Senator Clinton tried to spend $1 million on the Woodstock Concert Museum. Now, my friends, I wasn't there. I'm sure it was a cultural and pharmaceutical event ... I was tied up at the time." Shot down in 1967,

Navy pilot McCain spent 5 ½ years in a North Vietnamese prison as a prisoner of war.

"No one can be president of the United States that supports projects such as these," McCain said of the Woodstock Museum project which he criticized as excessive Washington spending. McCain had responded to Senator Hillary Rodham Clinton's proposal for a Woodstock tribute when on June 22, 2007, she stated: "These funds will help the Bethel Woods Center for the Arts continue to promote education, the arts, culture and tourism in the region." Clinton's website further explained that the exhibits would focus on "the post-WWWII period and cultural, political, social, and significant historic events during this period including, in particular, the period of the 1960's and its continuing legacy." Clinton and fellow New York Senator Chuck Schumer had earlier lobbied the Senate Labor, Health and Human Services and Education Committee Appropriations for the $1 million earmark to be used to commemorate the Woodstock music festival of 1969. The funding would have been used to construct a Performing Arts Center on the site.

In answer to McCain's attack, the Clinton camp responded "Senator McCain should focus more on explaining … why he supported the fiscally irresponsible Bush policies that squandered a federal surplus and left us with the largest deficit in American history. As president, Senator Clinton will reverse these policies and restore the nation to fiscal responsibility." The Museum at Bethel Woods is due to officially open in the spring of 2008, but without federal monies.

9

Anna Nicole Smith

o o o o o o o o o o o o o o o o o o o o o o o o o
"I want to be the new Marilyn Monroe."

—*Anna Nicole Smith*

On February 8, 2007, the front desk staff at the Seminole Hard Rock Hotel and Casino in Hollywood, Florida made a desperate 911 call: "We need assistance to room 607 at the Hard Rock. It's in reference to a white female. She's not breathing and not responsive ... actually, it's Anna Nicole Smith." Anna Nicole Smith was found lifeless in room 607 after bodyguard "Big Moe" Brighthaupt called the hotel front desk from Smith's sixth floor room. Maurice Brighthaupt, a trained paramedic, administered CPR before Smith was rushed to Memorial Regional Hospital at 2:10 p.m. TV reality star and former Playboy Playmate of the Year Anna Nicole Smith was pronounced DOA at 2:49 p.m.

In the aftermath of her demise, and after a seven week investigation, the official death report and autopsy were publicly released 46 days later. The March 26, 2007, report stated that Smith's death was not considered to be due to homicide, suicide, or natural causes, but was caused by an accidental drug overdose. During his press conference, Dr. Joshua Perper, Broward County Medical Examiner and Forensic Pathologist, stated that Smith died of "combined drug intoxication," with the sleeping medication chloral hydrate being the "major component" in her death. There were no illegal drugs but there were a total of seven prescription drugs, usually prescribed for anxiety, depression and insomnia, discovered in her bloodstream. Smith, it was revealed, had also injected herself with shots of Vitamin B-12 (cyanocobalamin) and human growth hormone, as an anti-aging strategy, which brought the total number of substances in her bloodstream to nine.

CHLORAL HYDRATE

Perper revealed that Anna Nicole Smith had developed an increased tolerance to the sedative chloral hydrate and took more than the average prescribed dosage. Smith ingested about three tablespoons, whereas the normal dosage is between one and two teaspoons. In his report Perper noted: "She may have taken the dosages she was accustomed to but succumbed because she was already weakened. Miss Smith has a long history of prescription drug abuse and has self-medicated in the past."

Chloral hydrate, first synthesized in 1832, was the first depressant developed for the specific purpose of inducing sleep. The infamous "Mickey Finn" or "knockout drops" was a solution of alcohol and chloral hydrate that was popular in Victorian England and in that era's literature. When used properly, and without the introduction of alcohol or other depressants, chloral hydrate is effective in easing sleeplessness due to pain or insomnia. But according to Avis (1990) the effective dose and lethal dose of chloral hydrate are so close that the sedative should be considered dangerous. Today, the use of chloral hydrate has declined as other agents, including barbiturates and benzodiazepines, have largely replaced them. In the death of Anna Nicole Smith, chloral hydrate became increasingly lethal when mixed with other prescription drugs in her system, specifically four benzodiazepines: Klonopin (Clonazepam), Ativan (Lorazepam), Serax (Oxazepam), and Valium (Diazepam). In addition, Smith had taken

Benadryl (Diphenhydramine) and Topamax (Toprimate), an anticonvulsant GABA agonist, which likely contributed to the tranquilizer effects of the chloral hydrate-benzodiazepine combination. Although the individual levels of any of the benzodiazepines in her system would not have been sufficient to cause death, their combination with a high dose of chloral hydrate led to her fatal overdose. The autopsy report indicated that chloral hydrate was the "toxic/lethal" drug, but it is difficult to know if chloral hydrate ingestion would have killed her alone. And in a bizarre footnote to this tragedy, Chloral hydrate also contributed to the mysterious 1962 death of actress Marilyn Monroe, Smith's idol.

Despite rumors of methadone use (due to its involvement in her son's death) Dr. Perper stated that it was not a contributing factor. Perper only found methadone in Smith's bile, indicating that the drug could only have been ingested 2-3 days prior to her death. Smith's autopsy report indicated that abscesses of buttocks (presumably from prior injections of vitamin B-12 and human growth hormone), and viral enteritis were contributory causes of death.

On Friday, October 12, 2007 Dr. Khristine Eroshevotz found herself at the center of a Drug Enforcement Agency investigation as California authorities served eight search warrants in connection with the death of Smith. Dr. Perper acknowledged that Eroshevitz wrote all eleven prescriptions. According to California State Attorney General Jerry Brown, detectives had collected over 100,000 computer images, files, patient profiles and other important documents associated with Smith's death probe. FOX News anchor Greta Van Susteren acquired paperwork from Perper's office that indicated eight of the 11 drugs in Smith's system, including the chloral hydrate, were prescribed to Howard K. Stern, not Smith. Additionally, two of the medicines were written for Alex Katz and one was written for Smith's friend and psychiatrist, Dr. Khristine Eroshevitz. Los Angeles physician Sandeep Kapoor, who prescribed the methadone, used the pseudonym "Michelle Chase" during his treatment of Smith. Dr. Eroshevich, Smith's personal psychiatrist, also used the name and requested a variety of drugs to be couriered to the Bahamas to an "M. Chase." The assortment of painkillers included two milliliter bottles of Lorazepam (Ativan); four bottles of two mg Dilaudid; two bottles of 350 mg Soma, containing 180 tablets; one bottle each of 30 mg Dalmane and 400 mg of the British drug Prexige; and one bottle of methadone, 300 5mg tablets.

VICKIE SUE HOGAN

A curious member of Generation X, Anna Nicole Smith appeared to materialize out of nowhere to become, at least for a brief, explosive moment, one of the most captivating icons of celebrity culture. Vickie Sue Hogan, a high school dropout and former topless dancer from Houston, made her first appearance in *Playboy* in 1992 and was named the 1993 "Playmate of the Year." But it was Smith's marriage to Texas oilman and billionaire J. Howard Marshall that riveted the public. Smith, 26, and Marshall, 89, were married in Houston on June 27, 1994. Marshall, who was 63-years older that the actress/model, died thirteen months after the marriage. His estate and holdings were worth a reported $1.5 billion and triggered a highly publicized court battle between Smith and Marshall's sons E. Pierce Marshall and James Howard Marshall lll. After changing her name to the more glamorous "Anna Nicole Smith," she eventually became a model for Guess jeans and spokesperson for TrimSpa. For a short period of time, Smith's reality television show, *The Anna Nicole Show,* was the highest-rated program on the E! Entertainment cable network. Smith unveiled that project in 2002. Since Smith's death, various legal battles have ensued, regarding the will, the paternity of her daughter Dannielynn, and her final resting place, which resulted in a delay in her burial. Even though Smith's attorney-boyfriend Howard K. Stern had been listed on the child's birth certificate, a much-publicized paternity suit to determine the father of Dannielynn was initiated. In April 2007, a DNA test determined that photographer and ex-boyfriend Larry Birkhead was the biological father.

Filed in Los Angeles County Superior Court, Smith's will listed Stern as the executor of her estate. The will did not name Larry Birkhead as a beneficiary, but listed him as a party with interest to Smith's estate. The will had been the focus of a contentious Florida court proceeding that involved Stern and Birkhead, among others. Released on February 16, 2007, and made public by Florida's Broward County Court, the will left all of Smith's belongings to her (deceased) son Daniel, but did not specify a living beneficiary. Smith's will, written in 2001, stated "I have intentionally omitted to provide for my spouse and other heirs, including future spouses and children and other descendants now living and those hereafter born or adopted." In the will, Anna Nicole Smith was listed to have personal property valued at $10,000 and real property valued at $1.8 million. After her death it was determined that she still had a $1.1 million mortgage remaining.

GRADUATION CLASS OF BAD GIRLS

The plus-sized Anna Nicole Smith was unique as she was the largest Playboy Playmate in terms of height, weight and overall measurements. Smith was the epitome of that classic voluptuous "look," and represented the opposite polarity of the current anorexia-chic image. Still, the reality-TV actress helped forge a culture that mindlessly worshipped instant fame, impulsivity and notoriety. Often referred to as the "girls gone wild," this group included a cadre of dubious role models such as Lindsey Lohan, Britney Spears, Paris Hilton, Nicole Richie, Drew Barrymore, Anissa Jones, Christina Aguilera and others. Madonna's 1990 Blonde Ambition tour, the antics of individuals like Courtney Love, Pamela Anderson and Carmen Electra and the celebrity of Anna Nicole Smith were all part of that toxic landscape, but it was a host of younger acts, including the Pussycat Dolls, who took it to a greater extreme. It was this graduation class of bad girls who promoted themes of false celebrity, sexual dress, anorexia, substance abuse and self-destructive excess to their younger sisters. It has become obvious that girl culture has taken a dramatic shift towards the left. The incidence of girls going wild has become more prevalent and predictable in our increasingly violent society. On August 14, 1998, in Clovis, NM, population 35,000, 13-year-old Regina Apodaca was stabbed to death. Both her jugular vein and carotid artery were severed causing her to bleed to death. She was brutally slain by Ruby Guerra, 14, while Felicia Duran, 15; Mariana Gallegos, 15; and Francesca Lopez, 13, bit and beat her. The violence had erupted over a shared boyfriend and demonstrated the disturbing trend of young girls involved in violent crime.

According to the National Center for Juvenile Justice, arrests of girls have skyrocketed at a higher rate than those for boys. Between 1992 and 1996, the violent crime arrest rate for girls increased by 25 percent while the boy's rate remained steady. And, among girls under 18, the arrest rate for violent crimes between 1983 and 1992 increased by 85 percent. In their most recent study of girls' violence, the U.S. Justice Department reported that between 1992 and 2003, the number of girls arrested for assault rose by 41 percent. The increase among boys was only 4.3 percent in this troubling example of extreme role reversal that has carried over from the mainstream to the Hollywood set.

Spontaneous violence became part of the implicit and explicit messages gleaned from endless hours of television and magazine indoctrination, coupled with the message that young girls could have it all, without hard work, preparation or sacrifice. They could have it all, just like Anna Nicole Smith or Paris Hilton and Nicole Richie (b. 1981). From 2003 to 2007, Hilton and former-heroin addict Richie starred in a TV reality series called *The Simple Life*. It was a contrived attempt to merge the opposite worlds of the rich and famous with the down-to-earth realities of those less fortunate. And even though the acting, articulation and talent were far from superb, it did promote the celebrity status and notoriety of these two individuals. Richie's two DUIs and mandated alcohol education classes and Hilton's jail term and 40-minute sex video with ex-boyfriend Rick Solomon, did little to discourage their faithful audience. Hilton had been placed on house arrest after serving three days of her shortened 23-day jail sentence for alcohol-related reckless driving. After violating terms of her probation, Hilton was sent to Century Regional Detention Center where she completed her sentence.

Lindsey Lohan, former Disney girl and CK model, has made a very public transition from child star to that of a sexual and adult image. Part of that image revolved around her party-girl nightclub adventures. In 2007 actress Linsey Lohan (b. 1986) was arrested twice on DUI charges. She was also cited for possession of cocaine, the transport of narcotics and for driving with a suspended license. The 21-year-old celebrity, as part of her plea bargain for misdemeanor drunken driving, spent two months in rehabilitation. She was later instructed to work in a morgue as part of her mandated community service. Lohan's *Mean Girls*, released in 2004, was prophetic as Lohan's character joined the Plastics, the alpha female group in a public high school.

Once called "the most powerful celebrity in the world" by *Forbes magazine*, Britney Spears, at age 21, seemed to have everything going her way. The former Mickey Mouse Club regular, with talent, charm and charisma, worked her way to the top of teen pop-stardom. Her "Baby One More Time" offering sold over 14.6 million copies. Unfortunately, for the youthful superstar, her rise to the top was fleeting as the stage of pop celebrity was soon replaced by the reality of a self-destructive mission. Five years later, Spears (b.1982) found herself in a very public meltdown triggered by poor judgment and reckless behavior. The troubled pop star spent a month at Promises Treatment Center in Malibu, CA, then emerged with shaved head and damaged image. Spears briefly entered into treatment for her substance abuse several times. She was criticized for excessive partying, reckless driving with her son on her lap, and for allowing herself to be photographed without underwear. Spears then defied court orders and refused to comply with her custody agreement. Forced to hand over her two sons to former husband and L.A.-based actor/rapper Kevin Federline, Spears barricaded herself inside her $7 million Beverly Hills mansion. On January 3, 2008, police and paramedics were called and scenes of Spears being carted out on a gurney, with news helicopters hovering overhead, were repeatedly played on national television. The singer was then taken to Los Angeles' Cedars-Sinai Medical Center for an emergency psychiatric evaluation under a California statute known as the 5150 Hold. *OK.Magazine* covered the event with a front-page expose entitled, "Last Day With Mommy." Almost immediately Spear's visitation rights with 2-year-old Sean Preston and 1-year-old Jayden James were suspended.

Britney was a questionable role model for her younger sibling Jamie Lynn Spears, who, at age 16, announced her pregnancy to the world. Jamie Lynn Spears was the star of the popular *Zoey 101*, featured on the Nickelodeon network. More than 7 million people tuned into an episode called "Goodbye Zoey," which marked the end of *Zoey 101's* third season. That viewer reaction was significant as it represented more than double the usual numbers for the program and the appeal of the talented Jamie Lynn. Keeping it all in the family, mother Lynne inked a one million dollar deal with *OK. Magazine* for a tell-all story about her youngest daughter.

The Spears Family was a unit in crisis. Father Jamie, a recovering alcoholic, searched for answers, while Britney and mother Lynne endured months of silent, hateful estrangement, ironically as Lynne Spears agreed to write a book on celebrity parenting. Britney, who suffered from obvious drug addiction and a possible bi-polar disorder, found herself alone without a true self-concept. The only persona that Spears knew was the one that was contrived and created by the entertainment industry, a false, empty mask that lied to her and the world. Spears continued to spin out of control. Even her purported comeback during the 2007 *MTV Video Music Awards* was met with criticism from fans and media critics, partially due to her untoned abs and her soft and out-of-shape physique. Yet despite Spear's continued downward spiral, her latest album was met with rave reviews (October 2007) and provided Spears with her first No. 1 record in years, "Gimme More."

And across the pond, English R&B singer Amy Winehouse (b.1983) eerily followed in Spears' bizarre footsteps. Winehouse, also stalked and tormented by the unrelenting *paparazzi*, watched as her own struggles with drug and alcohol addiction, eating disorders, cancelled tour dates and ensuing legal troubles were all shamelessly revealed to the tabloid-crazed public. Ironically songwriter Winehouse's first North American hit (They tried to make me go to) "Rehab" was a #7 single in the UK and won the 2007 Ivor Novello award as it detailed a painful aspect of her life. Winehouse ironically, in her first Grammy appearance, won the 2008 Record of the Year Grammy, for "Rehab."

ANOREXIA CHIC

Ranked high on *Forbes*' "Under 25 Rich List," Mary-Kate and Ashley Olsen are multimillion-dollar moguls and examples of successful young women with a complicated message to their peers. "You can never be too rich or too thin" was the quote attributed to the Dutchess of Windsor Wallis Simpson (1896-1986), wife of former-King Edward Vlll, but a message that the Olsens have embraced. With their spectacular wealth and fame, these women have chosen, in an act of willful starvation, to reshape their bodies into anorexic versions of their former selves.

This sisterhood has celebrated actresses often proffering skeletal image and style above their talent. Their heroines included young women such as Jessica Alba, Jennifer Aniston, Victoria Beckham, Cate Blanchett, Kate Bosworth, Laura Flynn Boyle, Hilary Duff, Calista Flockhart, Terri Hatcher, Angelina Jolie, Keira Knightly, Brittany Murphy, and Nicole Richie; rail thin models and actresses well practiced in the art of restrictive eating. The unfortunate examples of Karen Carpenter (1950-1983) and Terri Schiavo (1963-2005) did little to discourage this life-threatening behavior, much of it fueled by perceived societal expectations and the $30 billion a year diet industry.

The attitudes of unhealthy body image, espoused by teenage girls, are troubling. Researchers pointed out that developing a strong and realistic body image is all-important for adolescent women. A negative self-image can lead to a lifetime of low self-esteem and resulting eating disorders. According to an *ELLEgirl* survey of 10,000 readers, 30 percent said that they would rather be thin than healthy while 90 percent of teenage girls believed that they were overweight, even though they were in the normal weight range. That number was 24 percent in 1995. Over 50 percent of women, between the ages of 18 to 25, preferred to be "run over by a truck" than to be fat. According to a Colgate University study, nearly half of nine to 11-year-olds were "sometimes" or "very often" on diets. Another national study of "tween" girls revealed that forty-two percent of first to third-grade girls wanted to be thinner. Although approximately 7 million women and girls suffered from eating disorders, their illness had often been viewed as a type of positive empowerment. Value was placed on the perfection of the physical body through exercise, self-control and restrictive eating. Overweight individuals were often viewed as lazy, sickly and lacking in self-control. Anorexia and bulimia were positively transformed into a combined psychotherapy and religion, its altar situated in the citadel of the internet temple and at the feet of Goddess Ana. Self-described *"anas"* or pro-EDs (people who advocated eating disorders) organized contests that promoted creative and dangerous weight loss. Some cybernet participants called *skin n' bones* and *anorexiarocks* boasted to their peers of an existence on 500 calories a day.

Characterized by a distorted body image, anorexia nervosa has one of the highest mortality rates of all mental disorders. An estimated five to 20 percent of afflicted individuals will die from complications of this condition. Specific traits of this disorder include an extreme fear of obesity, refusal to maintain a minimally normal body weight and, in women, absence of menstrual periods. Individuals in late adolescence and early adulthood meet the full Diagnostic and Statistical

Manual of Mental Disorders criteria for anorexia nervosa at a rate of 0.5 percent to 1.0 percent.

Anorexia can affect both men and women, although the disorder is more widespread among girls and women (90 to 95 percent) and especially those who live in Western countries. According to 2006 data from the Anorexia Nervosa and Related Eating Disorders group, the rates in women in Western countries ranged from 0.1% to 5.7% of the population. Recent data has indicated that 40 percent of newly identified anorexia cases are in girls ages 15 to 19. The average age of onset for this disorder is 17, according to the American Psychiatric Association. Over the past forty years, the incidence of anorexia has tripled among young women as reported in a 2004 University of Maryland Medical Center study. In addition, as stated by the Eating Disorders Coalition (2006), 30 to 40 percent of junior high school girls were concerned about their body image, while 40 to 60 percent of high school girls had dieted. This dangerous trend has reached younger girls in the fourth grade as 40 percent of nine-year-old girls reported having dieted. Several websites, including The Proanasanctuary Club and Proanorexia, promote restrictive eating as a positive means of purification of the body and self-control.

Young women are getting plastic cosmetic surgeries in greater numbers. ABC News reported that, in an eight-year span, a 465 percent increase in corrective cosmetic procedures occurred from 1997 to 2005. And in 2008, the American Society for Aesthetic Plastic Surgery stated that surgical procedures were sought out not just for older individuals but for those 18 and over. In a new ASAPS study, men and women ages 18-24 had the highest approval rating for cosmetic surgery. According to the report of 1000 teens and young adults ages 18 and above, 69% of respondents were in favor of cosmetic surgery, which is a 7% increase from 2006. Men and women ages 65 and older had the lowest approval rating of cosmetic surgery with 41%.

THE MARKETING OF GENERATION TWEEN

According to researchers Strauss and Howe, Generation Y has been deemed the fourteenth or Civic Group, with anticipated parallels to the G.I. Generation so many years before. Their population explosion will eclipse any contributions from the withering Generation X and the aging-out Boomers as Generation Y will have reached a tremendous milestone by pure numbers alone. This Generation Y cluster is represented by about 71 million individuals born since 1979 and is the largest block of consumers since the post-World War ll baby explosion. Those numbers are expected to dramatically increase until the teen demographic group swells to 34 million around 2010. That will give us the largest number of teenagers in this country ever, a significant event in many ways. With large amounts of disposable income, the spending power of American teens has grown at an astonishing rate.

Scenting blood, corporate America stalked and hunted down their most vulnerable prey. Generation Y, comprised of the older Echo Boomers (also called Generation Next and Clickeratti) and the younger "tweens," is now recognized as the most desirable and impressionable demographic group. Corporate America has also squarely focused on "tween consumers." This sub-group of Generation Y, ages 8 to 14, has been described as being more than "just a kid" but not "quite a teenager." Tweens, represented by 39.9 million individuals, have directly influenced the selection of approximately $110 billion in food and drink products and possessed over $60 billion in purchasing power of their own. With a spending allowance of about $ 50.00 per week, "tweens" are an invaluable group in the market place. Tweens are responsible for the success of such acts as 98 degrees, Christina Aguilera, Back Street Boys, Brandy, Aaron Carter, Hillary Duff, Hanna Montana, Britney Spears, Jessica Simpson, and 'N Sync.

The heavy media attention to the tween group has often incorporated the use of controversial images to market a sexual, sophisticated tween look. But these types of sexual marketing strategies drew criticism when Abercrombie & Fitch launched its summer catalog in 2001. Geared towards the increasingly sophisticated tastes of youth ages 18 or older, the popular publication was under attack for using sex, including group sex, to enhance its street image. Called a "soft porn magazine," the publication was also accused of promoting " unrealistic body types." Among those pointing fingers at the 300,000 catalogs were the National Organization for Women and Concerned Christian Americans. Even J.C. Penney took some flak after they aired a commercial that promoted a sexy, midriff-baring look for teenage girls. The commercial was withdrawn on August 10, 2001 after only one week on the air.

American women have been indoctrinated into pursuing a body image that is unattainable and unrealistic yet reflective of what the patriarchal system has mandated. This stereotyped feminine image is best symbolized by the Mattel Corporation and its Barbie and Ken figurines. Invented by Ruth Handler in 1959, Barbie has influenced girls' awareness of their body image for over 50 years. Mattel's Barbie line, which also includes Teresa and Christie, is directly aimed at Generation Y female tweens ages three to ten. Marketed in 150 countries, the assortment of voluptuous plastic dolls has commanded an impressive two billion dollars worth of revenue. A 2001 promotional campaign had Barbie promoting 'N Sync in a polished marketing strategy that combined tween puppy love with child fantasy.

In a sense, Anna Nicole Smith was able to transform herself into a real-life version of the Barbie doll. According to reports, Smith had breast augmentation that consisted of two implants placed into each breast. Over the last two years she also had a face lift and other facial procedures. Moreover, it had been speculated that her dramatic weight loss, attributed to Trimspa X32, may have actually been due to gastric bypass surgery or a similar process.

It was impossible to have known the real Anna Nicole Smith. She said that she wanted to be "the next Marilyn Monroe" but had been known variously as Vickie Lynn Hogan, Vickie Lynn Marshall, Anna Nicole, Vickie Smith, Vicki Smith, Michelle Chase and M. Chase. Smith was only two-years old when her father, Donald Eugene Hogan, deserted the family. Her life was a series of painful and tragic events, and it was against almost impossible odds that the platinum-blonde reality star climbed her way to the top of the celebrity world. Even with her success there were many who considered her a garish, ignorant and crude individual. *New York* magazine featured a degrading photograph of Smith eating potato chips in its 1994 issue that was titled *White Trash Nation*. That same year Smith appeared in *Naked Gun 33 1/3* and *The Hudsucker Proxy* and then filmed 2006's *Illegal Aliens*. Her appearances were met with little media acclaim. *The Anna Nicole Show* was another pathetic attempt at entertainment, with Smith often dazed, confused and possibly in a drug-induced condition. That show stayed on the air for almost two seasons due to the morbid curiosity of viewers and perhaps in anticipation of the star's expected self-destruction. Much like Britney Spears, both women never really knew who they were. Both were false creations of empty beauty and empty promise, both products and victims of the celebrity machine with each providing us with equal glimpses of hope and despair.

Three days after the birth of her daughter Dannielynn Marshall, Smith's 20-year-old son, Daniel Wayne Smith, overdosed in his mother's hospital room. Autopsy results indicated that he died from a drug combination of Zoloft, Lexapro and methadone. The tragedy of Anna Nicole Smith did not end there. On February 7, 2007, a woman filed a lawsuit against Smith, who was a spokeswoman for the weight-loss supplement Trimspa X32. The lawsuit accused Smith of making "false and misleading" statements about the product. That event may have been the final blow to Smith's damaged and tortured psyche. The following afternoon, after ingesting a deadly combination of chloral hydrate and benzodiazepines, she drifted off into her final sleep. Smith was buried March 2, 2007 at Nassau's Lakeview Memorial Gardens and Mausoleum in a plot adjacent to her son even as Virgie Arthur, Smith's estranged mother, attempted to have her daughter's remains exhumed and reburied in their home state of Texas. The merciless turmoil that defined much of Anna Nicole Smith's life continued even after her unfortunate death.

10

Post Columbine

Even as it signaled the end of another decade and reflected the dark mythology of Generation X, there was something terribly wrong about the year 1999. And as it began with the mindless anarchy of the Los Angeles Riots it ended tragically with blood running in the hallways of the Columbine High School.

Eric Harris and Dylan Klebold, possibly emulating the sadistic dream sequence in *The Basketball Diaries*, called themselves "The Trenchcoat Mafia." On April 20, 1999, at the Columbine High School, and on the anniversary of Adolph Hitler's birthday, Harris and Klebold systematically executed 12 schoolmates and a teacher before taking their own lives. The killers provided ample clues of the impending carnage on their violent website: "It'll be like the anarchy of the LA Riots, the Oklahoma Bombing, WW ll, Vietnam, Duke and Doom all mixed together," warned Eric Harris in 1998. "I want to leave a lasting impression on the world." Six months before the Columbine attack Harris outlined in a premeditated *manifesto* that during his deadly rampage he only wanted to spare "about 100 people max."

Dylan Klebold wrote a minute-by-minute schedule for the imminent shootings in his day planner. "Walk in, set bombs at 11:09, drive to park,??? gearup, get back by 11:15, park cars, set car bombs for 11:18, get out, go to outside hill, wait, when first bombs go off, attack?????????" At the time, Columbine was the most horrific school massacre in American history, yet, even before the bloodletting of Eric Harris and Dylan Klebold, there were ominous signs, easily recognized but subtlety ignored, that something evil lurked in the dark recesses and corridors of America's classrooms.

Like real-life video games, a slew of copycat school shootings began to wound communities across the nation. In 1996 Barry Loukaitis, 14, dressed in long coat and black clothing, killed two classmates and his algebra teacher in Moses Lake, WA. Luke Woodham, 16, stabbed his mother to death and then killed two students and wounded seven others in Pearl, MS. In West Paduca, KY, in 1997, 14-year-old Michael Carneal killed three girls and wounded five others. Consumed with hatred and rage, these misguided individuals were all members of Generation Y, the most violent gang of school killers encountered by society. From 1985 to 1995, violent crimes committed by juveniles doubled to 67 percent with perhaps a fifth of all violent crimes committed in the U.S. being the work of teens. And, according to the Justice Department's Bureau of Justice statistics, in 2002, of the 1,200,203 state prisoners, 3,055 were younger than 18 years old, while adult jails incarcerated 7,248 inmates under the age of 18. "In America today, no population poses a greater threat to public safety than juvenile criminals," said Representative Bill McCollum, the Florida Republican who wrote the House version of the Violent Youth Predator Act.

After Columbine, the response to the mass shootings was swift. Numerous school boards across the country enacted Draconian measures that enforced a strict dress code and limited personal expression. Some educators theorized that when all students wore pre-approved school uniforms it somehow reduced violence by an increased conformity to standards. Among the other proposed measures were a banning of traditional school garb, including khakis and camouflage-style dress, large earrings, oversized shirts and jeans, book bags, bulky purses and handbags. Some went even so far as to forbid the wearing of shirts that depicted images of professional wrestlers, beer and cigarette logos and controversial shock-rockers such as Marilyn Manson,

Rob Zombie and Nine Inch Nails. But those restrictive measures may have been in vain, according to associate professor of sociology J. William Spencer of Purdue University. He said: "We know that the quality of the parent-child relationship is a good predictor of whether a teen-ager will participate in delinquent behavior. That's why all the discussion following school shootings about installing metal detectors, or even banning backpacks because weapons can be hidden, is off the mark."

Legislative proposals became even stranger as a large number of dramatic resolutions sought to prevent violence in our nation's schools. Alabama Republican Rep. Robert Aderholt introduced an amendment to allow states to display the Ten Commandments in all schools and state-owned facilities. The final House vote on June 17, 1999, was 248 to 180, along party lines. Aderhold stated that his measure would "promote morality and work toward an end of children killing children." Georgia Congressman Bob Barr introduced the Juvenile Justice Reform Act that provided schools the individual option to display the Ten Commandments. Barr called it an open expression of freedom of religion, as protected by the Constitution and the First Amendment. Defying political correctness, Barr argued that these moral values were important Judeo-Christian tenants significant enough to preserve and pass on to America's youth. Missouri Republican Jo Ann Emerson proposed an amendment condemning the entertainment industry for their promotion of violence. Her amendment passed in the House. Ironically Congress failed to pass gun-control legislation of any kind, but did uphold a Senate bill that tightened restrictions on gun show sales. And in May, 2000, Alabama Sen. Jeff Sessions, along with eight other senators, sent letters to several retailers asking them to remove violent video games from their stores or restrict their sales to youth over 17. Sessions argued that "intense involvement" in these games could cause a child to become violent.

In the wake of the Columbine High School shooting, President Clinton ordered the Federal Trade Commission to study the marketing practices of the entertainment industry. The report, announced in October 2000, chastised the industry for enticing children with adult material and called for expanding the existing voluntary codes. Both presidential candidates Al Gore and George W. Bush searched for ways to quell the violence in the media.

Although censorship in this country is nothing new, it has assumed many, varied forms. In 1996 Congress passed the Telecommunications Act that required all television sets over thirteen-inches wide to be fitted with a V-chip, touted as a means to censor violent or sexual themes from the curious eyes of children during the absence of their parents. As explained by President Bill Clinton "If every parent uses this chip wisely, it can become a powerful voice against teen violence, teen pregnancy, teen drug use, and for both learning and entertainment." The V-chip solution to the problem of unrestricted television watching produced a curious effect. Even though 77 percent of parents approved of the use of the chip, few of them understood the complicated television rating system and failed to utilize the system in their homes, according to The Kaiser Family Foundation.

In 1985 Tipper Gore testified before a Senate hearing on the questionable lyrics of rock music. As co-founder of the Parents' Music Resource Center, Gore was able to force the industry, despite harsh criticism and resistance from the art community, to place warning labels on music CDs deemed too violent or sexually explicit. Many in the art community felt that the entertainment industry should have the ability to police itself and, ironically, on May 25, 1999, Warner Brothers Cable TV did pull the season finale "Graduation Day, Part Two" from the popular series *Buffy the Vampire Slayer*. The episode depicted school violence, right after the killings in Littleton, Colorado, and during the period of traditional school graduations. In an obvious compromise Warner Brothers rescheduled the chilling episode for July 13, 1999.

The cartoon-film *South Park: Bigger, Longer and Uncut* was released on June 30,1999. It's release was significant as there was a renewed public interest in the motion picture rating system, a process negotiated between President Bill Clinton and major theatre owners in the aftermath of the Littleton tragedy. Clinton stated that the youth of America were being subjected to "too much violence through media and cultural contacts." *South Park*, filled with vulgarities, bodily functions and graphic scenes of death and destruction, carried an R rating, which allowed an individual under the age of 17 to view the movie if accompanied by an adult. The more restrictive NC-17 rating meant that no one under the age of 17 would be allowed to view the movie, even with an adult present.

Baby Boomers were the first generation to grow up watching television, a visual primer of untainted white Anglo images of a perfect world order. But over the decades the images of picture-perfect innocence became darker in their cruel realism. It became a different *Ozzie and Harriet* and *I Love Lucy* that Generation X was being offered. Theirs became a visceral onslaught of violence, vulgarity and sexuality as evidenced by such popular programs as *Beavis and Butt-Head, Saturday Night Live, Married With Children, NYPD Blue, Sex and the City, Queer as Folk,* and *The Shield*.

They were young and pure and untainted, but the innocence of our children has faded fast. Our children have matured into a society that is addicted to and worships violence in act and deed. The ritual of TV watching is part of that maturation, yet regrettably, violence is also a part of that experience. During prime time TV viewing, there are an estimated five to six violent acts per hour especially in cartoon shows. Compare that with an estimated 25 violent acts per hour during children's programming and we begin to understand the confused mindset of our children and our teenagers.

Television steals valuable time from our youth and prevents them from growing up and developing healthy relationships, adequate coping skills and maturing in a manner where a connection with the child's community is forged. A child in the United States watches three hours of TV per day, more than any other country. Teens watch 18 to 22 hours per week and 17 percent of youths ages 18 to 24 watch an average of five hours of television per day, or 35 hours per week.

The American Psychological Association projected that by the end of elementary school, a child had viewed 8,000 murders on television and 100,000 acts of violence.

BEYOND THE 1990'S

Regarding to the incidence of high-school shootings, the 1990's are largely recognized as one of the deadliest ten-year spans, with the shooters being overwhelmingly members of Generation Y. But the Generation Y Gang have continued their copycat bloodletting far beyond the decade of the 1990's. In September 2006, Kim Veer Gill, 25, killed a young woman and wounded 20 others before taking his own life when cornered by police at Montreal's Dawson College, a campus of 10,000 students.

Blacksburg, VA, home of Virginia Tech, has become the site of the deadliest mass shooting in modern U.S. history. On April 16, 2007, South Korean English major Cho Seung-Hui, 23, shot to death 32 people before firing a bullet into his head. The attack came in two stages that were separated by a two-hour span. Seung-Hui, armed with a Glock 9 mm and a .22-caliber handgun, with the phrase *"Ismail Ax"* written in red ink on his arm, began his apocalypse of rage at 7:15 a.m. in one of the college dormitories. Prior to the shooting he had created numerous pieces of disturbed writings about violent attacks and rants against rich kids, women and religion.

And on October 26, 2007, 14-year-old Dillon Cossey, believed to have been the victim of protracted peer abuse, admitted to having plotted a Columbine-style assault on the Plymouth Whitemarsh High School in Norristown, PA. Among the weaponry discovered in his home were a 9 mm semi-automatic rifle with laser scope, homemade grenades, a bomb-making instruction book and several .22 caliber guns. According to authorities Cossey's mother, Michele, was believed to have purchased the weapons for her son Dillon, who had stated to a friend, "The world would be better off without bullies."

On November 7, 2007, in southern Finland and in a country where the legal age for owning a firearm is 15, eighteen-year-old Pekka-Eric Auvinen, described as "a bullied outcast," opened fire at his high school, killing six students, a school nurse and the school principal. He then turned his .22-caliber Sig Sauer Mosquito pistol on himself. Just hours before his rampage the shooter had uploaded a home-made video entitled "Jokela High School Massacre," using KMFDM's "Stray Bullet" in the background. "I am prepared to fight and die for my cause. I, as a natural selector, will eliminate all who I see unfit, disgraces of human race and failures of natural selection," he threatened on a You Tube posting.

COMPLEX PTSD

There have been many terms for the unrelenting sensory assault on our psyche such as *shell shock, combat fatigue, compassion fatigue, war neurosis* and *post-traumatic stress disorder.* Shell shocked from the continued bombardment of violence paraded before its eyes, society has been increasingly assaulted and traumatized. Collectively, a classic Post Traumatic Stress Disorder, with ensuing symptoms of helplessness, frustration, isolation and depression, has been experienced.

As horrible bloodshed is witnessed on the daily news, many have accepted this revulsion as part of the permanent cultural landscape. Continuously bombarded with instantaneous graphic images during the morning, noon and evening news, many have built up a tolerance where the violence becomes muted, affecting us in a less palpable manner. Even our children have become conditioned to the ongoing event as they are entertained by extreme video games that normalize violence.

Stu Gilhelm, in *Lifetime Guarantees,* illustrated this by utilizing a device he called a "feeling meter." Usually our meter, according to Gilhelm's theory, is resting at point zero, but after having witnessed trauma upon trauma, our meter begins to inch higher and higher, until our "normal" resting point is well above zero and closer to the proverbial ten. Hence, omnipresent death, destruction and carnage have been accepted as a normal part of our lives. Contaminated by this onslaught of violence in both real life and by the media, one begins to consider that violence has become a constant, that it will only get worse and, most importantly, that one has no control over it. In surrender, a fatalistic persona and desensitization towards the carnage are adapted. It is a collective numbing experience shared by large numbers of our society.

Instant communications have been a boon and a curse as vivid, in-depth coverage of national and global carnage follows directly after the event. Like adrenaline junkies and blood voyeurs, society will have relived these horrors in an immediate, vicarious manner. Note the following horrendous events that transpired in the 1990's. They are but a small portion of the grim realities experienced by our nation but are unique in their importance and relationship to the group Generation X:

1992: Hospital technician Brian Stewart, 32, of Columbia, IL, injected his 11 month-old son with AIDS-tainted blood during a hospital visit. Stewart was convicted on December 6, 1998, and sentenced to life in prison. Stewart admitted that he injected his son, who was later diagnosed with AIDS, to avoid paying child support.

1994: After she strapped her two small boys in her Mazda Protégé, Susan Smith, 23, watched as the vehicle slid into South Carolina's John D. Long Lake. Smith later admitted that she drowned her sons, Michael Daniel Smith and Alexander Tyler Smith, to win the love of a married man. Smith was sentenced to life in prison.

1995: In an example of extreme domestic terrorism, 168 people are killed after an explosion devastated the Alfred P. Murrah Federal Building in Oklahoma City. Among them are 19 children. The terrorist act occurred at 9:02 a.m. on April 19, 1995. Timothy McVeigh and Terry Lynn Nichols are convicted of the bombing.

1996: Ronald Shanabarger, 30, confessed to using plastic wrap to smother his 7-month-old boy, Tyler, to punish his wife for not cutting a vacation short after Shanabarger's father died in 1996. Although Shanabarger, from Franklin, IN, had also taken out a $100,000 life insurance policy on his son, authorities believe that his true motive was revenge. Shanabarger's atrocity is part of an evil trend as a study by the National Institute of Child Health and Human Development reported that of the 35 million babies born during the years of 1983 to 1991, a total of 2,776 died of homicide during their first year. And according to the NICHHD, homicide is the leading cause of infant death, usually due to neglect, physical injury or child abuse.

1997: Scott Falater, 43, was convicted of brutally stabbing his wife 44 times and then holding her head under water in their Phoenix, AZ, swimming pool, until her life was extinguished. Falater, a Mormon, claimed that he had been sleepwalking and had no recollection of the murder.

2001: Andrea Yates, 36, drowned her five children, ages 6-months-old to seven years, in a bathroom in their Clear Lake, TX, home. She had a history of depression and was being treated for post-partum depression, and was on medication at the time of the incident. Authorities discovered four of the lifeless bodies neatly on a bed under a sheet. The remaining victim, a 7-year old boy, was found in the bathtub. Jurors rejected her insanity defense finding her guilty of capital murder.

THE CYCLE OF HOMICIDE

The cycle of homicide has continued, each crime appeared even more wicked than the previous one as each confronted us with images more horrific than the last. This has become society's norm, watching numbly as this grim reality is accepted. Bessel van der Kolk, an authority on posttraumatic stress disorders, noted that the numbing sensation has been associated with a number of similar experiences, all connected with a significant thread of violence. "This consistent pattern of hyper arousal alternating with numbing has been noticed following such a vast array of different traumas, such as combat, rape, kidnapping, spouse abuse, natural disasters, accidents, concentration camp experience, incest, and child abuse." Van der Kolk has suggested a new classification, a new diagnosis that he called "Complex PTSD." Ironically, van der Kolk and Gilheim have arrived at the same conclusion: that our society has suffered from an ongoing trauma brought on by vicarious and ongoing images of violence. As a society, the negative repercussions of this invasive flow of violence are felt. As a result, an increased rash of symptoms, usually reserved for those suffering from posttraumatic stress disorder, are evidenced. These include a sense of hopelessness and despair, persistent distrust, isolation and withdrawal, a sense of helplessness and the loss of sustaining faith. And, as our sense of community vanishes, it is replaced by a world filled with rapid technology and impersonal communications. Many of those supportive interpersonal relationships that have forged this great society, including our interrelated network of family, church and community, have vanished and much of that important sense of community, that extended family structure, has been gutted. A recent NPR *All Things Considered* described the prison system in the state of Maryland. Although Baltimore represented about 13 percent of the state's population, that city is disproportionately representative of approximately 57 percent of Maryland inmates currently behind bars. The NPR program concluded that the important community support network, especially important for children in need of positive role models, has been effectively dismantled and perhaps even destroyed in locales such as Baltimore.

Moreover, according to Generation United, in the year 2000, 6 percent of our children were being raised by their grandparents because of the tremendous number of incarcerated parents, many due to substance abuse issues. The 2000 U.S. Census estimated that 6.3 percent of children under 18 were living in a grandparent-headed home. In that survey, 42 percent of the nearly 5.5 million grandparents (2.4 million) were responsible for "most of the basic needs" of a grandchild in the home. (The U.S. Census Bureau estimated the number of children under 18 living in a grandparent-headed home to have been 3.2 percent in 1970, 3.6 percent in 1980, and 5.5 percent in 1990).

In less than a decade, the prison population of the United States has doubled. The US, along with countries such as Russia, China, Iran and the Republic of South Africa, had a greater percentage of its population in prison. In 1999 there were 1.8 million individuals, one of every 150 Americans, sitting in prison. Over half of these were incarcerated for drug related crimes as the number of individuals serving time for drug offenses tripled from 1990 to 1999. As this country passed tougher and more punitive laws, with the resulting incarceration of young males, the majority of them black and Hispanic, we devastated significant portions of select demographic groups. According to a new report from the Justice Department's Bureau of Justice Statistics (BJS), America's prison population topped two million inmates for the first time in history on June 30, 2002. The 50 states, the District of Columbia and the federal government held 1,355,748 prisoners (two-thirds of the total incarcerated population), and local municipal and county jails held 665,475 inmates. By midyear 2002, America's jails held 1 in every 142 U.S. residents. Males were incarcerated at the rate of 1,309 inmates per 100,000 U.S. men, while the female incarceration rate was 113 per 100,000 women residents.

In 2000 two percent of American children had to visit a prison in order to see their mother or father. And in a *Newsweek* article entitled "The Prison Paradox," writer Ellis Cose noted that "In 1999 nearly 1.5 million children had at least one parent in state or federal prison (up from less than one million in 1991)." The choice of prisons over rehabilitation, of steel bars winning over education and prevention, has effectively bypassed the role of the community as an important safety network. The extended community is no longer called upon to shape, define and nurture the behavior of its children. The extended community has effectively been destabilized and made ineffective as so many of its children, and its children's parents, are locked behind bars.

THE ROOT CAUSE OF VIOLENCE

Scientists continued to debate the root cause of violence. Was the Y chromosome to blame, or could it be attributed to an excess of the hormone testosterone and a type of testosterone poisoning that led to violence? Some facts were obvious. Violent crimes and drug experimentation by juveniles peaked immediately after school, usually around 3:00 p.m., and decreased during the evening hours, while juvenile crime tripled between the hours of 3:00 p.m. to 8:00 p.m. A record number of single parents and an unfortunate lack of parental supervision had spawned a nation of latchkey children forced to survive on the streets in any way they could.

Homicides rose from the late 1980s and throughout the decade of the 1990s. According to a Justice Department survey, crime jumped in 1991 by eight percent from the previous year. There were 2,612,150 violent crimes in 1991 compared to 2,421,530 in 1990. In 1991, in the country's 75 largest counties, 92 percent of the juveniles in Criminal Court were male and 96 percent of them had been charged with murder. In a ten-year span, during the period from 1985 to 1995, the number of youths murdered by firearms rose 153 percent. For Generation X, life on the mean streets was increasingly dangerous, as homicide, accidents and drive-by shootings became part of the bloody equation.

The epidemic black-on-black violence, as evidenced by fallen brothers Tu Pac Shakur and the Notorious B.I.G., has been another disturbing trend. As articulated by William Oliver, in 1995 "Black-on-Black violence has emerged as the most significant social problem threatening the survival and quality of life among Blacks since slavery." In 1993, 94 percent of black murder victims were killed by black offenders (as compared to 84 percent of white murder victims killed by white offenders). In 1991 death rates for homicide were eight times higher for black males (72.5 per 100,000) as compared to white males (9.4 per 100,000) and almost five times higher for black females (13.9 per 100,000) as for white females (3.0 per 100,000). The death rate in 1991 for black males 15 to 24 years of age (159.9 per 100,0000) was nine times greater than the rate for white males in that age group. Then, too, in 1993 blacks represented 58 percent of persons arrested for murder, 41 percent arrested for rape, 62 percent arrested for robbery, and 40 percent arrested for aggravated assault, even though blacks constituted only 12 percent of the U.S. population.

School violence, suddenly front-page news, had been traditionally underreported due to fear of bad publicity and immediate public reaction, but in the 1990's an ominous trend emerged. Parents had been less accessible than in past decades; working, divorcing, and existing. They were less connected to the extended safety network of neighbors, teachers, religious leaders and social workers resulting in a generation of isolated and scared young individuals falling into a black hole. This silent and lonely void was a place of home-alone desolation where survival, not nurturing and mentoring, was the goal. These feral children, a vulnerable population with the least amount of coping skills, were being forced to grow up too fast. They were the hurried children, the after school youngsters being asked to act like adults. It wasn't long before the predictable response of anger took hold. School shootings, from 1996 to 1999, were a likely byproduct of this horrible experiment in child rearing with Dylan Klebold and Eric Harris, shrouded in alienation, repressed anger and Nazi mythology, leading the charge.

11

Concerning their Legacy

○ ○
"The longer you look back, the further you can look forward."

—*Winston Churchill*

In the mid 1930s, Ruth Fulton Benedict, anthropologist and author of *Patterns of Culture*, noted that, "From the moment of his birth, the customs into which (a child) is born shape his experiences and behavior. By the time he can talk, he is the little creature of his culture." According to many experts, the outcome was predictable, as man is a product of all those earlier variables, variables that have shaped his collective being. As long as children received love and consistent structure and parenting, they could go out into the world as adept and healthy individuals striving toward their potential. Those individuals, having a strong self-concept and positive outlook, would have the ability to adapt to traumatic, unforeseen events in a successful and resilient manner. But for those unfortunate others, that life journey could be shrouded in pessimism, uncertainty and fear.

The members of Generation X, arguably more than any other generation since The Lost Generation, were psychologically disturbed by the world that surrounded them. Although not mentally ill, these individuals experienced the subtle effects of mental, physical, and social trauma due to the blatant scapegoating and marginalization that they endured from a larger and more affluent socio-economic class. This group, many of whom were members of the Baby Boomer demographic, rejected and excluded the members of Gen X. What would eventually become a critical and destructive self-fulfilling prophecy was systematically presented to them from all aspects of society. And, as detailed by both Crosby and Namka, Generation X responded with predictable feelings of anxiety, insecurity and vulnerability.

Generation X had been marginalized and scapegoated, society's very tidy way of dealing with groups they would much rather ignore. That devaluation was reflected in a *Time Magazine* article that noted, "so far they are an unsung generation, hardly recognized as a social force or even noticed much at all ..." And in Great Britain Jane Deverson co-authored a book titled *Generation X* that described a cluster of teenagers who "sleep together before they are married, don't believe in God, dislike the Queen, and don't respect parents." They were "Category X," a nameless group who viewed themselves in terms starkly outside traditions of position, wealth and social status; an amorphous group who didn't even know who they were.

That identity crisis was expressed in Generation X's negativity, isolation, rebelliousness, and extremism. Unable to adopt society's pre-scripted role, they responded by shutting down, an instinctive mechanism used to protect the traumatized self. After this protective mechanism there was then a shifting of energies to rediscover ways to feel once again. This shift, accomplished by engaging in excessive behaviors, became one of Generation X's cultural trademarks. To that end, the Generation X response to harsh, intense stimuli was not a well-conceived plan for self-destruction, but a hard-wired shift to the extreme. Consider Generation X's attachment to grunge, Goth, heroin, mosh pits, body modification and extreme sports as their embodiment of the aforementioned identity crisis and response to trauma.

The psychologist B.F. Skinner also observed that behaviors were determined by proceeding events and that we have responded to those stimuli. Even though there was cognition sandwiched between stimuli and response, our fates have been predetermined. Should Skinner's thesis be accepted, we could understand the misfortunes that Generation X suffered. With Kurt Cobain it had started early with a conflicted relationship with his mother, Wendy, her divorce, and the low expectations that apparently others had for him. Kurt Cobain's troubled persona, and let there be no doubt that this boy was indeed troubled by ghosts he would never conquer, was wrapped around a self-loathing, what he called a "negative creep" mentality. Even as the media attempted to coronate him as spokesperson for his generation, Cobain raged and refused to "sell out" to corporate America. A perceived problem child, Cobain was also a drug addict with a victim persona and suicidal tendencies. Percodan became Cobain's drug of choice as he eventually, pill after pill, became hooked on the pharmaceutical opiate. Later, a small-time drug dealer gave Cobain his first shot of heroin, which provided the ultimate escape and the ultimate euphoria Cobain had longed for his entire life. At that point, to that end, Cobain's aspirations were to become the best junkie that he was capable of becoming.

YOUTH SUBCULTURES

Up until the 1970s social scientists debated whether the existence of youth subcultures was theoretical or factual. But a more careful inspection of the past revealed that the older beatniks of the 1950s and Hell's Angels biker gangs of the 1960s were indeed new subcultures, outside the traditional mainstream. Generation X fit into this sociological model as they created their unique youth counter-culture, predicated on the influence of hippie role models, including Dylan, The Beatles, Rolling Stones, Timothy Leary, Jimi Hendrix, and all those who preached the religion of sex, drugs, and music. For many, inspiration was derived, not from politicians and world leaders, but from the anti-war and civil rights protest messages of the time. To negate or minimize the influence of music on this group was to ignore a basic tenet of youth culture. Songs such as "We Shall Overcome," "Blowing In the Wind," "Joe Hill," "Turn, Turn, Turn," and "We Shall Be Released" helped to mobilize a nation demanding change from an oppressive past.

Music also played a key role in defining the bleak attitude of Generation X. Bands including Nirvana, The Pixies, Pearl Jam, Alice In Chains and others utilized grunge as a cathartic musical therapy that examined the pathos of their generation. Generation X'ers, caught between our loss in the Vietnam Conflict and the false bravado of the Reagan Years, understood that American industrial prowess was being challenged. As a larger international certainty unfolded, the fear of being overeducated and underemployed became part of an increased global competition and technological maelstrom. Thousands of Gen-X-ers witnessed the massive lay off of their parents in the early 1990s. The optimism of their Boomer parents was replaced with the reality of a limited scope of our superpower status and the lingering Vietnam syndrome. Despite massive losses, military commander General William C. Westmoreland, who orchestrated the Vietnam Campaign from 1964 to 1968, refused to admit defeat. Westmoreland rationalized, "It's more accurate to say our country did not fulfill its commitments to South Vietnam." That distortion of the truth was yet another reminder of the vestiges of Vietnam as retold through countless Hollywood films in the 1970's and 1980's. In addition to the Vietnam syndrome with its themes of surrender and failure were the "devil child films" and the zero population movement, all pointing to the lack of value in our evil children. To create music from this melancholy that also included broken homes and latchkey kids became the alternative music genre known as grunge. What Generation X created was not unlike the artistic expression of the Lost Generation, the Beat Generation or the Hippy Generation, a cyclical phenomena that was recycled once every 30 years or so. What was unique to Generation X were their icons, wrapped not in revolutionary zeal and a call to action, but a group steeped in despondency, violence and death, reflected in the legacies of Kurt Cobain, Layne Staley, Marilyn Manson, Notorious B.I.G. and Scott Weiland.

Still there were other more resilient personalities that sounded in the void. The voices of Beck, Billy Corgan, Eminem, Dave Grohl, Natalie Merchant, Moby, Trent Reznor, TuPac Shakur, Gwen Stefani, Michael Stipe and Eddie Vedder preached from a platform of strength and insightful perspective as they rose above the hopelessness. The media's strangulation hold on society was of particular concern to singer-songwriter Natalie Merchant. In "River," a song from *Tigerlily*, she castigated the *paparazzi* for their role in savaging the life of child actor River Phoenix. Much of their sensationalized reporting was about Phoenix' alleged drug-using lifestyle and fatal overdose. And on the CD *Motherland*, Merchant put together one of her best lyrical efforts in the dark and ambiguous song "Golden Boy," as she lashed out at a media that bestowed martyrdom upon serial killers and psychopaths. "We're all fools for this factory fame and you've got the brand new face," Merchant observed of the media's enshrinement of deviants, such as those who perpetrated the Columbine tragedy.

Merchant's protest represented a significant facet of 1990's women's liberation. From 1995 to 1998 the movement grew, swelled and then peaked. 1998 was THE year of the female artist, young, insightful and angry. These women drew upon the female voices of the past, from Joan Baez to Ann and Nancy Wilson's Heart to the hard-edged rock of Pat Benatar. It was the counterpoint to the predominance of white, male rock stars in the music industry. Now, it was the ladies turn. After decades of musical experimentation, the collective voice of women was finally heard.

Alanis Morissette was the heavy hitter. Leading the charge she raised social awareness for this new generation. Her 1995 *Jagged Little Pill* album sold over 28 million copies with angry personal expressions of relationship neurosis. The recording became the second best-selling album of the 1990s and one of three albums to remain in the top ten for over a year. Morissette was 21 years old at the time as she stormed the charts making both an economic and cultural impact. Her follow-up *Supposed Former Infatuation Junkie* pulled in a respectable 2.4 million buyers.

There were a host of others who followed in the creative social wake. Jewel made her 1995 impact with *Pieces of You*, a collection of works including "Who Will Save Your Soul?" that sold 12 million copies in the United States. Former lead singer of 10,000 Maniacs Natalie Merchant, in her initial 1995 solo endeavor, *Tigerlily*, sold 3.5 million units and another 1.2 million with the follow-up *Ophelia*. Shawn Colvin, intelligent and sensitive singer-songwriter, swept the 1996 Grammy Awards with her haunting ballad "Sunny Came Home." It won both Song and Record of the Year, with *A Few Small Repairs* to become Colvin's first platinum album. Paula Cole, another ambassador to a generation of women who demanded to be heard, took to the commercial airwaves with 1996's ubiquitous *This Fire*. The album sold 1.6 million copies on the strength of the hit "Where Have All the Cowboys Gone?" That same year Tori Amos, although not able to capture the large numbers of her more successful sisters, still was able to watch her *Boys For Pele* album reach #2 on the Billboard Top 200 list. Merideth Brooks continued the rage with 1998's "Bitch," while Fiona Apple's "Criminal" helped launch 1999's *Tidal* to the 2.5 million sale mark.

Female singers captured center stage in 1997 after Sarah McLachlan's Lilith Fair was launched. Canada's McLachlan organized an experimental event that demonstrated women had, not only star power, but also economic drawing power. Lilith Fair was an immediate success. It grossed over $16.4 million and was financially better received than the male dominated H.O.R.D.E. and alternative Lollapalooza festivals. Billed as "a celebration of women in music," Lilith Fair was marketed to the female demographic group and donated two million dollars to rape-crisis centers and women's shelters. The all-female (with a few exceptions such as the backing musicians of The Pretenders) touring troupe featured a 40-date bill and an ever-changing lineup. Among the musical luminaries were Beth Orton, Bif Naked, Cibo Matto, Deborah Cox, Dixie Chicks, Luscious Jackson, Monica, Mya, Sarah McLachlan, Shawn Covin, Sheryl Crow and rapper/actress Queen Latifah. But those splendid examples of the feminist voice were only a small portion of the Generation X gestalt.

The social experiment that became Generation X evolved from the primordial juncture where Goth, grunge and heroin intersected and coagulated into a chemical mass of muck and ooze. It was a psychological and visceral convergence that unrelentingly descended upon Generation X from all sectors as it begat the shared chemistry of the Tipping Point Theory, the Butterfly Effect, and the Paradigm Shift. Although the Boomers helped to create it, Generation X became the first of the post-modern groups who espoused a dramatic paradigm shift. Their rejection of previous values and formation of a new cynical manner of perceiving the world resulted in "post-modernism," a philosophy that insisted upon instant gratification, a mistrust of individuals and institutions of authority, an opposition to the traditional Protestant work ethic, an attitude of entitlement, excessive consumerism and a re-evaluation of the religion of their parents.

SELF-EMPOWERED COUNTER-CULTURE

In the 1960s the self-empowered counter-culture evoked hope and expectation as they protested against conventional beliefs. The 1960s was a radical and violent period that demonstrated our country's extreme divisions. Blood ran in the streets as those who carried the banner of change were gunned down, having paid the ultimate price for their convictions. With powerful numbers and an outrage against the Vietnam War as their focal point, Baby Boomers had an enormous impact on American society. Woodstock and Kent State were the bookends that encapsulated the anti-war, civil rights and feminist movements and demonstrated the scope of this generation's reach. Bolstered by sheer numbers, they expressed a passion for self-exploration, self-expression and self-improvement, seldom seen in one group of individuals. Boomers believed that they had altered the course of world events, even as they anticipated being "forever young." Underground hippie author Alan Bisbort defined the hippie-boomer culture as "the possibly naïve belief that a better world is possible." The hippies expected the values of society to match those values espoused in the eclectic sociopolitical mindset of the times, reflective of their vision, idealism and protest and created with input from, among others, the Free Speech Movement, Bob Dylan, Betty Friedan, Jack Kerouac, Ken Kesey and Martin Luther King Jr. Others of equal importance included J.D. Salinger, Gloria Steinem, Hunter S. Thompson, Kurt Vonnegut, Brian Wilson and Malcom X. Boomers believed that with their active involvement a better world was possible. Searching for meaning and inner consciousness—what Boomers perceived as "enlightenment"—also became an integral part of their professed legacy. That expectation was dramatically different from the apolitical Generation X who lacked the numbers, empowerment and optimism. On that score Generation X, unlike the three proceeding generations, stood starkly alone.

But being "enlightened" and more experienced has not netted the Boomers the respect that Aretha Franklin sang about. The Boomers have been criticized for having peaked too early and for being culturally frozen in time. Their critics also chastised them for betraying their youthful anti-establishment, anti-materialistic idealism, for choosing power over nurturing and for becoming fat and lazy. A current rash of books has been critical of self-centered Baby Boomers' lax attitudes, inability to save for retirement (almost 25 percent have not adequately prepared for life after career), high debt, excessive consumerism, a supposed lack of computer skills and their "economic and policy imperialism." These negatives resulted in a collection of essays all critical of the Baby Boom generation: *Bobos in Paradise,* by David Brooks; *Balsamic Dreams: A Short but Self-Important History of the Baby Boomer Generation,* by Joe Queenan; *Stiffed: The Betrayal of the American Man,* by Susan Faludi; and Marty Asher's *The Boomer.*

As parents, many Boomers did not lay a solid foundation and clearly were at fault for being poor mentors. The Boomers' permissive parenting style, where parents had little or no control over their children, demonstrated a lack of disciplinary measures and guidance. In many cases there were no complex sets of rules established or the use of rewards as an incentive. Boomers could have modeled those behaviors they wanted to instill upon Generation X. Unfortunately their anti-establishment attitudes, public drug use, and inability to maintain a stable family unit may have accomplished just the opposite. Had Generation X developed a stronger sense of self through a more positive upbringing, they could have viewed their troubled world as an opportunity to resolve conflict—rather than as a miserable world without end.

Still, other barometers that have been sorely neglected and overlooked were the darker aspects of the Baby Boomer group. Just as this book has looked at Generation X through the pessimistic eyes of Kurt Cobain, Marilyn Manson, Anna Nicole Smith, Layne Staley and River Phoenix, we could just as easily have viewed the Baby Boomers through the eyes of other, less respected members of their clan. Boomers had Woodstock, but they also had Altamont. They had the Kennedys, but they also had Charles Manson, David Berkowitz, Richard Ramariz, Jeffrey Dahmer, Ted Bundy and other social pathogens whose sickness infected much of the psychedelic hippy dream.

Although researchers Strauss and Howe have predicted that the youthful Generation Y will be the next Greatest Generation, similar to those American heroes who fought during World War ll, there is still much left to assess. That assumption may not be correct. Generation Y has been the most aggressive generation in recent years. Their behaviors at the violence-prone Woodstock 1999 and their horrific incidence of high school killings, especially during the bloody years of 1997 to 1999, which peaked during the Columbine massacre, has established their dark and ugly side. The discounted Generation X may have more in common with the GI Generation, the Greatest Generation, as they too have mustered their forces, grouped together and bonded in order to withstand tremendous external challenges and to survive. For the GI Generation it was the depression and World

War 11, and for Generation X it was all that has been discussed in these pages. Generation X continued that passionate search for the keys to the kingdom; a search for identity and empowerment. It continued the search of the previous generation for hope, optimism and change. They have their heroes, too. The valor of Todd Beamer, 32, who led the attack against the terrorist-controlled United Airlines Flight 93 cockpit, was a perfect example. Shouting "Let's roll," Beamer and his fellow passengers succeeded in eventually bringing down the Boeing 757 aircraft in rural Shenksville, PA.

While Generation X has remained on the sidelines, Generation Y, our most pampered and spoiled group, have received intense media attention and admiration. Much of this media awareness has been driven by Generation Y's estimated 76 million headcount and sizeable financial assets. Geared towards Generation Y tastes and sensibilities, the aforementioned Woodstock 1999 is a perfect example of intense media attention. Despite corporate rip-off prices, consumer anger and rioting, even the vile and ill-fated Woodstock '99 produced positive and uplifting moments, although largely ignored by the media. An exposition of art, photography and sculpture was an integral part of the festival, as was the three-mile "peace wall" that provided a brilliant contrast against the former Rome, New York, military fortress. Buddhist Monks designed an intricate and beautiful sand *mandala* that was painstakingly created before it was destroyed. The destruction was not acted out in anger, but reflected a peaceful acceptance that all things are but fleeting glimpses of time.

The legacy of Generation X should be a curious one as researchers attempt to decipher the never-ending progress and essence of this group. Although saddled with the reputation of being non-productive slackers, Gen X'ers have actually been impressive in their aspirations. During the 1990's, Generation X students took out more college loans than did their counterparts in the 60's, 70's and 80's combined. Having made their mark on the labor force, Generation X's workplace enthusiasm has replaced Boomers' fear, trepidation and past glory. One immediate difference is that Generation X'ers have moved quickly from one company to the next, changing jobs often to secure better benefits and opportunities for professional growth. They believed in teamwork, but distrusted hierarchy and believed in job promotions based on performance and not longevity. Boomers have long associated themselves with one or two employers, a lifetime commitment that some have suggested is reflective of their loyalty and sense of "fair play." While Generation X'ers appear to have reached the top ranks faster and easier, Boomers have arrived the traditional way, through long, arduous and consistent job performance. Many observers have noted that Baby Boomers are more process-oriented while Generation X workers are more results-oriented.

With the emergence of the technological highway, it has been Gen X, in the true spirit of wanderlust, who stuck out their eager thumbs and hit the road. Having been born into it, Generation X understood the computer technology and adapted to it with savvy and innovation. Many excelled as day traders, software developers, headhunters and innovators in a computer-driven world. They have enjoyed the advantage, as witnessed by youthful creativity in San Jose's "Silicon Valley" and with innovations such as You Tube and Google. That entrepreneurial spirit could be the legacy of Generation X and their ongoing work-in-progress. It is but another example of the power and resilience of this special group of individuals, a cluster of highly skilled and adaptive individuals intent upon survival. Their ability to embrace resilience is in itself amazing and is the one true marker of their identity.

To many it appeared that the passive indifference of Generation X was about nihilism and about the absence of a well thought-out series of philosophies and discourses and, in that regard, was reflective of a group of people still searching for meaning. Jean-Paul Sartre may have defined this generation with his existentialist belief that existence precedes essence. According to Sartre, "... man first of all exists, encounters himself, surges up in the world—and defines himself afterwards. If man, as the existentialist sees him, is not definable, it is because to begin with he is nothing ... will not be anything until later, and then he will be what he makes of himself."

As our first postmodern generation, the group known as Generation X is much different than their parents in attitude, expectation and work ethic. For those who have been watching, the signs have always been there. From *The X-Files* FBI agent Fox Mulder's warning to "Trust no one" and Kurt Cobain's "here we are now, entertain us," his personal take on Generation X entitlement, it has all been laid out before us. The Baby Boomers will not live long enough to see the conclusion of the grand Generation X Experiment, and what they will experience they may not be able to comprehend. Despite having awakened from their personal nightmare, what will ultimately unfold will be the result of Generation X's collective effort and an increased optimism. Unlike the self-fulfilling prophecy that society attempted to bestow upon them, Generation X will ultimately assume what they will themselves to be.

The 1990's Political and Sociocultural Timeline

The following are a brief list of both political and sociocultural events that occurred in the decade of the 1990's—collectively what will be remembered as the decade of Generation X. They are intended to represent but a small part of the X'ers experience.

1990   Iron Mike Tyson, controversial professional prizefighter and member of Generation X, reigned as undisputed heavyweight champion for over two years before losing in a shocking upset to James "Buster" Douglas. By knocking out Tyson in Tokyo, Japan, Douglas scored one of the biggest upsets in the history of boxing. Tyson was at that point considered *the pound-for-pound best boxer on the planet* and was a 42 to 1 favorite by The Mirage Casino in Las Vegas. (02/11/1990).

1990   Andrew Wood, 24, died from a heroin overdose. Wood was the flamboyant front man for Mother Love Bone, the pioneering grunge band that evolved into Pearl Jam and captured the attitude of a generation. (03/19/1990).

1990   In a significant demographic shift, The U.S. Census Bureau estimated that 5.5 percent of all children under 18 lived in a grandparent-headed household. That number was estimated at 3.6 percent in 1980.

1990   According to the Bureau of Justice Statistics in 1990, more than half of federal inmates who served mandatory minimum sentences were first-time offenders.

1990	The Uniform Crime Reporting Program (UCR) of the Federal Bureau of Investigation (FBI) reported that in 1990, 6.7% of the 20,273 homicides in which circumstances were known were narcotics related.
1990	Iraq invaded Kuwait and seized control of the oil-rich emirate. The Iraqis were later driven out in Operation Desert Storm. (08/2/2007).
1990	The Clery Act, originally enacted by the Congress and signed into law by President George H.W. Bush as the Crime Awareness and Campus Security Act of 1990, was championed by Howard and Connie Clery after their 19-year-old freshman daughter Jeanne was murdered at Lehigh University in 1986. (11/08/1990).
1990	The Food and Drug Administration warned consumers of the dangers of the sedative Gamma-hydroxybutyrate. (11/08/1990).
1991	President George Bush and the White House announced the beginning of Operation Desert Storm to drive Iraqi forces out of Kuwait. (01/17/1991).
1991	Motorist Rodney King became a reluctant symbol of police brutality after amateur photographer George Holliday's videotape showed several white Los Angeles police officers using batons to beat King, who was later suspected of being on the hallucinogen PCP. King had led police on a high-speed car chase after they tried to stop him for speeding. The video was viewed internationally and triggered the Los Angeles riots after the police officers were acquitted. (03/03/1991).
1991	TV's *L.A. Law* features a brief innocent lesbian kiss during its 10:00 pm time slot.
1991	Canadian author Douglas Coupland published *Generation X: Tales For An Accelerated Culture* and, in doing so, named a generation searching for its identity. (03/11/1991)
1991	Supreme Court Justice Thurgood Marshall, the first African-American to sit on the nation's highest court, announced his retirement. (06/27/1991).
1991	During the Persian Gulf War 28 Americans are killed after an Iraqi Scud missile strikes a U.S. barracks in Dhahran, Saudi Arabia

1991	The Uniform Crime Reporting Program (UCR) of the Federal Bureau of Investigation (FBI) reported that in 1991, 6.2% of the 21,676 homicides in which circumstances were known were narcotics related.
1991	George Hennard drove his pickup truck into a Luby's Cafeteria in Killeen, Texas and then proceeded to shoot 23 people to death before taking his own life. It was, at the time, the deadliest mass shooting in modern U.S. history. (10/16/1991).
1991	*The Beauty Myth: How Images of Beauty Are Used Against Women* by Naomi Wolf, argued that women in Western culture are damaged by the pressure to conform to an idealized concept of female beauty. The text became a bestseller.
1991	Justin Achilli, developer of the White Wolf Games, creates *Vampire: The Masquerade*, a successful role-playing game.
1991	A worldwide financial scandal erupted as regulators in eight countries shut down the Bank of Credit and Commerce International. (07/05/1991).
1991	The Lollapalooza Festival began to tour the U.S. and Canada. Organized by Perry Farrell of Jane's Addiction, the music fest promoted "alternative music" to the masses. (07/18/1991).
1991	NBC re-released the series *Dark Shadows*, as a minimalist Goth-inspired soap opera. (01/13/1991).
1991	Nirvana released the "grunge rock" LP *Nevermind,* their second album. The album on Geffen Records sold three million records within a four-month period as it captured the despondent attitude of a lost Generation X. (09/24/1991).
1991	American jazz trumpeter and composer Miles Davis died in Santa Monica, CA, at the age of 65. (09/28/1991).
1991	According to the National Institute on Alcohol Abuse and Alcoholism there were 13.8 million individuals who abused alcohol or were alcohol dependent for the period 1991–1992.

1991	A graduate student from China shot and killed five employees of the University of Iowa and wounded two others. He then killed himself. (11/01/1991).
1992	*Nevermind* becomes Nirvana's first #1 album, as it replaced Michael Jackson's *Dangerous* at the top of the Billboard charts and signaled the beginning of a new musical era. (01/11/1992).
1992	The Los Angeles Riots ensued after three police officers are acquitted by a jury of ten whites, one Latino, and an Asian, of the Rodney King beating. (The jury could not agree on a verdict for one of the counts on one of the officers.) The acquittal was based in part on a 13-second segment of the video tape that was edited out and largely unknown to the public. There was an estimated one billion dollars in damage and 53 killed during the Los Angeles Riots and over 8,000 arrested. (4/29/1992).
1992	The murder trial of serial killer Jeffrey Dahmer began. Dahmer, officially indicted on 15 murder charges, pleaded insanity, arguing that he could not control his necrophilia urges. Dahmer was found guilty and sane on 15 counts of murder and sentenced to 15 life terms, totaling 937 years in prison. It was one of the harshest prison sentences ever imposed in Wisconsin's legal history. (4/1992).
1992	On a cliff overlooking Waikiki Beach, *the King and Queen of Grunge*, Kurt Cobain and Courtney Love, were married in a ceremony performed by a female non-denominational minister. (02/24/1992).
1992	Marc Jacobs, *the Guru of Grunge,* won the Women's Designer of the Year award from the Council of Fashion Designers of America. That same year Jacobs is laid off by Perry Ellis who felt that his fashions were too radical.
1992	Prizefighter "Iron Mike" Tyson is convicted of raping a beauty pageant contestant in an Indianapolis hotel room. Desiree Washington, Miss Black Rhode Island, was named as the victim of the sexual assault. Tyson is sentenced to six years in prison. (03/26/1992).

1992　　Produced and directed by Francis Ford Coppola, *Bram Stoker's Dracula* was the 9th highest grossing film worldwide ($215,862,692) for the year. The Gothic horror film won 3 Academy Awards and featured Gary Oldman, Keanu Reeves, Anthony Hopkins and Winona Ryder.

1992　　Anna Nicole Smith, b. Vickie Lynn Hogan, (1967-2007), former topless dancer, landed on the cover of the March 1992 issue of Playboy and was recognized as the Playmate of the Month in May 1992. Smith is also the Playmate of the Year for 1993. (03/1992).

1992　　The Justice Policy Institute (2001) reported that from 1992 to 1996 there was a 721% increase in coverage of homicides on network evening newscasts despite a 20% decline in America's homicide rate.

1992　　The Uniform Crime Reporting Program (UCR) of the Federal Bureau of Investigation (FBI) reported that in 1992, 5.7% of the 22,716 homicides in which circumstances were known were narcotics related.

1992　　In its Annual Report the National Highway Traffic Safety Administration reported that almost half of all traffic fatalities were alcohol-related.

1992　　In Mineola, N.Y, Amy Fisher was sentenced to five to 15 years in prison for shooting and seriously wounding Mary Jo Buttafuoco. Fisher eventually served seven years for the crime. (12/1/1992).

1993　　*TIME Magazine* named President William Jefferson Clinton as *Man of the Year* for 1992. (01/4/1993).

1993　　Mir Aimal Kasi shot to death two CIA employees outside agency headquarters. Captured in Pakistan four years later, he is sent back to the United States to face trial in the state of Virginia. Kasi was eventually found guilty and executed by lethal injection in 2002. (01/25/1993).

1993　　Actress Anna Nicole Smith divorced husband Billy Smith in Houston. Sixteen months later she married Texas oilman and billionaire J. Howard Marshall. (02/03/1993).

1993	After agents of the Bureau of Alcohol, Tobacco and Firearms attempted to serve warrants on the Branch Davidians cult, a gun battle erupted at the Waco, Texas compound. Six Davidians and four agents were killed as a 51-day standoff began. (02/28/1993).
1993	Hollywood celebrity River Phoenix, 23, overdosed and died outside Johnny Depp's *Viper Room* on Sunset Strip. A multi-drug cocktail of heroin, cocaine and GHB was suspected to have caused his death. (10/31/1993).
1993	Islamic terrorists exploded a bomb in the parking lot of New York's World Trade Center, killing six people and injuring over one thousand others. (February 26, 1993).
1993	According to the Department of Justice (February 1994) 21% of the total federal prison population in 1993 were low-level drug violators with no history of violence or prior incarceration. Another 17% were drug offenders with no criminal histories.
1993	The Uniform Crime Reporting Program (UCR) of the Federal Bureau of Investigation (FBI) reported that in 1993, 5.5% of the 23,180 homicides in which circumstances were known were narcotics related.
1993	Controversial shock rocker Marilyn Manson and the Spooky Kids get their big break as they are signed to Trent Reznor's *Nothing Records*.
1994	Leona Helmsley, the "Queen of Mean," is released from prison after serving 21 months for income tax evasion. Helmsley, after an eight-week trial, was convicted of evading $1.2 million in federal taxes. In 2007, Forbes magazine ranked her as the 369th richest person in the world, with an estimated net worth of $2.5 billion. (01/1994).
1994	The DEA estimated that 20 tons of heroin were shipped into the United States, an increase of from 4 to 6 tons in the early 1980's.
1994	Kurt Cobain, founder of Nirvana, is rushed to a hospital in Rome, Italy after having overdosed on a combination of 60 sedatives and champagne. (3/27/1994).

1994	Kurt Cobain, in what was to be his final attempt at getting clean, is admitted to the Exodus Recovery Center in Marina Del Ray, CA. (3/30/1994).
1994	Kurt Cobain is reported missing after leaving the Exodus Recovery Center after only 48 hours. (4/01/1994).
1994	California state-licensed private investigator Tom Grant is hired by Courtney Love to locate Kurt Cobain. (4/03/1994).
1994	The genocide in Rwanda began and lasted another bloody 100 days. Hutu militia, in this example of tribal bloodletting, killed over 800,000 Tutsis, who represented over one-tenth of the nation's population. (04/6/1994).
1994	The body of rocker Kurt Cobain is discovered at his home in Seattle. Cobain had injected himself with significant amount of heroin before committing suicide with a 12-guage shotgun. His body and suicide note are not discovered until several days later. (4/08/1994).
1994	The Eagles kick off their long-awaited "Hell Freezes Over" reunion tour which produced a #1 live album for the band. The tour took in a reported $1.5 million per week in one of the most successful concert series in history. (05/27/1994).
1994	The state of Illinois executed serial killer John Wayne Gacy Jr. for killing 33 young boys and men. The bodies were later discovered under the floorboards of Gacy's home and in the local river. (05/10/1994)
1994	A U.S. Air DC-9 crashed in poor weather at North Carolina's Charlotte-Douglas International Airport, killing 37 of the 57 passengers aboard. (07/02/1994).
1994	The genocide in Rwanda ended after armed Tutsi rebels, invading from neighboring countries, attacked the Hutu militia. Over 800,000 Tutsis were slaughtered with clubs and machetes during the tribal bloodletting. It was estimated that over 10,000 Tutsis were killed each day. (07/1994).

1994   Jesse Timmendequas, a twice-convicted sex offender, lured 7-year-old Megan Kanka into his New Jersey house where he brutally raped and killed her. Her death resulted in Megan's Law, intended to warn communities of resident pedophiles. (07/29/1994).

1994   Nine Inch Nails performs their "industrial rock" at Woodstock '94 (billed as *"2 more days of peace and music"*), 25 years after the original festival, in Saugerties, New York, about 100 miles north of New York City. Other bands included Aerosmith, Blind Melon, Green Day, Peter Gabriel, Primus, Red Hot Chili Peppers and also several bands from the original Woodstock 1964: Bob Weir, Crosby, Stills and Nash, Joe Cocker, Joe McDonald, John Sabastian, Santana and The Band. (08/12–14/1994).

1994   Neil Young, called the "Godfather of grunge," dedicated his LP *Sleeps With Angels* to Kurt Cobain. Young had never met the deceased star but admired his music and songwriting abilities. (08/16/1994).

1994   *New York* magazine featured a degrading photograph of Anna Nicole Smith eating potato chips and wearing a short skirt and cowboy boots in an issue titled *White Trash Nation*. Smith later claimed that the article damaged her reputation and sued the magazine for $5,000,000 (08/22/1994).

1994   *Natural Born Killers* is released with the tag line "The media made them superstars." Directed by Oliver Stone, the film centered on two psychopathic serial murderers that are irresponsibly glorified by the media. Written by Quentin Tarantino. (08/26/1994).

1994   *Pulp Fiction*, made on a shoestring budget of only 8 million dollars, is released. The violent film went on to gross over 100 million dollars in ticket sales as it promoted heroin themes to the curious masses. Directed by Quinton Tarantino. (10/14/1994).

1994   The Uniform Crime Reporting Program (UCR) of the Federal Bureau of Investigation (FBI) reported that in 1994, 5.6% of the 22,084 homicides in which circumstances were known were narcotics related.

1994	Ritalin-related visits to hospital emergency rooms increased 214 percent over 1993, according to the Substance Abuse and Mental Health Services Association.
1994	Marijuana use among teenagers nearly doubled from 1992 to 1994, even as adult's use of all illegal drugs leveled off.
1994	Susan Smith placed her two small boys in her 1990 Mazda Protégé and watched them drown in South Carolina's John D. Long Lake. Smith later admitted that she murdered her sons, Michael Daniel Smith and Alexander Tyler Smith, to win the love of a married man. (10/25/1994).
1994	Serial killer Jeffrey Dahmer, serving time at the Columbia Correctional Institution in Portage, Wisconsin, and another prisoner, Jesse Anderson, are brutally beaten to death in the prison gym by fellow inmate Christopher Scarver. Dahmer later died from severe head trauma en route to the hospital. (11/28/1994).
1994	The Uniform Crime Reporting Program (UCR) of the Federal Bureau of Investigation (FBI) reported that in 1994, 5.6% of the 22,084 homicides in which circumstances were known were narcotics related.
1994	The Coalition for Federal Sentencing Reform (1997) noted that in 1994, 92% of federal inmates were incarcerated for a non-violent crime.
1994	Anna Nicole Smith married 89-year-old oil tycoon J. Howard Marshall II, head of oil-based Koch Industries. He died in 1995, setting off a feud with her former stepson, E. Pierce Marshall, over whether she had a right to his estate worth at least 400 million dollars. A California federal court awarded Smith 474 million dollars in a complicated legal twist that was later overturned. (06/27/1994).
1994	Nirvana's appearance on MTV's *Unplugged* is released and is the first Nirvana product to appear following Kurt Cobain's suicide. (11/1/1994).
1995	The 104th United States Congress convened, the first entirely under Republican control since the Dwight Eisenhower era. (01/04/1995).

1995	The space shuttle Discovery lifted off with Air Force Lt. Col. Eileen Collins in the pilot's seat. Collins would be the first woman in NASA history to hold that position. (02/03/1995).
1995	The U.S. Sentencing Commission, Cocaine and Federal Sentencing Policy reported in 1995 that whites account for 52% of all crack users and African-Americans, 38%. However, 88% of those sentenced for crack offences are African-American and just 4.1% are white. (02/1995).
1995	"Iron Mike" Tyson is released from prison after being convicted and sentenced for the raping of a beauty pageant contestant Miss Black Rhode Island, Desiree Washington. Tyson was sentenced to six years but is released after serving three. (03/1995).
1995	*The Basketball Diaries*, based on the book by Jim Carroll, is released. Director Scott Kalvert's violent dream sequence draws criticism after the Columbine school shootings. (04/21/1995).
1995	Deborah Curtis, widow of Joy Division's lead singer Ian Curtis, published the biography *Touching From a Distance: Ian Curtis & Joy Division*. Her husband, a Goth rock pioneer, committed suicide at age 23.
1995	At 9:02 a.m. a truck filled with 5,000 pounds of ammonium nitrate, an agricultural fertilizer, and nitro methane, a highly volatile motor-racing fuel, exploded in the street in front of the Alfred P. Murrah Federal Building in Oklahoma City, OK. Timothy McVeigh and Terry Nichols are formally charged with the domestic terrorist attack killing 168 individuals. McVeigh is executed by lethal injection on June 11, 2001 and Nichols sentenced to life in prison. (4/19/1995).
1995	The troubled Stone Temple Pilots lead singer Scott Weiland is arrested for cocaine and heroin possession. (05/1995).
1995	According to the Federal Bureau of Prisons ("Quick Facts," September 1996) in 1995, the average drug sentence was 82.4 months. The average sentence for a first-time, federal drug offender is 82.4 months, compared with 66.9 months for firearms offences, 73.8 months for sexual abuse, 33.4 months for assault and 26.8 months for manslaughter.

1995	The Uniform Crime Reporting Program (UCR) of the Federal Bureau of Investigation (FBI) reported that in 1995, 5.1% of the 20,232 homicides in which circumstances were known were narcotics related.
1995	According to the Drug Abuse Warning Network (DAWN), emergency room admissions for heroin rose 58 percent from 1992 to 1995.
1995	The U.S. Centers for Disease Control estimated that 11 million women suffer from eating disorders.
1995	President Bill Clinton spoke out against advertisements depicting photographs of half-dressed adolescents used to promote Calvin Klein fashions. The White House claimed that the ads demeaned the fashion industry.
1995	High on methamphetamine for 24 hours, a psychotic Eric Starr Smith decapitates his son and then tosses the head onto a New Mexico highway. (07/1995).
1995	Susan Smith of Union, South Carolina, was found guilty of drowning her two sons, 3-year-old Michael Daniel Smith and 14-month-old Alexander Tyler Smith. (7/22/1995).
1995	Canadian singer-songwriter Alanis Morissette released her *Jagged Little Pill* album. The recording became the second best-selling album of the 1990s with twenty-eight million copies sold by 2000. It became one of three albums to remain in the top ten for over a year. (06/13/1995).
1995	Scott Weiland of the Stone Temple Pilots walks out of a mandatory drug rehabilitation program. The following day, after a warrant is issued for his arrest, Weiland turned himself in. (6/26/1995).
1995	Oil billionaire J. Howard Marshall died in Houston, Texas. Marshall had been married to actress Anna Nicole Smith for thirteen months. (08/4/1995).
1995	Jerry Garcia, leader of the cultish San Francisco Grateful Dead band, died from a heart attack at age 53. (08/9/1995).

1995	The U.S. Justice Department reported that in 1994 state and federal prisons incarcerated another 83,000 inmates, the second-largest increase ever. The total prison population was at a record 1.5 million. (08/8/1995).
1995	The jury in the O.J. Simpson murder trial announced its verdicts, finding the former football star and motion picture actor not guilty of the 1994 slayings of his former wife, Nicole Brown Simpson, and Ron Goldman. (Simpson was later found liable in a civil trial). (10/03/1995).
1995	Shannon Hoon, lead singer of the alternative band Blind Melon, is discovered dead on his tour bus from a cocaine overdose. Hoon had previously attempted to quit heroin use. After the release of the Blind Melon album in 1992, Hoon was arrested on drug charges and, over the next three years, was in various rehab clinics. Despite the birth of his daughter, and a tour to support Blind Melon's second album *Soup*, Hoon relapsed back into drug use. (10/21/1995).
1996	Dressed in long coat and black clothing, Barry Loukaitis, 14, kills two classmates and his algebra teacher at the Moses Lake, Washington Frontier Jr. High School. He quoted from Stephen Kings 1977 novel, *Rage* "This sure beats Algebra, doesn't it?" *Natural Born Killers* was one of his favorite films. (02/2/1996).
1996	Statistics from the Bureau of Justice Statistics (Prisoners in 1996, 1997) demonstrated that the growth rate in the prison population among women was 9.1% in 1996 compared with 4.7% for men (1996,1997).
1996	President Bill Clinton signs the Telecommunications Act of 1996 which included the use of the V-chip. This device allowed parents to block programs containing excessive violence, sex and language. (02/8/1996).
1996	The Uniform Crime Reporting Program (UCR) of the Federal Bureau of Investigation (FBI) reported that in 1996, 5.0% of the 16,967 homicides in which circumstances were known were narcotics related.

1996	According to the National Household Survey on Drug Abuse (1997), an estimated 171,000 people tried heroin for the first time. The estimated number of new users and the rate of initiation for youth were at the highest levels in 30 years.
1996	A U.S. Government report demonstrated that overall drug use among those 12 to 17 years-old had risen about 80 percent since 1992.
1996	Northeastern University Professor James Allen Fox warned of a "teenage time bomb" that could explode into a "blood bath of teenage violence."
1996	Electricity and phone service was knocked out for millions of customers from Canada to the Southwest after power lines throughout the West failed on a record-hot day. (07/02/1996).
1996	*Trainspotting*, directed by Danny Boyle, is released. Critics immediately charged that the film glamorized the heroin subculture of addicts living around Edinburgh, Scotland. (07/19/1996).
1996	Due to Managed Care, the average number of patient bed days dropped from 35 to 17 between 1988 and 1993, causing many inpatient treatment programs in substance abuse clinics to reinvent themselves.
1996	Former Black Sabbath lead singer Ozzy Osbourne launches the heavy metal Ozzfest, as an alternative to Lollapalooza. (10/25/1996)
1996	Protease inhibitors began becoming available to enable HIV-positive individuals to lead normal, and extended, lives.
1996	The diet drug Redux is approved by the FDA as an appetite suppressant for obese individuals. It is voluntarily taken off the market the following year at the request of the FDA, citing studies reporting heart valve disorders.
1996	Former model and heroin addict Zoe Fleischauer revealed in an *Allure Magazine* interview that she, like many other models, began snorting heroin at the start of her career. (06/1996).

1996	The Citadel, a South Carolina military academy, voted to admit women, ending a 153-year-old men-only policy. (06/28/1996).
1996	The FBI claimed that there was "direct evidence of Iran's complicity" in the terrorist attack on Khobar Towers, a military barracks in Saudi Arabia, that killed 19 individuals. (06/25/1996).
1996	A pipe bomb exploded at Centennial Olympic Park during the Atlanta Olympics, killing one person and injuring 111 others. Anti-government extremist Eric Rudolph later pleaded guilty to the terrorist bombing. (07/27/1996).
1996	Shortly after takeoff from Miami an Atlanta-bound ValuJet DC-9 caught on fire and crashed into the Florida Everglades. All 110 passengers were killed. (05/11/1996).
1996	Rep. Bill McCollum, R-Fla., reintroduced the Violent Youth Predator Act to the full House under the more subdued title the Juvenile Crime Control Act. The controversial bill called for confining children as young as 13 with adult offenders, denying federal funds to states that do not try 13-year-olds who commit certain crimes as adults and abolishing the federal agency charged with preventing juvenile crime.
1996	A troubled graduate student at San Diego State University killed three professors with a handgun while defending his thesis. (8/15/1996).
1996	The Night Stalker, serial killer Richard Ramirez, married one of his groupies, 41-year-old Doreen Lioy, while on San Quentin's Death Row. Lioy had described herself as a virgin prior to her marriage to Ramirez. (10/03/1996).
1996	After winning the Grand Jury Prize at the Sundance Film Festival the previous January, the motion picture *Hype* is released. Directed by Doug Pray, the documentary explored the roots of the grunge movement. (11/08/1996).
1996	The Mars Pathfinder lifted off from Cape Canaveral and began speeding toward Mars on an odyssey of 310 million miles. The Pathfinder arrived on the Red Planet in July 1997. (12/04/1996).

1996	In a troubling sign of continued drug use, heroin-related emergency room visits were up more than 150 percent since 1990.
1997	Coca-Cola introduces Surge, a high-calorie, high-caffeine soda, to compete against PepsiCo's popular Mountain Dew. Mountain Dew has 37 milligrams of caffeine per eight ounces, while Surge boasted 35 milligrams. (01/1997).
1997	White House drug czar Barry R. McCaffrey stated that American patients would have access to marijuana and other illegal drugs if scientists concluded those drugs had proven medicinal uses. (01/10/1997).
1997	Scott Falater, 43, killed his wife by stabbing her 44 times and then holding her head under water. Falater claimed to have been sleep-walking and offered no recollection of the brutal crime of which he is convicted. (01/16/1997).
1997	Davide Sorrenti, fashion photographer known for his "heroin chic" method, dies of a heroin overdose at the age of 20. It brought about a response from the Clinton Administration and signaled the end of the dark fashion industry trend. (02/4/1997).
1997	The average cost of housing, clothing and feeding a federal prisoner for one year is $23,000, according to estimates from the Coalition for Federal Sentencing Reform. (03/1997).
1997	39 members of the Heaven's Gate cult killed themselves in the upscale San Diego community of Rancho Santa Fe. The mass suicide was directed by eunuch leader Marshall Appelwhite and a psychiatric nurse, known collectively as "Bo and Peep." They encouraged cult members to die in shifts as they drank lethal cocktails of Phenobarbital and vodka. Plastic bags were then secured around their heads to induce asphyxiation. (03/26/1997).
1997	In yet another school copycat shooting, Mitchell Johnson, 12, and Andrew Golden, 11, pulled the school fire alarm before they slaughtered four middle-school classmates and a teacher. The attack took place in Jonesboro, AK. (03/1997).

1997 Charles Dederich, founder of the tough-love Synanon drug rehabilitation group that evolved into a cult-like religion, died of heart and lung failure, at the age of 83. Dederich, a recovering alcoholic, started the group in Santa Monica in 1958. The controversial group disbanded in 1991. (03/5/1997).

1997 The New York Times publishes article about the heroin overdose death of fashion photographer Davide Sorrenti. (5/20/1997).

1997 President Bill Clinton attacked the destructive "heroin chic" trend during a meeting that was organized by the United States Conference of Mayors. (5/21/1997).

1997 Prosecutors urged the jury at the Oklahoma City bombing trial to sentence Timothy McVeigh to death. They called relatives of the victims to testify about their agonizing loss. (6/4/1997).

1997 Harold J. Nicholson is sentenced to more than 23 years in prison for selling defense secrets to Russia after the Cold War. Nicholson was the highest ranking CIA officer ever caught spying against his own country. (6/5/1997).

1997 Timothy McVeigh's lawyer pleaded with the jury to spare the life of the convicted Oklahoma City bomber. He held up his dress uniform and portrayed McVeigh as a model soldier who was deeply disturbed by his government's role in the disaster near Waco, Texas. (6/6/1997).

1997 A special presidential commission, comprised of 18 members, approved a report that stated cloning a human being was "morally unacceptable," but added that research using cells from humans and animals should be allowed. (6/7/1997).

1997 America's premier long distance runner, Mary Slaney, is suspended by the U.S. Track & Field Association for alleged ergogenic drug use. That suspension made Slaney ineligible for the National Championships. (6/12/1997).

1997 A 1939 comic book that featured the first appearance of *The Batman* was auctioned off for $68,500 at Sotheby's in New York. (06/14/1997).

1997   Mir Aimal Kasi is brought back to Fairfax, Va., to face trial after being arrested in Pakistan. He was later convicted and sentenced to death for the 1993 killing of two CIA employees outside agency headquarters. (06/17/1997).

1997   In a rematch with Evander Holyfield, Mike Tyson, in an attempted comeback, bit off a portion of Holyfield's ear in retaliation for what he perceived as deliberate head butts. The incident, which led to Tyson's disqualification, occurred during the third round of the Las Vegas fight. In an upset decision Holyfield retained the WBA heavyweight boxing championship. (06/28/1997).

1997   In his first formal response to charges from Paula Jones of sexual harassment, President Bill Clinton denied all allegations in her lawsuit, and asked a judge to dismiss the case. (07/03/1997).

1997   NASA scientists brain-stormed to fix problems that left Mars Pathfinder's robotic rover stuck aboard the lander. (07/05/1997).

1997   The U.S. Senate Governmental Affairs Committee opened politically charged hearings into fund-raising abuses, with chairman Fred Thompson accusing China of trying to influence the 1996 U.S. elections. (07/8/2007).

1997   The Mayo Clinic and the government warned the diet drug combination known as "fen-phen" could cause serious heart and lung damage. (07/8/2007).

1997   American boxer Mike Tyson was banned from the ring and fined three million dollars for biting opponent Evander Holyfield's ear. (07/9/1997).

1997   President Bill Clinton visiting Warsaw, Poland told cheering Poles that "never again will your fate be decided by others" following his successful drive to bring Poland, Hungary and the Czech Republic into NATO by the year 1999. (07/10/2007).

1997   London scientists announced that DNA from a Neanderthal skeleton supported a theory that all humanity had descended from an "African Eve" 100,000 to 200,000 years ago. (07/10/1997).

1997   Carl Drega, a 67-year-old resident of Colebrook, NH shot and killed two state troopers, a newspaper editor and a part-time judge before being killed in a gun battle with police. (08/19/1997).

1997   Writer and heroin addict William S. Burroughs, the godfather and seminal figure of the "Beat Generation," died in Kansas City, MO, at age 83. He was the author of *Naked Lunch* and *Junkie*. (08/02/1997).

1997   Andy Green, a British Royal Air Force pilot, twice drove a jet-powered car in the Nevada desert faster than the speed of sound, and officially shattered the world's land-speed record. (10/15/1997).

1997   Thirteen members of the London-based Designers Against Addictions signed a statement condemning "heroin chic". (10/1997).

1997   Hungarian-born U.S. financier and philanthropist George Soros announced he would donate as much as $500 million in aid to Russia over the next three years. (10/20/1997).

1997   The stock market shut down for the first time since the 1981 assassination attempt on President Reagan, after the Dow Jones industrial average tumbled 554.26 points. (10/27/1997).

1997   Nushawn Williams, an HIV-positive man who traded drugs for sex with young women and teens, had infected a number of them with the AIDS virus according to Chautauqua County, N.Y. officials. Williams was later sentenced to four to twelve years in prison. (10/27/1997).

1997   Marc Jacobs, called the Guru of Grunge," appointed the creative director of the world-renowned fashion empire, Louis Vuitton. Jacobs was a fashion student at New York's acclaimed Parsons School of Design and developed a grunge-inspired collection for the fashion runway.

1997   The Uniform Crime Reporting Program (UCR) of the Federal Bureau of Investigation (FBI) reported that in 1997, 5.1% of the 15,837 homicides in which circumstances were known were narcotics related. (For these statistics murders that occurred specifically during a narcotics felony, such as drug trafficking or manufacturing, are considered drug related.)

1997	Michael Flutie, head of Company Management, filed a 5 million dollar breach of contract law suit against model Amy Wesson claiming that due to her excessive use of drugs she missed assignments. Flutie had been a leader of the anti-drug campaign within the fashion industry.
1997	A survey of more than 1,200 public schools by the U.S. Department of Education found that 79 percent had zero tolerance policies against violence, 88 percent for drugs, 91 percent for weapons and 94 percent for firearms. Zero tolerance became a popular concept during the waning days of the Ronald Reagan administration's "War On Drugs."
1997	Diet drugs Redux and fenfluramine are voluntarily taken off the market at the request of the FDA, citing studies of reported heart valve disorders.
1997	American rapper, actor and record producer Calvin Cordozar Broadus, Jr. (born 1971) changes his name to Snoop Dogg after leaving his original record label Death Row Records and signing with No Limit Records. Dogg, called "America's lovable pimp", has sold over 18.5 million albums in the United States.
1997	Lilith Fair, billed as a celebration of women in music, is launched, grossing $16.4 million dollars and besting other festivals such as Lollapalooza and H.O.R.D.E. Founded by singer Sarah McLachlan, the lineup featured acts including Beth Orton, Deborah Cox, The Dixie Chicks, Luscious Jackson, Monica, The Pretenders, Sheryl Crow and Queen Latifah.
1997	Apple Computer and Microsoft agreed to share technology in a business deal giving Microsoft a stake in Apple's survival. The deal ended years of rivalry between the two computer giants. (08/6/2007).
1997	In a high-profile trial, an unrepentant Timothy McVeigh was formally sentenced to death for the Oklahoma City bombing. (08/14/1997).

1997   Luke Woodham stabbed his mother to death and then drove to the Pearl, MS. High School where he killed his former girlfriend and another student. The sixteen-year-old also wounded seven others in this example of rampant school violence. Woodham was sentenced to serve three life sentences plus 140 years in prison for his crime. (10/1/1997).

1997   President Bill Clinton, setting the stage for an upcoming summit, rejected calls for a confrontational approach to communist China. Clinton argued that isolating the Chinese would be "potentially dangerous." (10/24/1997).

1997   In Philadelphia, hundreds of thousands of black women joined the Million Woman March in a show of solidarity. (10/25/1997).

1997   A jury in Cambridge, Massachusetts convicted British *au pair* Louise Woodward of the second-degree murder in the death of 8-month-old Matthew Eappen. (10/30/1997).

1997   British *au pair* Louise Woodward received a mandatory life sentence, a day after a jury in Cambridge, Mass., convicted her of second-degree murder in the death of 8-month-old Matthew Eappen. The judge, Hiller B. Zobel, later reduced the verdict to manslaughter and set Woodward free. (10/31/1997).

1997   The U.S. Supreme Court let stand California's groundbreaking Proposition 209, which banned race and gender preference in hiring and school admissions. (11/03/1997).

1997   Opening statements were presented in the Oklahoma City bombing trial of Terry Nichols. Timothy McVeigh had been sentenced to death two months earlier. (11/03/1997).

1997   Michael Carneal, 14, killed three girls and wounded five others outside a prayer circle in West Paducah, KY. Prevention experts pointed to a copy of Stephen King's *Rage* found in Carneal's school locker. (12/1/1997).

1997   *Mode,* a glossy fashion magazine for women "size 12 and above", won the Ad Week's Start-up of the Year award for business performance and innovation.

1997   Activist Patricia Pulling, founder of Bothered About Dungeons and Dragons (B.A.D.D.) died of cancer. Her son Irving "Bink" Pulling had committed suicide, after playing the role playing game. (09/18/1997).

1997   Concerned with American youth, Princeton Professor John Dilulio warns of a "rising wave of super predators" primed to prey on society. The media-savvy Dilulio, wearing a leather jacket, posed against a graffiti-covered wall to illustrate a story on "A Teenage Time Bomb" for *Time magazine.*

1997   One day after moving to halt the import of modified assault weapons, President Bill Clinton defended the action in his weekly radio address, stating that such weapons did nothing but "inspire fear and wreck deadly havoc on our streets." (11/15/1997).

1997   According to Join Together, the overall number of estimated heroin users rose from 68,000 in 1993 to 325,000 in 1997.

1998   During his weekly radio address President Bill Clinton denounced Chicago physicist Richard Seed's call to clone human beings, calling the statement "morally unacceptable. (01/10/1998).

1998   Inside New York's World Trade Center, three masked men robbed two Brink's guards of $1.7 million. Three suspects were quickly arrested as the robbers removed their masks while under surveillance video cameras. (01/13/1998).

1998   Working for the FBI, secretary Linda Tripp wore a hidden microphone and recorded a conversation with former White House intern Monica Lewinsky. Tripp's information led to the impeachment and subsequent acquittal of U.S. President Bill Clinton. (01/13/1998).

1998   The Uniform Crime Reporting Program (UCR) of the Federal Bureau of Investigation (FBI) reported that in 1998, 4.8% of the 14,276 homicides in which circumstances were known were narcotics related.

1998   For a generation too young to have appreciated "90210", the WB Network introduced "Dawson's Creek," a teen-angst, sex-obsessed drama that launched the careers of Katie Holmes and Michelle Williams. (01/20/1998).

1998	Terrorist Theodore Kaczynski, the "Unabomber," pleaded guilty in Sacramento, CA., in return for a sentence of life in prison without parole. (01/22/1998).
1998	"I did not have sexual relations with that woman, Miss Lewinsky," President Bill Clinton forcefully told reporters as he denied charges that he had an affair with a former White House intern. (01/26/1998).
1998	Karla Faye Tucker was executed by the state of Texas for the pickax murders of two people in 1984. Tucker was the first woman executed in the United States since 1984. (02/03/1998).
1998	Eric Rudolph is officially declared a suspect by authorities in the bombing of a Birmingham, Alabama abortion clinic. A $100,000 reward was offered for information leading to his capture. (01/14/1998).
1998	The Dow Jones Industrial average closed above 9,000 points for the first time in its volatile history. (04/6/1998).
1998	"Seinfeld," the cultural phenomenon that was about "nothing," presented their much-anticipated finale. In their last episode the foursome are jailed for having violated a small town's Good Samaritan Law as they did "nothing" to stop a car jacking. (05/14/1998).
1998	In Jasper, Texas, James Byrd Jr., 49, an African American, was stripped, chained to a pickup truck and dragged for miles until he was decapitated. White supremacists John William King and Lawrence Russel Brewer were sentenced to death for the barbaric act. Shawn Allen Berry was given a life sentence. (06/7/1998).
1998	*There's Something About Mary*, directed by Bobby and Peter Farrelly, a wacky romantic comedy, emerged as the year's highest-grossing comedy. It starred Matt Dillon, Cameron Diaz and Ben Stiller. (07/15/1998).
1998	Director Steven Spielberg paid tribute to America's greatest generation, the GI Generation, in his epic film *Saving Private Ryan*. (07/24/1998).

1998 Thirteen-year-old Regina Apodaca was stabbed to death with both her jugular vein and carotid artery severed. She was brutally slain by Ruby Guerra, 14, while Felicia Duran, 15; Mariana Gallegos, 15; and Francesca Lopez, 13, bit and beat her. The violence erupted over a shared boyfriend. The incident demonstrated the troubling trend of young girls involved in violent crime. (8/14/1998).

1998 Britney Spears, a 17-year old ex-Mouseketeer, released her first single "Baby One More Time." She would go on to experience both dramatic highs and lows in her troubled pop-star career. (10/23/1998).

1998 Brian Stewart, 32, is convicted of injecting his eleven month-old son with AIDS-tainted blood, as a means of avoiding child support. Stewart received a sentence of life in prison. (12/6/1998).

1998 An expelled seventeen-year-old Kip Kunkel killed two and wounded 22 others at the Springfield, Oregon Thurston High School cafeteria. Kunkel had murdered his parents prior to the school shooting. (05/21/1998).

1999 Amadou Diallio, a 23-year-old immigrant from Guinea, was killed by four New York Police Department plain-clothed officers after reaching for his wallet. The officers, part of the now-defunct Street Crimes Unit, fired a total of 41 rounds and hit Diallo 19 times. The tragedy occurred at 1157 Wheeler Avenue in the Southview section of the Bronx. Bruce Springsteen later wrote a song about the killing. (02/4/1999).

1999 The Uniform Crime Reporting Program (UCR) of the Federal Bureau of Investigation (FBI) reported that in 1999, 4.5% of the 13,011 homicides in which circumstances were known were narcotics related.

1999 Considered to be among the best 21st century motion picture directors, Stanley Kubrick died in Hertfordshire, England at the age of 70. Among his films were *Lolita* (1962), *Dr. Strangelove* (1964), *2001: A Space Odyssey* (1968), *A Clockwork Orange* (1971), *The Shining* (1980), and *Full Metal Jacket* (1987). (03/7/1999).

1999	The FDA issued a public alert about the potential dangers of GHB precursors, and also asked for a voluntary recall. Their press release stated, "The Food and Drug Administration is alerting consumers not to purchase or consume products, some of which are labeled as dietary supplements, that contain gamma butyrolactone (GBL). FDA has also asked companies that manufacture these products to voluntarily recall them. The agency has received reports of serious health problems—some that are potentially life-threatening—associated with the use of these products."
1999	Eric Harris, 18, and Dylan Kleibolt, 17, unleashed the Columbine school massacre on April 20th, the cryptic birthday of Adolph Hitler. The shooters killed twelve fellow students and a teacher before taking their own lives. The media blamed Marilyn Manson and Nine Inch Nails and motion pictures *The Basketball Diaries* and *The Matrix* for possibly influencing the murderous acts. (4/20/1999).
1999	Warner Brothers Cable TV pulled the season finale "Graduation Day, Part Two" from the popular series *Buffy the Vampire Slayer*. The episode depicted school violence, ironically right after the killings in Littleton, Colorado and during most school graduations. The controversial episode was rescheduled for July 13, 1999. (05/25/1999).
1999	Controversial Christian-right leader Jerry Falwell suggested "Teletubbies" character Tinky Winky is gay and morally damaging to children. In 1979 Falwell founded the Moral Majority, a conservative Christian lobbying group.
1999	John F. Kennedy Jr., his wife Carolyn, and her sister, Lauren Bessette, died when their single-engine plane, piloted by Kennedy, plunged into the Atlantic Ocean near Martha's Vineyard, Mass. (07/16/1999).
1999	Woodstock, 1999, a music festival that was held at Griffiss Air Force Base near Rome, NY ended in violence and tragedy. Propane tanks were exploded and there were incidents of "serious vandalism." Half a dozen women claimed that they had been sexually assaulted. It was called "Woodstuck '99" and "The night the music died." (7/23-25/1999).

1999	Stone Temple Pilots lead singer Scott Weiland was sent to the Los Angeles County Men's Central Jail for violating his probation. Weiland had been hospitalized in July after a heroin overdose. The singer was also kicked out of a rehab center in April for treatment noncompliance. (08/13/1999).
1999	Cellansene, an herbal remedy made of ginko biloba, sweet clover and grapeseed extracts, is marketed commercially in America. The Australian herbal product claimed to reduce cellulite in women.
1999	The U.S. Commerce Department reported that the 1999 trade deficit was up a sharp 65.1 percent (an all-time high of $271.3 billion) from a 1998 deficit of $164.3 billion, the previous record.
1999	The National School Safety Center reported there was a one-in-2 million chance of being killed in one of America's schools in 1999.

References

Chapter 1: The Dark Prophesy

Anderson, R. (2003). Smack is back. *Seattle Weekly.* Retrieved from http://www.seattleweekly.com/news/0302/news-anderson.php

Andrew Wood—Star Dog of the Celestial. Retrieved from http://members.tripod.com/Kuriakon))/andy/index.html

Andy Wood (person) (2005). Retrieved from http://www.everything2.com/index.pl?node_id=1730172&display ...

Darke, S. and Zador, D. (1996). Fatal Heroin Overdose: A Review. Addiction. Retrieved from http://www.lindesmith.org/library/darke2.cfm

Epidemiologic Trends in Drug Abuse. (1999). National Institute on Drug Abuse. Retrieved from http://www.drugabuse.gov/CEWG/AdvancedRep/699ADV/699adv.html

Heroin a Major Killer in Pacific Northwest. (2000). Associated Press.

Heroin Becoming Drug of '90s, Report Warns. (1994). Associated Press.

Heroin Overdose. (2006). Medline Plus. Retrieved from http://www.nlm.gov/medlineplus/ency/article/002861.htm

Kevin Wood Interview. (2005). Full in bloom music. Retrieved from http://www.fullinbloommusic.com/interviews.html

Kuhn, C., Swartzwelder, S. and Wilson, W. (2003). Buzzed. The Straight Facts About the Most Used and Abused Drugs from Alcohol to Ecstasy. New York: W.W. Norton.

Moon, T. (1996). Heroin Leaves Legacy of Lessons Ignored." Knight-Ridder Newspapers.

Murphy, K. Andrew Wood—Classic Rock. Retrieved from http://mysite.verizon.net/res8xin8/id12.html

National Institute of Drug Abuse InfoFacts. Heroin. (2004). Retrieved from http://www.nida.nih.gov/Infofax/heroin.html

Recent Drug Abuse Trends in the Seattle-King County Area. (2001). Community Epidemiology Work Group. Retrieved from http://www.metrokc.gov/health/subabuse/drugtrends2001.pdf

Talvi, S.J.A. (2000). Smack Down: Seattle's heroin treatment program may soon get the boot from downtown. Seattle Weekly. Retrieved from http://www.seattleweekly.com/news/0046/news-talvi.php

Welsh, I. (1993). *Trainspotting*. New York City: W. W. Norton & Company

Chapter 2: The Lost Tribes of Generation X

Anderson, K. (2001). Disillusionment in the 1990's. *Probe Ministries*.

Blake, M. and Halladay, J. (2000). They died protecting us. *USA Today*.

Brokaw, T. (1998). *The Greatest Generation*. New York: Random House.

Clubb, M. (2000). The Greatest Generation. *Liberty* .

Coupland, D. (1991). *Generation X*. New York: St. Martin's Press.

Crosby, S. (2003). Scapegoating Research and Remedies: Constructive Inquiry Into The Nature and Neutralizing Of Blame. *The Scapegoat Society.* Retrieved from http://www.scapegoat.demon.co.uk/

Dacey, J. and Travers, J. (1991). *Human Development Across the Lifespan.* Dubuque, IA: William C Brown Publishers.

D'Innocenzio, A. (2001). Sexy kids clothes cause debate. *Times Leader.*

Franklin, S. (1998). New Generation Works Hard, Has Different Outlook. *Chicago Tribune.*

Gladwell, M. (2002). *The Tipping Point.* Boston: Little, Brown and Company.

Graff, J. L. (1996). High times at New Trier High: A model school struggles with a vexing national issue: kids on pot. *Time.*

Holtz, G. T. (1995). *Welcome to the Jungle: The why behind 'Generation X.'* New York: St. Martin's Griffin.

Hood, T.V. (2003). Teen Icons: Cultural Images and Adolescent Behavior. Retrieved from http://www.smu.edu/ecenter/discourse/Teens.htm

Hornblower, M. (1997). Great Expectations. *Time.*

Howe, N. and Strauss, B. (1993). *13th Gen: Abort, Retry, Ignore, Fail?* New York: Vintage.

Jacobson, M. (1999). The Generation Gap in my Living Room. *New York.*

Kantrowtz, B. and Wingert, P. (2001). Unmarried With Children. *Newsweek.*

Ling, L. (2000). Talkin' 'bout my generation: Why Gen Xers don't care about Election 2000. *USA Weekend*.

Lowry, R. (1996). Our Hero, Heroin. *National Review*.

Namka, L. (2003). Scapegoating—an Insidious Family Pattern of Blame and Shame on One Family Member. Retrieved from http://www.angriesout.com/grown19.htm

Peck, M. S. (1978). *The Road Less Traveled*. Clearwater,FL: Touchstone Books Limited.

Sacks, P. (1996). *Generation X Goes to College*. Chicago: Open Court.

Strauss, W. and Howe, N. (1997). *Generations: The History of America's Future 1584 to 2069*. New York: Quill.

Stern, L. (1999). The Next Big Thing. *Newsweek*.

Zernike, K. and Nieves, E. (2001). New Generation Confronts Notions of War and Peace As Their World Changes. *The New York Times*.

Chapter 3: Kurt Cobain

Alice in Chains. (1992). *Dirt*. [CD]. New York: Sony Music.

Alice in Chains. (1990). *Facelift*. [CD]. New York: Columbia Records.

Alice in Chains. (1996). *Unplugged*. [CD]. New York: Sony Music.

A northwest music timeline.1991-1994. The grunge years. (1994). *Soundcheck*. Retrieved from http://cycletheory.tripod.com/history/4.html.

Azerrad, P. (1993). *Come as you are: The story of Nirvana*. Main Street Books/Doubleday.

Brite, P. (1997). *Courtney Love: The Real Story.* New York: Touchstone Books.

Crisafulli, C. (1996). *Teen Spirit: The Stories Behind Every Nirvana Song.* New York: Fireside Books/Simon and Schuster.

Colapinto, J., Boehlert, E. & Hendrickson, M. (1996). Who are you? Pearl Jam's Eddie Vedder. *Rolling Stone*.

di Perna, Alan. (1994). Cast a Giant Shadow: The Story of Nirvana and Kurt Cobain. *Guitar World.*

Farley, J.F. (1998). Love in Bloom. *Time.*

Gaar, G. G. (2000). Hendrix's Seattle: Seattle is to Jimi Hendrix fans what Liverpool is to Beatles fans. *Goldmine*.

Gilbert, J. (1996). Go Ask Alice. *Guitar World.*

Gold, T., Chiu, A. and Green, M. (2004). Remembering Kurt. *People.*

Grant, T. (1998). Cobain Murder Investigation. Retrieved from http://tomgrantpi.com/

Halperin, I. and Wallace, M. (2000). *Who killed Kurt Cobain? The mysterious death of an icon.* New York: Citadel.

Henderson, D. (1983). *'Scuse Me While I Kiss the Sky: The Life of Jimi Hendrix.* New York: Bantam Books.

Jacobs, P. (1990). *Rock and Roll Heaven: Legendary music stars who died in their prime.* New York: Gallery Books.

Jane Says by Jane's Addiction. (1988). *Songfacts.* Retrieved at http://www.songfacts.com/detail.php?id=4269&

"Jane Says, and We Still Listen" (2001). *The Washington Post.* Retrieved at http://www.washingtonpost.com

Kenneally, T. and Bloom, S. (1996). Who Killed Kurt Cobain? *High Times.*

Kitts, J., Tolinski, B. and Steinblatt, H. (1998). *Nirvana and the Grunge Revolution.* Milwaukee, WI: Hal Leonard Corporation.

Knopper, S. (2004). 2004 Summer Tours in Trouble. *Rolling Stone.*

Kurt Cobain Killed by psychiatry. (2007). Citizens Commission on Human Rights Investigating and Exposing Psychiatric Human Rights Abuse. *Scientology Against Drugs.* Retrieved from http://www.cchr.org/index.cfm/5319

Kurt Cobain Tribute. (1994). Retrieved from http://www.hotshotdigital.com/WellAlwaysRemember.2/KurtCo...

Laird, J. (1999). Forever in Debt: The Death of Kurt Cobain. Retrieved from http://www.angelfire.com/pa/freezinchick/cobainresearch.html

Layne Staley. (2006). *Wikipedia.* Retrieved from http://en.wikipedia.org/wiki/Layne_Staley

Lollapalooza Festival—Grunge Music (2003). Retrieved from: //home.att.net/~grungehistory/Lollapalooza_Festival.htm

McNeil, L. and McCain, G. (1997). *Please Kill Me: The Uncensored Oral History of Punk.* New York: Penguin Books.

Moon, T. (2000). Pearl Jam perfects 'bootlegging' for own ends. *The Philadelphia Inquirer Magazine.*

Neely, K. (1998). *5 Against One: The Pearl Jam Story.* Penguin Books.

Nirvana. (1991). Smells Like Teen Spirit. On *Nevermind* [CD]. Los Angeles: DGC.

Nirvana. (1994). *Unplugged in New York.* [CD]. Los Angeles: Geffen Records.

Pareles, J. and Romanowski, R. (1983). *The Rolling Stone Encyclopedia of Rock and Roll. New York:* Rolling Stone/Summit Books.

Pearl Jam. (1981). *Ten.* [CD]. New York: Sony Music.

Petrillo, T. (2001). Ramones inspired a whole generation. *Associated Press.*

Prato, G. (1998). A Special Tribute: Nirvana, the early years. *Circus.*

Pray, D. (Director). (1997). *HYPE, Surviving the Northwest Rock Explosion.* Motion picture and lecture. Kirby Theatre, Wilkes-Barre, PA.

Punk rock superstar Joey Ramone dies at 49. (2001). *Associated Press.*

Rossi, M. (1996). *Courtney Love: Queen of noise.* New York, New York: Pocket Books.

Stack, R. [Narrator]. (1997). The Death of Kurt Cobain. *Unsolved Mysteries.* New York : National Broadcasting Company.

Rogers, S. (1997). Kurt Cobain. *Laserlight Audio Book* on CD. Westwood One Entertainment: 12827.

Rubio, A. (2003). *Layne Staley: Angry Chair: A Look Inside the Heart and Soul of an Incredible Musician.* Evansdale, IA: Xanadu Enterprises.

Soundgarden. (1994). *Super**k*om*.* [CD]. Hollywood, CA: A&M Records.

The Tragedy. (1994). *Kurt Cobain Suicide Note.* Retrieved from http://ourworld.compuserve.com/homepages/gracefyr/greatone.htm

Thompson, D. (1999). *Better to Burn Out: The Cult of Death in Rock and Roll.* Thunder Mouth Press: New York City.

Thompson, D. (1994). *Never Fade Away.* New York: St. Martin's Press.

Ward, E., Stokes, G. and Tucker, K. (1986). *Rock of Ages. The Rolling Stone History of Rock and Roll:* New York. Rolling Stone Press/Summit Books.

Chapter 4: The Culture of Goth

Alice Cooper: Musician Info. *Metrotimes.* Retrieved at http://www.metrotimes.com/guide/musicians/artistprofile.asp?id=3711

Bela Lugosi. *Answers.com.* Retrieved at http://www.answers.com/topic/b-la-lugosi

Bauhaus. (1998). Bela Lugosi's Dead. On Crackle. [CD]. New York: Beggars Banquet

Carlo, P. (1996). *The Night Stalker.* New York: Pinnacle.

"Columbine: whose fault is it?" (1999). *Rolling Stone.*

Count Pauper—Bela Lugosi. (2006). *Artrepreneur.* Retrieved from http://www.theartrepreneur.com/paupers_grave/bela_lugosi.asp

Bauhaus. (1998). Bela Lugosi's Dead. On *Crackle.* [CD]. New York: Beggars Banquet

Dansby, A. (2001). Manson Responds to Protest. Retrieved at http://www.rollingstone.com/news/story/5932217/manson_responds_to_protest/print

Dark Shadows official web site. Retrieved from http://www.mpimedia.com/darkshadows/index.html

Elwood, W.N. (2001). "Fry:" A Study of Adolescents' Use of Embalming Fluid with Marijuana and Tobacco. *Houston: Texas Commission on Alcohol and Drug Abuse.*

Eric Harris' Writing—Journals, Notebooks and Diaries. Retrieved from http://www.acolumbinesite.com/eric/writing.html

Fitton, K. (2000). Procession moves on, the shouting is over. *CLUAS.* Retrieved from 2000 http://www.cluas.com/music/features/iancurtis.htm

Gabler, M. (2003). Dungeons and Dragons—Concerns For The Christian. Retrieved from http://www.believersweb.net/view.cfm?ID=603

Gabriella. (2003). Marilyn Manson Gets Grotesque. *NY Rock.* Retrieved at http://www.nyrock.com/interviews/2003/mm5_int.asp

Joy Division: A History in Cuttings. Retrieved at http://joydivision.homestead.com/history.html

Larson, Bob. (1999). *Extreme Evil: Kids killing kids.* Nashville: Thomas Nelson Publishers.

Lovecraft, HP. (1973). *Supernatural Horror in Literature.* New York: Dover Publications.

Loviglio, J. (2001). Drug users now using embalming fluid. Harrisburg *Patriot News.*

Menu: Dungeons and Dragons and other fantasy role playing games. (2002). Retrieved at http://www.religioustolerance.org/d_a_d.htm

Mercer, M. (1997). *Hex Files: The Goth Bible.* Woodstock, NY: The Overlook Press.

McKaig, A. Christianity and Vampirism. Retrieved from http://www.angelfire.com/mi/Aleph/ar2.html

McNally, R.T. and Florescu, R. (1994). *In Search of Dracula: The History of Dracula and Vampires.* Boston: Houghton Mifflin Company.

NIN Bio. Retrieved from http://en.wikipedia.org/wiki/Nine_Inch_Nails

Ozzy Osbourne. (2007). *BlinkBits.* Retrieved from http://www.blinkbits.com/en_wikifeeds/Ozzy_Osborne

Patricia Pulling. Retrieved from http://en.wikipedia.org/wiki/Patricia_Pulling

Rice, A. (1976). *Interview With the Vampire.* New York: Alfred A. Knopf.

Russell, D. (1992). Reznor Nails Down Extreme Clip. *Billboard.* Retrieved from http://www.9inchnails.com/articles/articles.php?id=48

Robison, B.A. (2002). *Role-playing games: Attacks by conservative Christians.* Retrieved from http://www.religioustolerance.org/d_a_d2.htm

Ryan, E. (2004). *Blood Rites, Brocade and Bauhaus.* Retrieved from http://www.boiseweekly.com/gyrobase/Content?oid=oid%3A158492

Shadow of the Vampire. (2001). *Amazon.com.* Retrieved from http://www.amazon.com/Shadow-Vampire-John-Malkovich/dp/B00005B6L0

Stackpole, M. (1989). *Game Hysteria and the Truth.* Retrieved at http://www.locksley.com/6696/rpgsatan.htm

Strong, M. (1998). *A Bright Red Scream: Self—Mutilation and the Language of Pain.* New York: Penguin Books.

Taylor, C., Cole, W., Padgett, T. (1999). "We're Goths and not Monsters." *Time.*

The Issue: Audience Reaction to Art: Who is Responsible? Retrieved fromhttp://www.tjcenter.org/ArtOnTrial/ozzy.html

Tigriss. (1998). *Teen Goths, Vampires and Pagans.* Retrieved at http://www.witchvox.com/va/dt_va.html?a=usco&c=teen&id=2241

The Goth Culture: Its history, stereotypes, religious connections, etc. Retrieved from http://www.religioustolerance.org/goth.htm

Various Artists. (1996). *Goth Box.* [CD]. Los Angeles: Cleopatra Records.

Vampire Cults Targeting Teens. (1999).*Catholic PR Wire.* Retrieved from http://www.catholic.org/prwire/headline.php?ID=46

Velvet Underground & nico. (1967). Heroin. On *Velvet Underground & nico.* [CD]. New York: Polygram Records.

Waldron,D. (2004). Role Playing Games and the Christian Right. Retrieved at http://www.3rdedition.org/articles/viewer.asp?id=67

Wise, R. (1994). *Satanism: The World of the Occult.* Retrieved from http://www.probe.org/content/view/854/0/

Quinion, M. (1997). Heroin Chic. Retrieved September from http://www.worldwidewords.org/turnsofphrase/tp-her1.htm

Chapter 5: River Phoenix

Blum,D. (1985). "Hollywood's Brat Pack". *New York*.

Brat Pack. (2006). Retrieved at http://www.the bratpacksite.com/origin.html

Children of God. Retrieved from http://www.religioustolerance.org/fam_love.htm

Corliss, R. (1993). "His Own Private Agony". *Time*.

"Flight of the Phoenix." Retrieved from Rio's Attic at http://www.river-phoenix.org/flight/goodbye/

Frankel,M. (1994). "Fallen Angel." *Spin*.

Gilbey,R. (2003). "The Lost Boy." *The Guardian*. Retrieved at http://film.guardian.co.uk/print/0,3858,4780772-3181,00.html

Goldman, A. (1988). *The Lives of John Lennon*. New York: William Morrow and Company. 248-262.

Heller, K. (2003). *From assassination comes the celebrity death industry*. Knight Ridder Newspapers.

Kennedy,D., Appelo,T., Ascher-Walsh, R., Carter,A., Siegmund, H., A.J. S. Rayl, Seidenberg, R., Thompson,A., Walker, M. and Wells., J. (1993).The Young and the Restless. *Entertainment Weekly*.

Lemonick, M.D. (2000). "Downey's Downfall." *TIME*.

Merchant, Natalie. (1995). "River." On *Tigerlily*. [CD]. New York: Elektra.

Phoenix Before the Fire. Retrieved from Rio's Attic at http://www.river-phoenix.org/before/

Phoenix, River. Biography Resource Center. (2001). Retrieved at http://search.biography.com/print_record.pl?id=22520

Porrara, T. (2002). Gamma Hydroxy Butyrate. Old Drug—New Tricks.

Porrata, T. (2007). *"G'd Up" 24/7: The GHB Addiction Guide.* San Clemente,CA: LawTech Publishing.

Ritz, R. and D. (1995). "Strange Days." *US.*

Smolowe, J. (1993). "Choose Your Poison." *TIME.*

Schindehette, S., Stambler, L., Dodd,J., Benet, L. and Stone, J. *High Life.* (1994). People Weekly.

Smolowe, J. (1993). "Choose Your Poison." TIME.

Stephan, E. Biography for River Phoenix. Retrieved at http://us.imdb.com/name/nm0000203/bio

Van Sant, Gus. (2003). Retrieved from http://www.geocities.com/sunsetstrip/club/9542/vansant.html

Wayne, Gary. *The Viper Room* (2003). *Seeing Stars: Restaurants Owned by the Stars.* Retrieved at http://www.seeing-stars.com/Dine/ViperRoom.shtml

Chapter 6: Hollywood on Dope

1979: Sid Vicious dies from drugs overdose. *BBC News.* Retrieved from http://news.bbc.co.uk/onthisday/hi/dates/stories/february/2/newsid_2523000/2523601.stm

All-Time USA Box Office. (2006). Retrieved from http://www.imdb.com/boxoffice/alltimegross

Avis, H. (1990). *Drugs and Life*. William C. Brown Publishers: Dubuque, IA.

Byme, J. (2003). Crossing the Classes. *Village.IE*. Retrieved from http://www.village.ie/People/Interviews/Crossing_the_classes/

Caro, M. (1996). They're victims of its siren song. *Chicago Tribune*.

Cohen, J. (2002). Report: Staley Died of Heroin/Cocaine Overdose. *Billboard*. Retrieved from http://www.billboard.com/bbcom/news/article_display.jsp?vnu_content_id=1484995

Charles, R., Ritz, D. (2004). *Brother Ray: Ray Charles' Own Story*. Da Capo Press: Cambridge, MA.

Eastwood,Clint. Retrieved at http://www.clinteastwood.net/welcome.html

Feather, L. (1967). *The Encyclopedia of Jazz in the Sixties*. Bonanza Books: New York.

Ford, L. A Few Notes About The HBO Production Gia. Excerpt of an interview with Ilene Power-Kahn Executive Producer of "Gia." Retrieved at http://giacarangi.org/hboproduction.html

Furek,M.W. (2007). Heroin in the Cinema: The Glorification of the Junkie. *Counselor Magazine*.

Gia: Review. (1998). *TV Guide*. Retrieved from http://www.tvguide.com/movies/gia/review/133394

Haq,F. (1996). CULTURE-USA: Heroin Chic Comes Back. Retrieved from http://faramir.sangonet.org.za/misa/articles/1996/aug/ips/10875-ips.html

Heroin becoming drug of 1990's. (1994). *U.S. State Department Report*.

Heroin/Introduction. (2005). Retrieved at http://soc.enotes.com/heroin-article/introduction/print

Lowry, J.V. (1958). Treatment of the drug addict at the Lexington (Ky.) hospital. *Federal Probation.*

Lowr, R. (1996). Our Hero, Heroin. *National Review.*

Middleton, J. (1999). Heroin Use, Gender, and Affect in Rock Subcultures. *Echo.* Retrieved from http://www.humnet.ucla.edu/echo/Volume1-Issue1/middleton/middleton-article.html

Sid and Nancy: Never Trust a Junkie. (2003). Retrieved from http://www.geocities.com/Hollywood/Set/7601/sidnancy.htm

Sid and Nancy. (2007). Retrieved from http://en.wikipedia.org/wiki/Sid_and_Nancy

Sixx, N. (2007). The Heroin Diaries: A Year in the Life of a Shattered Rock Star. New York: VH1 Books.

The Genius of Ray Charles (2004). 60 Minutes. *CBS News.* Retrieved from http://www.cbsnews.com/stories/2004/10/14/60minutes/main649346.shtml

Chapter 7: Heroin Chic

Angelina Jolie. (2001). Biography of Angelina Jolie. Retrieved from http://www.cosmopolis.ch/english/cosmo16/angelina_jolie.htm

Another Supermodel Dies After Weight Loss. (2006). *NBC11.com.* Retrieved from http://www.nbc11.com/health/10345797/detail.html

Body as commodity. *Bodyicon.* Retrieved from http://www.jrn.columbia.edu/newsmedia/projects/masters/bodyimage/commodity/media_page5.html

Carpenter, E. (2007). *40 Years of Rock Style: Kurt Cobain. Thrift-Store Punk.* Rolling Stone.

Clinton Condemns "Heroin Chic" in Fashion Industry following New York Times Story. (1997). Retrieved from http://www.ndsn.org/JULY97/CHIC.html

Clinton Decries 'Heroin Chic' Fashion Look. He says, "You do not need to glamorize addiction to sell clothes." (1997). Retrieved from http://opioids.com/heroin/heroinchic.html

Cynical Trend: heroin chic. (1995). *US News and World Report.*

Drug use and crime. U.S. Department of Justice. (2005). Retrieved from http://www.ojp.usdoj.gov/bjs/dcf/duc.htm

Fried, S. (1993). *Thing of Beauty: The Tragedy of Supermodel Gia.* Pocket Books: New York.

Graham, J. (2001). Web sites promote anorexia. Press-Enterprise.

Gross, M. (1995). *Models: The Ugly Business of Beautiful Women.* Harper Collins Publishers, Inc. : New York.

Harris, R. (1997). Whiter Shade of Pale: Revlon, Urban Decay feud over grunge makeup products. Times Leader.

Haq, F. (1996). CULTURE USA: Heroin Chic Comes back. Retrieved from http://faramir.sangonet.org.za/misa/articles/1996/aug/ips/10875-ips.html

James King Biography. (2004). Retrieved from http://www.celebritywizard.com/james_king_biography.html

Karen Mulder. (2007). Retrieved from http://en.wikipedia.org/wiki/Karen_Mulder

Kate Moss emerges from scandal intact. (2005). *USA Today.* Retrieved from http://www.usatoday.com/life/people/2005-12-07-kate-moss_x.htm

Luisel Ramos. (2007). Retrieved from http://en.wikipedia.org/wiki/Luisel_Ramos

Madrid bans waifs from catwalks. (2006). *BBC News.* Retrieved from http://news.bbc.co.uk/1/hi/world/Europe/5341202.stm

Malik,S. (2006). Body of opinion backs model clampdown. The Sydney *Morning Herald.* Retrieved from http://www.smh.com.au/articles/2006/09/15/1157827140142.html

Marc Jacobs: he is not about selling clothes. Retrieved from http://www.lookonline.com/editor.html

Mechling, L. (2005). One Photo She Won't Want in her Portfolio. *The New York Sun.* Retrieved from http://www.nysun.com/pf.php?id=20400&v=0339122811

O'Hara, P. Minimum Mandatory Madness. Retrieved from http://www.drugtext.org/library/articles/minmad.htm

Pearl Jam—Satan's Bed. (2001). Retrieved from http://www.songmeanings.net/lyric.php?lid=32826

Piercy, M. (1973). *Barbie Doll.* Retrieved from http://www.poemhunter.com/marge-piercy/

Sapsted, D. (1997). Model is sued for $5 million over drug use. *International news.* Retrieved from http://www.telegraph.co.uk/htmlContent.jhtml?html=/archive/1997/10/02/wmod02.html

Skinny models banned from catwalk. (2006). *CNN.com* Retrieved from http://www.cnn.com/2006/WORLD/europe/09/13/spain.models/index.html

Sullum, J. (1997). Victims of Everything. *Reasononline*. Retrieved from http://www.reason.com/news/show/34337.html

Supermodels are lonelier than you think: Karen Mulder Special. (2002). Retrieved from http://saltyt.antville.org/stories/230180/

Thomas, P.W. (2007). Grunge: *Fashion Era 1800-2000*. Retrieved from http://www.fashion-era.com/fashion_eras.htm

Transcripts. (2007). *CNN Showbiz Tonight*. Retrieved from http://transcripts.cnn.com/TRANSCRIPTS/0705/07/sbt.01.html

Twiggy. Click! Click! (1967). *Newsweek*.

Quinion, M. (1997). Heroin Chic. Retrieved September 22, 2001 from http://www.worldwidewords.org/turnsofphrase/tp-her1.htm

West, L. (2007). Designer Marc Jacobs in Rehab. *Entertainment News*. Retrieved from http://www.entertainmentwise.com/news?id=29171

Yeoman, F., Asome, C. and Keeley, G. (2006). Skinniest models are banned from catwalk. *Timesonline*. Retrieved from http://www.timesonline.co.uk/tol/news/world/europe/article633568.ece

Chapter 8: Woodstock Burning

Bauder, D. (1999), Woodstock '99: fine-tuning its act. *Associated Press*.

Corbett, S. (1999). Woodstock long dead. Wilkes-Barre *Times Leader*.

Doup, L. (1994). Woodstock Revisited. *Knight-Ridder Newspapers*.

Dowling, G., Foglino,C.A., Hofler, R. and Simon, J. (1989). Woodstock. *Life*.

Elliott, P. (2007). McCain Mocks Clinton's Woodstock Project. Retrieved at http://www.time.com/time/printout/0,8816, 1675257,00. html

Furek, M. W. (1999). Woodstock: Going Back to the Garden. *Professional Counselor.*

Gates, D. (1994). Twenty five Years Later, We're Still Living in Woodstock Nation. *Newsweek.*

Goldman, P., Garabedian, J., Kuflik. A., Cumberbatch, E., & Mathews, T. (1969). A Whole New Minority Group. *Newsweek.*

Gunderson, E. (1999). 4 rape cases surface in Woodstock's wake. *USA Today.*

Gunderson, E. (1999). At Woodstock 99, they get back to the muddy garden. *USA Today*

Hampson, R., and McShane, L. (1989). Woodstock: 20 years later, a generation remembers. *Associated Press.*

Handy, B. (1994). Woodstuck. This is the Dawning of the Age of Déjà Vu. *New York.*

Hinckley, D. (1999). Preparations continue for third Woodstock festival. New York *Daily News.*

Maurice, B. (Producer), & Wadleigh, M. (Director). (1997*). Woodstock. 3 days of Peace and Music: The Director's Cut.* [Film]. (Available from Warner Home Video, 4000 Warner blvd., Burbank, CA. 91522)

McCollum, B. (1999). Woodstock '99: More power than '69. *Knight Ridder Newspapers.*

Modzelewski, J. (1969). Hippies Mired in Sea of Mud. *Sunday News.*

Modzelewski, J. (1969). Traffic Uptight at Hippie Fest. *Daily News.*

Moore, T. (1999). Whose Woodstock Really Was it? Harrisburg, PA., *The Patriot News.*

Rubin, D. (1999). Woodstock: What Happened? *The Philadelphia Inquirer Magazine.*

Schoemer, K. (1994). Woodstock '94: Back to the Garden. *Newsweek.*

Schoemer, K., Rogers, P. and Sparkman. R. (1994). By the Time They Got to ... *Newsweek.*

Soriano, C.G. (1999). Woodstock 99: To top it all off: Nudity, body painting. *USA Today.*

The Message of History's Biggest Happening. (1969). *Time Essay.*

Woodstock: 20th Anniversary Special. (1989). *Life.*

Various Artists. (1994). Woodstock 94. [CD]. Hollywood, CA: A&M Records.

Chapter 9: Vicki Sue Hogan

Avis, H. (1990). *Drugs & Life.* Dubuque, IA: William C. Brown Publishers.

Brand, R. (2001). Teens forcing retailers to take notice. *Valley Times.*

Body Image and "Eating Disorders." (1992). *The Barnard/Columbia Women's Handbook 1992.* Retrieved from _http://feminism.eserver.org/real-and-ideal-body-image.txt

California Attorney General: 'Serious Evidence' Uncovered in Anna Nicole Smith Death Probe. (2007). *FoxNews.com.* Retrieved at http://

www.foxnews.com/story/0,2933,301436,00.html?sPage=fnc.entertainment/smith

Cohen, S. (2007). Lindsay Lohan faces new charges. *The Associated Press.*

Farley, C.J. with Thigpen, D.E. (2000). Christina Aguilera: Building a 21st Century Star. *TIME.*

Friedman, R. (2007). The Truth About Anna Nicole Smith's Doctors. *Foxnews.com.* Retrieved from http://www.foxnews.com/printer_friendly_story/0,3566,301516,00.html

Guido, M. (1999). Crime statistics show girls going bad at growing rate. *Knight Ridder News Service.*

Gundersen, E. (2008). Amy Winehouse's sobering transformation could hurt her musical credibility. *USA Today.* Retrieved from http://www.usatoday.com/life/music/news/2008-01-28-amy-winehouse_N.htm?POE=click-refer

Heckel, A. (2007). In the mirror: Teens struggle with body image. *Boulder Daily Camera.* Retrieved from http://www.dailycamera.com/news/2007/jan/29/no-headline-30pbod/

Jayson, S. (2007). Gen Y's attitudes differ from parents. *USA TODAY.*

Martin, C.E. (2007). For girls who hate their bodies: a spiritual crisis. *The Christian Science Monitor.* Retrieved from http://www.csmonitor.com/2007/0424/p09s02-coop.htm

Mitchell, S. (1997). *Generation X: The Young Adult Market.* Ithaca, New York: New Strategist Publications, Inc.

O'Leary, K. (2008). "Can Britney Be Saved?" *US Weekly.*

Racy catalog spawns unlikely alliance of protesters. (2001). *The Associated Press.*

Reality TV star Anna Nicole Smith dies at 39. (2007). *CNN.com.* Retrieved from http://www.cnn.com/2007/SHOWBIZ/TV/02/08/anna.nicole.collapses/

Reaves, J. (2007). Mean Girls: Girl Scouts launch nationwide offensive against spreading bully culture. *Chicago Tribune.*

Relly, J. (2001). Generation Y: Corporations, local retailers focus on vast pool of teens, pre-teen buyers. *Tucson Star.*

Sedensky, M. (2007). Autopsy: Playmate died of accidental OD. *The Associated Press.*

Smallwood, L. (2001). 'N Sync 1 Fan Barbie struts into new ere with new role. *Chicago Tribune.*

Thomas, K. (2007). What has gotten into them? Young celebs' lives filled with drugs, clubs, DUIs and rehab. *USA Today.*

Tiemeyer, M. (2007). Anorexia Statistics. *About.com.* Retrieved at http://eatingdisorders.about.com/od/anorexianervosa/p/anorexiastats.htm

Chapter 10: Post Columbine

Brown, E. (1999). Teenagers and the City. *New York.*

Bureau of Justice Statistics. (1994). *Guns and Crime.* Washington, DC: Department of Justice.

Cose, E. (2000). The Prison Paradox. *Newsweek.*

Department of Justice. (1993). *Crime in the United States.* Washington, DC: Government Printing office.

Gilhelm, S. (1987). *Lifetime Guarantees.* Brentwood, TN: Wolgemuth and Hyatt.

Hall, M. (2000). Tipper Gore's warning label: Surprises ahead. *USA Today.*

Hancock, L. and Heinauer, L. (2001). Cops: Mom drowned 5 kids. The *Dallas Morning News.*

Herring, J. (1996). In today's society, we're all shell-shocked. *Knight-Ridder Newspapers.*

Kantrowitz, B., Wingert, P. and Underwood, A. (1999). Beyond Littleton: How Well Do You Know Your Kid? *Newsweek.*

Kettl, P. A. (2000). Our Violent Society: The Scope of the Problem. Symposium conducted at the meeting of Violence in Youth: Home, School and Community Perspectives, Harrisburg, PA.

Klinger, W. R. (2000). Stress as a Contributor to Violence. Symposium conducted at the meeting of Violence in Youth: Home, School and Community Perspectives, Harrisburg, PA.

Labi, N., Monroe,S., Baker, G., J.B., Bland,E.L. and Cole, W. (1998). The Hunter and the Choirboy. *Time.*

Lacayo, R. (1997). Teen Crime: Congress wants to crack down on juvenile offenders. But is throwing teens into adult courts—and adult prisons—the best way? *CNN Time all politics.* Retrieved from http://www.cnn.com/ALLPOLITICS/1997/07/14/time/teen.crime.html

Lacayo, R.and Rainert, V. (1998).Toward the Root of Evil. *Time.*

Larson, B. (1999). *Extreme Evil: Kids Killing Kids.* Nashville: Thomas Nelson Publishers.

Leland, J. (1999). The Secret Life of Teens. *Newsweek.*

Longley, R. (2008). U.S. Prison Population Tops 2 Million. *About.com: US Government Info.* Retrieved at http://usgovinfo.about.com/cs/censusstatistic/a/aaprisonpop.htm

Lott, J. R.(1998). *More Guns, Less Crime: Understanding Crime and Gun Control Laws.* Chicago: The University of Chicago Press.

Mulrine,A. (1998). Curriculum for Crisis. Why your children's school should have an emergency plan. *U.S. News & World Report.*

Nauroth, T. (2000). Expert Outlines Warnings of Workplace Violence. *Associated Press.*

Oliver,W. (1995). Black Males and Violence. Retrieved from http://www.dvinstitute.org/conferences/proceedings/1995/william1.pdf

Patterson-Neubert, A. (2005). Prof: Stop explaining 'why' when teens kill; instead reach out. *Pardue University News.* Retrieved from http://www.purdue.edu/UNS/html4ever/2005/050426.Spencer.violence.html

Philly-area boy admits planning Columbine-style attack. (2007). *Associated Press.*

Puig, C. and Chetwynd, J. (2000).Gore, Bush chide entertainment industry. *USA Today.*

Revell, G. (1995). Dream Massacre. On *The Basketball Diaries.* [CD]. New York: Island Records.

Rowe, C. (2000). Are killers born or made? Dr. Dorothy Lewis explains why people turn violent. *Biography.*

Shaw, J. E. (2000). *Jack and Jill: Why They Kill.* Onjinjinkta Publishing.

Teenagers Under the Gun. (1999). Arts & Entertainment. *Investigative TV.*

van der Kolk,B. (1996). *Traumatic stress: The effects of overwhelming experience on mind, body and society.* New York: The Guilford Press.

Chapter 11: Concerning Their Legacy

Armas, G.C. (2000). Boomers wealthier than parents. *Associated Press.*

Armour, S. (1999). New Kids on the Block: Younger Bosses Raising Workplace Issues. *USA Today.*

Benedict, R.F. (1934). *Patterns of Culture.* New York: Houghton Mifflin.

Brooks, D. (2000). *Bobos in Paradise: The new upper class and how they got there.* New York: Simon and Schuster.

Chester, B.L. (2005). Time Gen-X wakes up, smells Starbucks. *The Virginian-Pilot.*

Current Population Reports: Current Income. (1998). *US Bureau of the Census, US Bureau of Labor Statistics, US Bureau of Economic Analysis.*

Demographic Profile: American Baby Boomers. (2007). *Mature Market Institute. MetLife.*

Generation X. (2008). *Wikipedia, the free encyclopedia.* Retrieved from http://en.wikipedia.org/wiki/Generation_X

Gunderson, E. (1999). Something to Crow About. *USA Today.*

Hirshey, G., Bozza, A. and Grochowski, A. (1997). The Backstage History of Women who Rocked the World. *Rolling Stone.*

Krotz, J.L. (2007). Practical Research Report #16. Baby Boomers and Generation X: Bridging the Gap. *Employee Selection & Development Inc.* Retrieved from http://www.employeeselect.com/pr16.htm

Kuczynski, A. (2001). A Caustic Look in the Mirror From Boomers. *New York Times.*

Males, M. (1996). The Scapegoat Generation: America's war on adolescents. *Common Courage Press.*

Miles, B. (2003). *Hippie.* New York: Sterling Publishing Co., Inc.

National Center for Health Statistics. (1994). *Health United States-1993.* Washington,DC: Department of Health and Human Services.

Parker, T. (2001). *What if Boomers Can't Retire? How to Build Real Security, Not Phantom Wealth.* Berrett-Koehler.

Sartre, J.P. (1971). *Being and Nothingness.* New York: Pocket Books. Hall, M. (2000).

Schwartz, R. H. (1998). Adolescent Heroin Use: a Review. *Pediatrics Journal.*

Smith,G.P. (2008). Baby Boomers Versus Generation X: Managing the New Workforce. Retrieved from . http://www.businessknowhow.com/manage/genx.htm

Vieira, M. (1997). Heroin: The New High School High. Turning Point. New York: *American Broadcasting Company.*

Von Hoffman, N. (1968). *We Are the People Our Parents Warned us Against: A Close-up of the Whole Hippie Scene.* Greenwich, CT: Fawcett Crest Books.

About The Author

Maxim W. Furek is an exciting, dynamic speaker and noted researcher. Blending tenets of psychology, sociology and cultural anthropology, he offers a unique perspective to the post-modernist discourse.

His rich background includes aspects of psychology, addictions, mental health, music journalism and bodybuilding. For a 14-year period Maxim published *Steele Jungle Publications,* one of the leading anti-steroid magazines in the United States. He remains an outspoken advocate against dangerous, illegal and unethical ergogenic substances. Maxim's eclectic areas of interest include recovery from addictions, body modification and the Modern Day Primitive Movement, and heroin and "the junkie culture."

Maxim is a Vietnam Veteran and was an attendee at the legendary Woodstock Nation held in Bethel, New York. He is a published author and a member of the self-empowered and idealistic Baby Boomer Generation.

Maxim's quote, "Don't allow others to define who you are."

www.maximfurek.com

www.gardenwalkrecovery.com

978-0-595-46319-0
0-595-46319-3

Printed in the United States
205388BV00003B/118-288/P